TERROR ON PAN AM FLIGHT 110

B. J. GEISLER

Library of Congress Control Number: 2023916648

ISBN (Paperback) : 978-1-962313-41-4
ISBN (Hardback) : 978-1-962313-42-1
ISBN (eBook) : 978-1-962313-40-7

Book Ordering Information

Writers Book Fair
99 Wall Street Suite 181
New York, NY, 10005, USA

info@writersbookfair.com
www.writersbookfair.com

Printed in the United States of America

Quote by Helen Keller is from Helen Keller, "Letter to Mr. William Wade, Boston, February 19, 1899," in *The Story of My Life* (First Signet Classics Printing, 2010).

CONTENTS

Dedication

On December 17, 1973, Palestinian terrorists blew up Pan Am 'Clipper Celestial' Flight #110 while it sat on the tarmac at Rome's Leonardo da Vinci-Fiumicino Airport. Seventeen people I knew lost their lives that day. This book is for those souls whose stories they cannot tell.

Self-pity is our worst enemy and if we yield to it,
we can never do anything good in the world.

Helen Keller

CHAPTER 1

The Illusion

I grew up in Iowa on a farm surrounded by swaying summer cornstalks and barren winter fields. Winters were brutally cold, and the best part of the day was early in the morning lying under a pile of yarn-tied, used-clothing quilts and listening to the D-minor moaning of the electrical wires that were stretched taut from the weight of the ice that weighed their limits and the constant wind that wore at my nerves. Not even the birds sang on those mornings. I could not see through the windows because of the swirling, twirling, cornucopia-thick frost that covered the panes. I scratched at the ice with my gnawed-down fingernails, trying to make a hole to see through, but the hole I dug filled up with ice as fast as I could scrape it off.

Downstairs at 4:30 a.m., my mother yanked the cast iron skillet from the bottom of the pile to start burning the bacon, the sure-fired sign that it was almost time to get up. Soon my dad stumbled down the hallway in his jockey shorts and a white T-shirt to begin his routine day of milking the cows, feeding the pigs, and shoveling the wind-packed snowdrifts of snow.

An unhappier couple you could not meet. At best, my parents tolerated each other. My dad's parents wanted him to marry my mother as she came from a "good family." His was not so good. The extended family was comfortable and had made a fortune in hog bellies during World War II. However, Grandpa lost everything during the Great Depression and hated banks, the government, and Norwegians, but not necessarily in that order. He said that Norwegians had a scar behind their left ear where they filled them full of shit and then sewed them back up. (I surreptitiously checked behind people's left ears for years to ensure they didn't have that loathsome scar). My dad did not like Eisenhower, and he feared that he would get us into another war. My mom never had her own opinion, at least one that she expressed. She usually just stared out the window, even when it was utterly frosted over, and no one else could see through it.

I wouldn't say I liked breakfast. I was not fond of eggs. I hated reaching under the pecking, angry chickens to grab the eggs, and I hated what my mom did to them. After torching the bacon and just before the grease burst into flames, she tossed in the eggs. The edges browned to a crisp and looked like a brown tatted doily.

After the cows were milked, the chores were done, and the dishes were washed, dried, and put away, anything could happen, depending on the season and the weather. That was the routine of the 30 below zero winter morning. You could set your watch to it, and you precisely knew what would happen and exactly what time it was. The evenings never varied and kept the same weekly food menu, freezer defrosting, and floor-waxing schedule, depending on whether it was Monday or Tuesday, etc.

The summer changed somewhat but reached the opposite end of the weather spectrum. Morning's solace was split apart by the guinea hens screeching in the trees outside my open bedroom window. If my dad was one minute late getting to the barn, the cows' painful cries filled the air like a Tchaikovsky overture. Of course, it would not be until years later that I would hear that Tchaikovsky was who I heard in cartoons, as my dad would only listen to the market report on WHO radio and the Ronnie Reagan program. Strains of Hank Williams and the crooning of some pretty fretful country sounds emanated from our old Philco radio. He hated the "screeching" of opera and almost just hated everything and everybody. For the most part, he was mad at the world and set out to make us all angry, too.

I had grown fearful of the world, especially the man standing in the corner at the top of the stairs. My parents told he couldn't reach out and grab me because he wasn't really there, but I could see him nonetheless. I was terrified to go up those steps and scared to go down. I knew he would get me sooner or later, and God only knew what he would do to me.

I truly loved spring and fall, but those unbearably hot, humid summer days in Iowa drained the life right out of me. Looking out over the humming, swaying corn stalks, I could see the pollen dancing lazily, clouding the air. When people say you can hear the corn growing, they are not kidding.

Summers were more fun than winters. It was not nearly as lonely. My brother and sister were home from school, and the sound of the spring wind complaining through the pine tree in the front yard muted its moan. When I got old enough to join in, we played Indian ball and played in the grove of trees west of the house. We chopped down spindly Dutch elms, made forts, and pretended to be Davy Crockett, cowboys, and Indians. I rode a horse named Trigger and, on some days, mounted onto a horse named Flicka or Fury that I raced through the woods with my golden-haired, white-collared border collie Tippy yipping happily around me. They were cheap horses and ate very little since they were about four feet long and about two inches around. After tripping over them too many times and getting a splinter or a scraped shin, I used them in the fort's walls or tossed them aside to stumble over later when my new imaginary horse was just one that sailed through mid-air.

The other thing I loved to do was pretend I was blind. Sometimes I closed my eyes and groped my way through the house. Other times, I tied a bandana around my head and covered my eyes. I would start from point A and count the steps to point B. What a crazy thing for a child to do. Don't you think?

After the hay was cut, baled, and went into the mow, we made tunnels, crawled through the bales, and pretended we were on military expeditions.

I loved jumping off the roof of the house and couldn't figure out why I couldn't fly. I even tried dish towels and bed sheets tied or safety-pinned around my neck but to no avail. I just couldn't understand why I couldn't fly. Somewhere in the back of my mind, I knew that I used to.

Carnivals and parades, picnics and family reunions, 4-H fairs, and the Iowa State Fair dominated our summers, and, of course, we had to go to church weekly.

I had to wear those horrible stiff, squeaky ox-blood Buster Brown shoes with the buckle and strap that dug into my feet and the hand-me-down dresses that were always at least a size too large or too small. I just wanted to be a cowboy. I wanted cowboy boots, a cowboy hat, and a gun to shoot the bad guys. And I loathed those unsafe scratchy, starched dresses.

When I was four, we got a new wienie-wagging preacher. He couldn't preach without first convincing one of us little kids that we would go to hell if we told anyone what he forced us to do in the dusty, cob-webby furnace room behind the stage that had crumbling pellets of foundation scattered on the floor that crunched when we stepped on them. I hated church after that and squirmed in the pew when I was supposed to be sitting still. Dresses should have been outlawed. I drew my race-car finger around and around the four-leaf clover on the end of the golden-oak pew. I tried to modulate the sound of my low-profile screaming car as it tore around a curve. Out of the corner of my eye, I watched Mrs. Bartell's three-hundred-plus pound body perched on the edge of the pew in front of me. I wondered if the pew was going to break and crush my feet. Her husband was the tiniest man in the congregation. He wore his too-big pants hitched up four inches above his navel and had sunken cheeks and skin the color of tallow.

Church was as predictable as the morning tatted eggs. The congregation sang *Holy, Holy, Holy*, while two children lit the candles, followed by the *Doxology*, the rituals, and Lord's Prayer. The last words in the song *Holy, Holy, Holy* were "blessed Trinity," and I wondered if that meant God had three heads and was a monster of some type, and I started at that moment to fear scary God. My family sat beside the picture of Jesus praying at the door. Later in the sixties, I wondered what the fuss about the long hair was about. I also questioned what was behind the door.

When I listened, the central theme of the sermon was that we would be struck blind, deaf, or dumb by God if we sinned. We would burn in the fires of hell—the sulfur-smelling, putrescent, keening, wailing pit of despair with the three-headed God spitting fire out of his mouth and ears.

Well, praise Jesus, in about an hour, I would be able to get out of that scratchy dress and into my shorts and Red Ball Jets, which, apparent to everyone and especially to me, made my short little legs run fast, and I could jump so much further and higher. After church, we stopped by Cook's grocery store for the quart bottle of Coca-Cola (of which I would get nearly 2 ounces!), a package of wieners and buns, and a can of Hormel chili.

I loved Sunday lunches. It was such a change from the home-canned food we usually ate because I couldn't see where it came from. I avoided the canned beef mainly. It just put me into a depression when my dad blasted the face of an old, under-achieving Holstein cow with his rusty, bent .22-rifle. He usually didn't kill the cow with the first shot or even hit the poor thing. The cow just stood there and looked at him after it had jumped straight up in the air a few inches and landed back down on its now-rigid legs. He had to try at least one more time before he even hit it.

Dad always swore it was because the gun's barrel was bent like a knot, but I think it's because his heart wasn't in it. Like the cow, I vehemently disliked the sound of the gunfire and frantically looked around for a place to hide. Deep in my soul, I knew what had just happened wasn't right. After my first experience of watching my dad botch the slaughter, then actually hitting the cow after the second or third shot and seeing the confused cow fall on its front knees, then keel over sideways and hit the ground with a plop, I hated guns and no longer wanted even a toy one. I no longer wanted to be anywhere near the noisy, destructive things.

Then, add eating rabbit to the mix, and it's a wonder I'm not a vegetarian. After my dad and brother killed the rabbits by slitting their throats, the sound of the skin peeling from the carcass and the steam from its insides that drifted toward the barn ceiling caused my heart to ache. I ran away and cried. Eating our soft, furry, nose-wiggling pet rabbits was the worst, and I refused even to allow the meat to touch my fingers. Farm reality was too much to bear for a little girl. The world of make-believe seemed so much easier.

* * *

I loved the carnivals with the cotton candy, the Ferris wheel, and the merry-go-round that's music sounded like a wheezing oom-pah-pah-ing windpipe. My morbidly obese paternal Grandma was always there with her sawed-off German/Swiss husband, my grandfather, a womanizer, a play-by-ear-any-instrument he could get his hands on, jokester, and wife torturer. He had a bald spot on his head that formed a yarmulke and teeth trimmed with gold. He always had round, pink peppermints in the top pocket of his bib overalls, called me Blondie, and smoked foul, disgusting cigars with a band around them that he gave me to wear on my finger.

He was the wildest man I knew. He never owned a pick-up. He just stuffed pigs in the backseat of the car and crates of chickens in the trunk to take to market. On his way down the road, he might drive into someone's driveway, honking, hooting, and hollering, waving his hat out the window, spinning a few donuts, and driving out without stopping and saying hello. It was a while before the dust in the yard settled, and the squealing of the pigs and screaming of the terrified, bug-eyed chickens died away on the wind. It also took a while for the people in the yard, usually relatives or family friends, to close their gaping mouths and try to figure out what the heck just happened. As the besieged victims of Grandpa's latest assault looked around, they saw circles of deep ruts scored into their driveway that looked like the Oregon Trail run amok. When they looked up, all they could see over the road was a boiling cloud of dust that appeared to have nothing in it.

For some bizarre reason, one day, Grandpa decided he had to have a Brahma bull. No one ever figured out the logic of his decision, but I think he did it because he needed another critter other than Grandma and Norwegians to go into battle against. Many days we saw him out in the cattle pen slapping his hat against his hip with one hand and with the other hand waving his red bandana at the bull and taunting him. Then he plopped his hat back on his pate, settled it down with a few scoots around his head, and the game was on.

Grandpa started his bullfight by suddenly running around the pen, flapping his bandana, jumping around like a monkey, and calling the bull cowardly, dirty names. Then he stopped, stared at the bull, dove in, and either popped him on the nose with his fist or yanked his nose ring to rile him up. If the bull just stood and stared at him, snorting, tossing his head with his ears turned up and slavering a little bit, Grandpa suddenly raced around behind him and gave him a mighty goose.

Once Grandpa got the bull pawing at the ground, snorting clouds of dust, and tossing streamers of snot into the air, the bull and Grandpa, who was laughing and taunting him at the top of his lungs, tore around in circles until the bull realized he was getting nowhere. Grandpa stopped, panting as he backed away in a crouch from the bull, a smirk on his face, readying himself for the next assault. The bull stopped with his legs spread stiff; knock-knees bumped back. He turned, raised his head, perked up his ears, stared at Grandpa, then lowered his head, blew a few mighty bursts, pawed the ground a few times, and tore after him with clods of muddy manure flying into the air behind his thundering hooves. His tail cocked straight out behind him, the hair at the end of his tail pointing like the nib on a pen.

Grandpa was only about 5'4" tall, but, man, could those little arthritic legs move. Grandpa flew up over the fence rail every time, just as the bull's horns reached his rear end. Of course, that would put Grandpa into a triumphant mood, and with his gold-trimmed teeth flashing in the sunlight, he laughed as if he had just conquered Satan while the bull pawed and snorted his unhappiness and ripped holes in the ground with his hooves that blew clouds of dust into the air.

Grandpa always chuckled and shook his head as he walked away. The bull stood rooted to his spot, his head up, his eyes bulging, staring, flicked his tail a few times in a jagged arch, stomped his hoof several times, and looked like he'd developed a more profoundly severe psychosis.

When Grandpa came to our farm to help my dad with the milking, planting or harvesting, much to my mother's chagrin, Grandma went into the house to help with the housework. Grandma couldn't do anything until she chased me around, caught me, gave me a wet, noisy, slobbery kiss, and poked my face a few times with her chin whiskers. She always happily scorched big brown iron marks into the shirts, bras, and hankies while chattering away about her neighbors. It was frightening when Grandma got a hold of the iron. If she washed the dishes, she wiped clods of oatmeal and congealed eggs into the hand-embroidered dishtowels. My mom's lip curled up in disdain at the mess, and you could see just a thin line of her teeth, her lips held together with strings of bubbly, white saliva. After Grandma left, Mom rewashed the encrusted dishes. She got the bleach to decontaminate the towels she had sunk into a bucket of water and ran through the Maytag ringer washer the following Monday. Then she hung the towels on the clothesline so the bucking wind could dry them and the sun could bleach the stains.

When Grandpa was ready to go, he blasted the horn on their Ford car that he never changed the oil in or cleaned inside or out. Grandma hobbled out of the house as fast as her massive body allowed her to, tearing off her top dirty dress as she waddled down the sidewalk and through the yard gate, leaning forward like she was tearing into a hurricane wind. The wind flapped the dirty dress around as she tore it off, and it twisted and tangled and wrapped around her legs, arms, or head or sometimes got caught in the blood-red rosebush that guarded the yard. As she burst through the squawking yard gate, it slammed against the fence and sometimes ricocheted back into her. Grandma always had a clean dress underneath the top one and sometimes a dress under that one. She was always prepared for anything and hated not getting to "go to town."

As soon as Grandma got through the gate, Grandpa started the car rolling. I could hear the sound of rocks ticking on the rocker panels behind the wheels and see pebbles dropping in slow motion.

Just as Grandma grabbed at the door handle, Grandpa revved the engine just a bit, smirked just a glimmer, and as the car lurched forward, Grandma lost her grip on the handle. Then, Grandpa let up on the gas. The next time my left lower lip-biting, determined Grandma grasped the handle, he revved the engine a little harder, and this time his teeth popped through the smirk. By Grandma's third or fourth try, he always let her get a hold of the handle, and she swung the door open like a woman possessed. As soon as she got one foot in the door while the car was rolling down the driveway, Grandpa gunned it again. Somehow, Grandma always hefted herself into the front seat with a grin and a triumphant laugh just as Grandpa floored it. As Grandma excitedly sat forward in the car seat with eyes open wide and a big smile, Grandpa cackled like a madman and, with his hand nailed to the car's horn, fish-tailed the car out the driveway. The tires spat rocks up that flew unpredictably and tumbled helter-skelter, and I knew I better take cover. The last thing I heard coming through the car's rolled-down window was Grandpa yelling in a high-pitched voice, "Yeee-hawwww!" as he waved his sweat-stained-brim hat out the window.

I waved the dust away from my face and watched as the car shot down the road with its nose up and rear end down. Soon it disappeared in a cloud of dust, just like the horse at the end of the *Lone Ranger*.

Unfortunately, Grandpa was as mean as he was funny. And Grandma was as depressed as she was happy.

The white oak colonnaded living room and dining area of their house had leaded-glass cupboards and china closets full of carnival dishes. Grandma loved pitching nickels into the carnival glass plates, dishes, and glasses at the fairs. She loved that deep red and green and onyx yellow carnival glass and had plate racks around the dining room wall weighed down by it. She also had a vast collection of salt and pepper shakers and little flower-painted jelly glasses she served ice cream and cream soda or root beer if she happened to remember to buy groceries or even got to "go to town."

Grandma's false teeth clacked like castanets, which drove my dad to distraction. Shc was jolly if you could get her out of bed by noon but would shop-lift the Christmas presents, and shame was brought onto our family when her name appeared in the Des Moines Register or Tribune as an arrest. Sometimes she would give me a "lifted" *Golden Book of Prayers* or *The Little Brown Puppy*, and sometimes a pair of slick pink or powder blue socks that wouldn't stay up. Sometimes she skipped one of us and gave my cousin two or three pairs of socks and two books. Grandma couldn't seem to get it right.

She loved holidays. The dripping silver, green, gold, and white garland ropes hung and wrapped around the pillars and strung to the chandelier in the middle of the living room at Thanksgiving were still laden with Christmas ornaments and twirling colored metal icicles in April. The brittle green evergreen surrounded the now ivory-ed burbling candles in the window sills. The Santa, holly, candy cane, and reindeer leaded glass receptacle ornaments acted as nightlights and contentedly warmed the chill in the subdued light on the pink or mint-green newly-painted living room walls. Curls of red, green, and white-striped hard candies and little anise, cherry, lemon, licorice, and mint-tinted, now-hardened gumdrops still filled the candy dishes nestled in pillows of fallen-off granules of sugar. We always wondered when the day would come that the five-month-old tinder-dry Christmas tree would self-implode and burn down the house melting the bubbling icicle ornaments with it.

Sometimes, she served the stiff, rubbery left-over jello from Thanksgiving at Christmas. Every time I was at Grandma's, and I walked by the Jello, I gave it a poke to see how stiff it was getting until just before Christmas, when it stopped moving at all. Mom told us not to trust Grandma's food because she left it uncovered on a table on the back porch, and you just never knew what four-legged or six-legged critter had moved into it and perhaps left its calling card. Fortunately, everyone else brought food to the dinners.

At Easter time, Grandma always got in a big hurry to hide the Easter eggs. Weeks before the big event, she boiled, dyed, polka-dotted, and striped dozens of eggs and hid them around the yard. By the time Easter rolled around, some eggs were green or rotten or pecked through by some nefarious animal that sucked or licked out the insides. When we gripped an egg to put it in our Easter basket, the shell shattered and crumbled to the ground, void of anything inside it. Or it smelled so bad that we threw it as far we could and ran away shrieking in disgust. Fortunately, there were also little marshmallow chickadees, now-hardened gumdrops, and other candies hidden around the porch that wrapped clear across the front of the skin-ripping stucco house.

After any of Grandma's gay occasions, she took blinding light-bulb-popping pictures with her big black, boxy Kodak with a rounded silver screen behind the bulb. As soon as the spots in front of our eyes died away, we cousins raced off to explore the farm. The older cousins stole Grandma's grocery money by taking the eggs from the hen house and throwing them against the coop's walls. When they grew bored of that destruction, they threw brick-hard hedge apples against the barn to try and break the boards. We younger children rode ponies, one of which was a little white, brown-spotted pony named Sparky, sway-backed and already thirty years old. We could get five smashed-together-at-the-shoulders grandchildren on Sparky, but then he wouldn't move no matter how hard we kicked, begged, or tugged. He had carried my dad to school and didn't die until a 2x4 impaled him during a tornado in 1962. The tornado sucked the kitchen linoleum into a pile in the middle of the floor, uprooted the trees, gave us Grandpa's coffee cans stuffed with money hiding places, and leveled everything on the farm except the bottom two-thirds of the house.

Grandma survived the tornado while rocking away in her rocking chair in the living room. She said she finally got up to see what all the commotion was about and found her kitchen in disarray and rain pouring through the ceiling. Grandpa just stayed in his bed that had been dragged downstairs and plopped in the middle of the music room. He wasn't really aware of what happened because he had taken his hearing aids out.

After the tornado, my dad carried my ex-bull-teasing, arthritic, cancer-wracked grandfather up the stairs directly into the starry-night sky. In the bright moonlight, my grandfather looked over his flattened farm and said in his gravelly, weak voice, "God, Bill, I think we had a cy-y-yclone!" Gone and broken was the bull teasing, "Yee-haw!" donut-spinning man who tormented so many creatures, family, and friends.

* * *

If it was cold or rainy outside, we took all of Grandma's dresses out of the closet and blankets off the beds and tossed them down the laundry chute. And then, one by one, we slithered through the chute door and banged our way down the metal clothes chute from the third floor down onto the piled-up clothes on the basement floor, laughing and giggling all the way. Every time we did it, we got in trouble with one of the uncles who hid a slashing smile behind his scolding words, and every time it rained, got too cold outside, or snowed, we did it again.

Toward late afternoon and after the chores were completed and the fist fights between my uncles were over because my dad broke up the squabble, we all gathered in the music room. My family, cousins, aunts, and uncles played guitar, drums, accordion, trombone, trumpet, saxophone, tuba, coronet, and Grandpa played the banjo, fiddle, harmonica, or whatever instrument he decided to play, or he might choose just to sing. My aunt "Sis" played piano by ear, and her right hand flicked from alto to soprano notes, and her left hand bounced back and forth between tenor notes and bass notes as her feet danced on the pedals. I marveled at the tension in her sinewy forearms and watched the flabby skin in her upper arms that hung over her elbows dance and jiggle. At the same time, one or both of Grandpa's legs bounced too early to the rhythm of the piano's deep bass notes. None of my relatives seemed to be able to sit still when they played or heard music, and it seemed to me that their bouncing and tapping was always a fraction of a beat early for the note, as if they heard the song before it got there. We had a regular hoe-down, singing everything from honky-tonk to country to gospel while Grandma sat on the sidelines smiling and watching, her too-big false teeth clacking and banging to the music as she bounced her double chin up and down. My dad's brother and wife had a gospel radio program for years. Later I would learn to play the kazoo and the comb admirably.

A few years after the tornado, Grandpa died of cancer and weighed only seventy-eight pounds. Grandma died of a heart attack on Christmas morning when I was twenty-three and weighed about three-hundred fifty pounds. We wondered why she was late for Christmas dinner. When the phone call came from the nursing home that she had dropped dead, my dad irreverently quipped, "She always has to be the center of attention."

Poor Grandma was so big that the funeral home director didn't have a coffin big enough for her and said he would have to order one from Des Moines. One of my uncles piped up and said, "Just stuff her in the biggest one you've got." I remember the grunting and groaning of the pallbearers, even though they had added two extra ones than usual, and I was afraid she would drop through the bottom onto the ground.

Nothing seemed to have a gray area in that side of the family.

* * *

My mom's family was as opposite as the opposite could be. Grandpa and Grandma were quiet, loving folks who spent their Saturday nights dancing at the Moose Lodge and whirling and twirling their way to winning ballroom dance competitions as they glanced lovingly into each other's eyes.

Grandma never walked anywhere. She trotted. You never quite knew when she would break out singing an Irish tune and start dancing a jig while she flapped the hem of her dress with her hands. We spent many trips in the backseat of a car sitting next to each other, with her teaching me such tunes as "Barney Google" or "Danny Boy" or songs about how Jesus loved her.

Grandma had a genealogical paper that showed how her family descended from a King in Ireland with a family crest and all—I guess that made her a princess. The king and his family escaped to Germany during the Normandy Invasion, and their name was bastardized into a Germanic version. When they boated to America, they landed in Canada, migrated to Pennsylvania, and farm-steaded in an Amish enclave.

Grandma's house was immaculate—just the opposite of my other Grandma. This Grandma had an electric-powered noisy, bright-light Hoover that scared the crap out of me, and the other Grandma had one that you just pushed back and forth and, as the roller spun, was supposed to pick up the dirt. I could hear the pebbles rattling away as they spun up into the housing, but the sweeper usually spat the dirt right back out the front. Occasionally there was enough dirt to dump out.

This Grandma wore violet-flower-patterned dresses and homemade aprons that she looped over her head and tied in the back into a big starched bow that fell into collapse by the end of the day. Her stock shoes were black lace-ups with little patterns on the toes and round clunky heels. She said the shoes "provoked" her enormous, painful bunions, but every year she bought the same style that continued to provoke her bunions.

There was always a quilt hanging from a rack she worked on in her "spare" time or a ball of tatting string that she clicked doilies out of. I loved to watch her flying fingers as she stretched the yarn from the cotton reel that tumbled and rolled when she pulled on it and how she somehow could push the string through holes and weave shuttles and knots. She did not believe in idle hands and said idle hands were the devil's playground.

Every morning as the sun rose, Grandma pulled the green window shades up exactly one-half up the window. She sometimes called people "the English." She talked about how her dad was a carpenter and built barns and houses without nails and how her family moved west from Harrisburg, Pennsylvania, in a Conestoga wagon that turned over in a tornado near Rockford, Illinois. Decades later, it dawned on me that my great-grandfather was Amish. Boy, this apple fell far from the tree—meaning me!

Grandma was the funniest woman I knew when I was a child, and she just saw life as a bowl of cherries for the most part, except when she was trying to take her afternoon nap and I disturbed her. One Sunday, we were at a family picnic at my aunt and uncle's after church, and she came out of the outhouse laughing like a hyena. Grandma said that she had been in such a hurry not to be late for church that she had forgotten to put on her underwear. If she got undies at Christmas, she modeled them right over her clothes, danced around, and sang as she modeled her new enormous drooping satiny lingerie. Grandma constantly complained, however, about how "the stays" in her corset poked her in the ribs. Years later, she developed breast cancer and blamed the stays in her girdle. The morning after they lopped off her breasts, I asked her if she was in pain. She pumped both arms back and forth, then over her head, and said, "Nope, I didn't need them anymore anyway!"

Grandpa smoked a Big Red-packed pipe (or Prince Albert, depending on the time of day) and rolled his own cigarettes. All tobacco came out of a red can that he carried in the top pocket of his khaki green shirt with the big flaps on the pockets, or in the top pocket of his blue and white striped bib overalls that had multiple hidden pockets and a loop on the side for his hammer and brassy buttons that connected the suspenders to the bib and said, Osh Kosh. He was soft-spoken and patiently tried to teach me how to roll his cigarettes or tamp tobacco into his pipe and clean the stem with temperamental, bendy white pipe cleaners that usually were shaped like an "s" when I finished them. Unfortunately, when I rolled his cigarettes, they were shaped like a comma even after Grandpa tried to lick them into shape. When I packed his pipe and he lit it, a cloud of smoke and tobacco cinders shot toward the ceiling or onto the carpet. I couldn't quite tamp it tight enough, but the cigarette rolling and pipe-tamping lessons would be useful in the sixties.

After lunch and his can of Hamm's or Pabst Blue Ribbon beer, which he always let me sip, even though it always made me gag, Grandpa listened to the market report with the TV volume turned up to ear-splitting proportions. Then he turned the volume down, and we watched cartoons which he seemed to get a kick out of, but one never could tell because Grandpa rarely got past a grin, as if a full smile would take too much energy. (I did notice on occasion that his front teeth were sawed down from holding his pipe in his mouth.) Sometimes after the cartoons, we sat on the back porch, and he showed me how to whittle a stick while his yellow or black lab, whom he consistently named Pal, lay quietly next to him. (My other Grandpa always had a cur, lopsided, "I got the wrong part" dog that ripped, slobbered, snorted, and rabidly snapped at us so we couldn't get out of the car until Grandpa showed up and kicked it about ten feet away and told it to shut up.) On still, cooling-down evenings, Grandpa showed me how to sneak up on and grab slimy, wiggling worms for fishing.

Grandpa was double-jointed and could do strange things with his knees. His knees dropped backward when he walked, giving the illusion of a sleek, silky being walking smoothly in a glide. It took him a good ten seconds to think about even moving toward the other room.

Grandpa loved Grandma as much as she loved him, and he grinned at Grandma's antics, his eyes a-twinkle. (My other Grandpa would clobber his wife with his cane when she walked by him or trip her and say, "There, that's for when you do something wrong." She, of course, just giggled.) Grandpa made me feel safe and never raised his voice or hit or harmed a human or an animal other than at slaughtering time which he always seemed to pin on Grandma to do. That seemed odd because Grandma always caught flies and spiders that invaded the house and returned them to the outdoors without harming them.

Grandma baked cookies and bread, and when the bread came out of the oven, she sliced off a big hunk for me, spread butter on it, and sprinkled sugar on top. When she cooked tomatoes or made grape jelly, she skimmed the foam off the top into a sauce dish and said, "You have to get rid of the bad stuff. Just like in real life, you have to get rid of the bad stuff." She made goose or duck, turkey, ham or fried chicken, and boiled dumplings for dinners. She made cinnamon rolls baked in caramel syrup that ran down my fingers or covered them with frosting that I licked off my hands. She baked seven pies for family dinners and put out a spread of homemade fresh and home-canned food that looked like a buffet and tasted like something from heaven. She never served stiff month-old Jell-o. I never could understand why Grandpa ate pickled pig's feet and had horseradish with every meal when there were so many other good things to choose from.

We, youngsters, played badminton or softball or tag. These cousins never threw eggs or hedge apples or taunted the animals until they cried out and raced away. After our evening lunch of leftovers from the family buffet, my cousin played the accordion, trumpet, piano, or organ. We sang such gutsy songs as "Beyond the Sunset" and maybe a few tunes from *The Lawrence Welk Show* until Grandma got cranked up and demanded something more dynamic so she could waltz around the room with an imaginary partner and croon at the top of her lungs. My cousin finished each song with a flourish and kept getting into trouble with the old ladies at his church, where he played the organ, for ending each hymn with a Jerry Lee Lewis tickle.

Twice a year, we butchered chickens. Grandma was fearless. She had a big block of a sawed-off oak tree with two nails driven into it about an inch apart. After Grandma laid down newspapers on the stump, she grabbed a squawking chicken, stuck its scrawny neck between the nails, hoisted the ax, and unceremoniously chopped off its head. When she let go of the chicken, it flapped around for a while with blood squirting out the top of its neck, then fell over with a thud, its upside, outspread wing settling back down to its body in slow, jerky motion. I always turned away in horror and got physically ill from the stench when they sunk the chickens in boiling water to release their feathers.

We never knew where we would find Grandma. Sometimes she was out quietly wading through the hog lot, so she wouldn't scare the pigs, wearing Grandpa's oversized blue Osh Kosh coat over her "house dress" and tall, black rubber boots that slapped against the side of her bow-legs and flapped and squished when she walked. She toted five-gallon buckets of feed and water to the trough that were so heavy for her that they made her sway like a drunken sailor. She sometimes was at the top of an apple tree singing at the top of her lungs, picking apples to make sauces, pies, and apple butter.

Grandma's idea of a Christmas tree was the most spindly tree in the forest because she felt sorry for it. She decorated it with a few lights, scratched-up balls, and just one box of tinsel hanging from the branches. The tree went up a few weeks before Christmas and came down the day after New Year's. When the artificial trees came out, Grandma bought a silver metal tree that she set on top of the TV after she gently moved the potted vine that wrapped itself around and around the flower pot. From the side and behind the tree was a round gizmo with green, red, yellow, and blue plastic sections with a light behind it. When she plugged in the gizmo, it rotated, and the silver-needled tree changed colors. Grandpa hated the thing because it made the TV screen fuzzy and interrupted the sound, and caused the voices to muffle and growl, forcing him to race to the antenna in the slowest way possible and, in an almost audible voice, say, "Can't we turn that thing off?" At the same time, he twisted and turned the rabbit ears in resolute frustration.

Grandpa and Grandma always had a large garden and planted potatoes on Good Friday, come hell or high water. Sometimes they had to use the tractor to plow the snow off of the dirt so they could plant them, but those potatoes got planted. They used the *Farmer's Almanac* to plant all crops, including when to get a haircut. When the snap peas got ripe, Grandma plucked bushel basketsful and dishpans full of peas, and while she told stories about her childhood, we sat on the porch and scooped the peas out of the pods with our thumbs. When I shucked the peas, most of the peas zinged out of the pod and shot down through the boards on the porch or caromed off the sides of the dishpan with a ping! Or, they shot out into the yard. Grandma never said anything to me about the waste, but her left eyebrow always slightly twitched up in the air in disapproval, and it took a few extra twitches to balance itself even again. After shucking the peas, she dug up little round red-skinned potatoes and made creamed peas and potatoes that sent my taste buds heavenward.

Grandma had a mysterious razor strop that (she said) she kept in the attic and sang out that she would use it on me if I misbehaved. I never saw the razor strop and wondered if it really existed. My mother confirmed that it did, so I always did what Grandma said to do. Besides, I never wanted to disappoint her.

* * *

When things got rough for me, it was always Grandpa and Grandma who rolled into the place where I was. They whisked me away in their 1953 blue and white immaculate Chevy that had a hood over the windshield and a spotlight like a cop's car so Grandpa could see where to go when he was fishing.

I loved sitting between them in that safe car. I loved the sound of the newly-invented power-glide transmission as it shifted from low to medium to high and the grooves and knobs on the dashboard that I ran my fingers over. I felt special because I got to sit in the front seat and secretly resolved always carefully to choose where I sat.

CHAPTER 2
Preparation for Disaster

Strangely enough, I realized at a young age that I could see people who weren't "really" there. Often I saw someone shoot through the room and would tell my mom that so-and-so died. She seemed to know better than to say anything about what I had told her or to act startled. Shortly after telling her what dead person I saw, the phone rang and the person on the other end said that so-and-so had just died. Or I heard the phone ring early in the morning and told her who had died when I got out of bed. She would nod to affirm that I was correct, and she never uttered a word of dissent.

* * *

There was always a strange imbalance in our household. There was never a middle road. Saturday mornings were hell inside our home or any other day when my siblings and I were cooped up in the house together, and my dad, who scared us into good behavior with threats like, "I'll give you something to cry about," was nowhere to be seen. I tried to imagine what the "something" was, and I thought it corresponded similarly to the experience the preacher told us we would have if we sinned.

We watched cartoons and then tried to mimic the eye-gouging and hitting and anvil-dropping onto each other that we saw on the Zenith TV screen. My mother became so upset by the yelling and explosions, then crying outbursts, that she dragged us into the kitchen and made us sit on the chrome and red and gray vinyl chairs. She had a yardstick in her hand and said she would spank us. It usually became a tap, if even that, and we would laugh at her. Sometimes she threatened us with, "Just wait until your dad gets home!" Sometimes her actions against herself to make us feel guilty were worse than the threats she made to us to alter our behavior.

On snowy Sunday afternoons, my family and our friends walked about a half mile through the squeaky snow-covered fields dragging sleds to a hill that was short but treacherously steep. At the bottom of the hill was a barbed-wire fence, and the game was to get under the wire without hitting a post, ripping a groove down the top of our heads on a barb, or ripping a hole that squared itself into our coats. One Sunday, Craig, a friend of my brother's, and I went down the hill on the sled together. He couldn't steer very well, and I still cringe at the thought of him driving a car. We went down that hill faster than I had ever gone and ran smack-dab into the fence post. It knocked both of us out, and when I came to, I saw stars for several minutes. I concluded that day that cartoons were actually right.

Some days after a blizzard, we went out front into the ditch, chopped out blocks of drifted snow, built igloos and forts, and pelted each other with ice balls. Usually, the mittens I wore were held to the coat sleeve with stretchy attached to metal snaps. They weren't warm enough. Sometimes we wore socks over the mittens. When my fingers got unbearably cold, they turned red, then numb, and when I went into the house, my fingers and toes burned and tingled and hurt like crazy while they thawed out.

Some days in Iowa never got above twenty or thirty degrees below zero, and birds died trying to fly between the barn and the cattle shed. During blizzards, my dad often had to dig a tunnel through the snow that drifted up the side of the house and blocked the door so he could get out to milk the cows. When he tunneled to the dog house, the dog happily stretched herself out from behind the burlap feedbag door, icicles hanging off of her whiskers and shaking gratefully, her lips curled into a toothy, rattling smile.

A car or truck would disappear under a drift if left in the open. When dug out, it would not start without hooking the tractor to it via a chain, dragging it down the road, and popping the clutch. My parents' first car had a storm window for a windshield and no top. They went wherever they needed to, even if it was in the middle of a snowstorm, and were so bundled up in coats and blankets that they looked like two Oliver Hardy's bouncing down the road.

We sometimes went to my aunt and uncle's house, and my uncle chained a car hood to the back of his tractor. We wrapped up in snowsuits, tied scarves around our faces, bundled up in homemade quilts, and plopped down inside the frozen, rigid hood, always careful not to stick a wet part of our skin to the metal. He pulled us up and down the ice-packed roads as we listened to the rocks screeching under the metal of the hood and to the rhythm of the exhaust stack on the tractor humming a high-low, deep-based melody to the tap of the stack's bouncing exhaust cover while we choked on the exhaust fumes.

* * *

We were thrilled beyond words when we finally got indoor plumbing. I remember the pink conga wall with the black trim that lined the bathroom walls and the silver faucet that replaced the red hand pump at the kitchen sink. We had hot water for the first time, a bathtub, and didn't have to heat pots of water on the stove to wash the dishes or for Saturday baths that we took in a round galvanized tub. I was the last one in the tub on Saturdays because I was the youngest and didn't know what a clean bath looked like until I went to a public swimming pool. I didn't have to worry ever again about falling in the sharp-edged white "pot" that we used during the night, during storms, or if it was too cold to go outside. The pot had a thin red line painted around the rim and a silver handle with a black clasp to carry it with. I never again had to worry about something grabbing me from below in the smelly hole in the outhouse. There would be no more snakes or spiders to scare me into constipation and no more cold wind blowing up my butt that made me hurry faster than I should have and caused an incomplete project.

The first thing I did when I entered the new bathroom was curiously push the button that locked the door. I was locked in because I wasn't strong enough to turn the knob to unclick the lock. I was so scared that I would never get out that the constipation came right back. Besides, I was afraid I would fall into the water, and the swish, when I accidentally hit the handle while falling in, would carry me to a place I could not imagine—possibly to that big tank in the ground that Jack had covered with dirt. And I didn't know where that pipe sticking out the other end went. Possibly it went to hell. My dad had to crank up the old wall phone (our ring was two longs and a short) and have "central" connect him to the carpenter Jack so he could ask him to drive back out from town and get me out. I don't know which thing was more humiliating—locking myself in the bathroom or knowing a call had been made and that "central" and everyone on our party line had listened in and heard what had happened, thus adding to my humiliation.

* * *

When I went to kindergarten, I was four years old and terrified. I was the youngest in the class because of my birth date and the smallest one. Old Mrs. Hale came to the little white house twice a week where kindergarten was held and always wore the same blue with white polka-dot dress, thick nylons that I could barely see her hairy legs through, and clunky black shoes just like Grandma wore. Mrs. Hale played the autoharp and sometimes let the children try to play it. She found out I could sing, and soon, she had me singing solos even though I was so shy that I could barely squeak out a word, or so it seemed to me. With my left arm clamped tightly behind my back by my right hand, I twisted and turned and looked everywhere but where I was supposed to look. Somehow through my terror, I managed to sing the song. "Brahms' Lullaby" was the song I always sang. Sometimes Grandma and Grandpa came to the "concert." Grandma beamed as I stood singing at the piano as if she were hearing Pavarotti for the first time. Grandpa usually just looked like he wanted to nap or roll a cigarette. I wanted to race to him, crawl up on this safe, secure lap, and help him.

On Saturday afternoons, when *American Bandstand* came on, we "rolled up the rug" and danced to the music. My brother and sister always dressed for the show. My brother thought he was the coolest man-child ever and gooed up his dark-brown hair with Brylcream and curled it toward the top of his head into a jelly roll. He wore his short sleeves rolled up two rolls, or if he was wearing long sleeves wore an argyle light blue sweater vest over his shirt and pleated black pants held up with a skinny little black belt. And, of course, he always carried his pocket comb in his rear pants pocket. A gold chain looped from one of the belt loops and disappeared into his front pants pocket in a mock pocket watch disguise. His conversations with me consisted of him saying, "You don't know what you're talking about," or, my favorite, "No one cares what you think." He thought he was too cool to sit on his butt, so he sat on his back in a posture that stated, "I'm smarter than you are."

My sister wore saddle shoes with her socks rolled down two times, a poodle skirt with a way-too-wide belt that divided the skirt, and made her look like a midget (I know, offensive word, but no one knew the difference in 1955), and wore a white blouse. Over the blouse, she wore a cardigan sweater with just the top pearly-button buttoned, and she hung a big gold decorative pin over her bumpless left chest. I just felt lucky to be in the room, so it didn't matter what I wore, but I always wore red corduroy pants. I loved the color red, and it accentuated my white-blond hair.

While my brother and sister were dancing to Paul Anka, Frankie Avalon, Annette Funicello, and the other white Dick Clark-introduced sounds of bee-bop, I was freestyle dancing. Those dances would later become known as break-dancing and hip-hop. Sometimes I developed a Tourette's-like mind thought and pictured my brother and sister's legs as bowling pins, and I was the ball. Invariably my strikes would send out howls that would re-set my mother's permed hair straight and throw her into one of her fits. I really enjoyed that.

When *American Bandstand* ended and after "supper," we watched *The Lawrence Welk Show.* My dad had a sweet tenor voice and sang along with some of the tunes while my mom popped popcorn, pared apples, and peeled oranges for us to eat. Probably my mom's most humiliating moment was when my aunt and uncle were visiting. She got sick, went in the bathroom, threw up, and returned with four missing gaps in her mouth. Her teeth had gone somewhere down into the hole in the ground and probably out the tube at the end into hell.

I was seven when my beloved Grandpa died of prostate cancer. He had stopped farming, and he and Grandma had moved to Ames into a little yellow house with brown trim that he bought because it had a backyard full of night crawlers for fishing. The night crawlers hefted bumpy mounds in the grass, making the lawnmower's carburetor grumble, flap, and shimmy like a hula dancer on a dashboard. The mower did quarter-turn pirouettes and leaped from lump to lump, which caused the blade to scalp the grass in spots when the wheels slammed down between the humps. When I mowed their lawn for a dime, it took a half hour for my body to stop shimmying. I loved to stay with them on weekends, did jigsaw puzzles with Grandpa, and went shopping with Grandma even though I got lost every time we stepped foot in a department store.

When Grandpa died, my world seemed to turn upside-down. Grandma seemed to have died with him, and she sat and talked to his picture for hours. I was mortified when I was taken to the funeral home and saw his stiff and rubbery-looking body dressed in his brown dancing suit with the knot on his tie jacked way up with a tie pin. For some reason, I focused, wide-eyed, my head cocked back as far it would go away from where Grandpa lay in his casket, on the touchier lights, and to this day, hate touchier lights. My safety went into the ground the day he was buried, and for the first time in my life, I felt that I was truly on my own.

Grandma started eating "new" potatoes out of a can instead of the Good Friday potatoes, and I knew she was gone, too.

* * *

When I got old enough to play in the band, even though I wanted to play the piano after watching my Aunt Sis and my cousin "Snort" have so much fun playing it, my dad determined that I play the trombone—at least it was not a tuba. That was not a good choice since I was so short. The horn was taller than I was. I could only get the slide out to the fifth note and would lose it right off the end of the horn if I tried to push it further and missed stopping it with my foot. I had band last class of the day. One afternoon, I couldn't get the thing apart to put it in the case and missed the bus. I was sure I would be in that school in the middle of the country all alone for the whole night. I refused to play the thing again. I never got past playing "Twinkle, Twinkle Little Star," anyway.

My dad had a big fight with his dad, sold the cows, pigs, and chickens, and quit farming. We moved into town shortly after the trombone incident, and my mom stopped being so crazy—well, at least until later. My dad started making money and never again had to go to the bank to borrow money to buy us shoes so we could go to school. When the crops came in, or he sold a cow or some pigs, he paid back the loan.

After we moved to town, I rarely saw either of my parents because of basketball, softball, tennis, school, and riding around town on my bike, hanging out with friends. Sometimes I snitched a nickel out of my mom's purse to go uptown and buy a comic book or to get a strawberry ice cream cone with a candy maraschino cherry plopped right in the middle of the top. I loved that chewy maraschino cherry.

My brother and sister were in a state of Nirvanic bliss. They no longer smelled like cows' milk or manure. A couple of years later, Dad bought their first house. We knocked down walls, moved doorways, refurbished it from top to bottom, inside and out, and my brother, sister, and I got our own bedrooms. Mom replaced our home-canned beef, chicken, ham, and potato-laden guest table with fake cut-glass artist's palette-shaped party dishes with a circle on the plate for the matching punch cup. A cut-glass punchbowl with an ice ring that had maraschino cherries or oranges frozen into it floated on the 7-up and lime sherbet punch. Mom also replaced the big juicy beef burgers the 4-H and church youth group kids lined up for when we lived on the farm with ridiculous little sandwiches with the crust trimmed off the edges and cut into four pieces. She lightly nestled the sandwiches onto the plate with a nut cup and a mint green, pink, or yellow mint that my aunt made by squeezing some goo out of a bag. I was a nervous wreck trying to balance that damn plate and not spill the punch onto the new wall-to-wall carpet. No one in this new group of friends seemed to appreciate the outfits I wore that announced I was a cowboy or the cape safety-pinned around my neck that said Clark Kent was in the room with his power over kryptonite. And my dancing was way out of line.

The first living-in-town summer before the State Fair, the FFA boys took over the main street and had a hog show. The ag teacher Mr. Harper pulled the school buses out of the bus barn, and the boys set up pig pens in the garage. The pig pens overflowed and dotted the main street. I couldn't believe what I saw the first year this happened, and the downtown area, with its five stores, one gas station, and COOP elevator, never seemed the same to me after that.

In sixth grade, my friend Donna, an Irish Catholic, talked about and wore buttons for John F. Kennedy's election. I didn't know that a Catholic or an Irishman, for that matter, could become president. Eisenhower had been the President all my life, and this big change came. I thought my dad would become apoplectic if Kennedy were elected, but he voted for him anyway because he hated Nixon and said he was a liar. My dad, of course, had a prejudicial opinion about Catholics that involved their hats and beer drinking.

It was my first introduction to actually thinking about politics and prejudice. Before we moved to town, the school I went to was in a town where "Negroes" had to be out of the city limits by sundown. I never understood that thinking and was always baffled when we drove to Des Moines. As soon as we entered the northwest part of the city, he told us to roll up the windows and lock the doors because he said the blacks would knife us, the "Spics" would steal our hubcaps, and the Jews would steal our money. And, of course, the Norwegians were full of shit. I just didn't get it.

After the world became unstable with Khrushchev's and Cuba's threat of global nuclear obliteration, and after Khrushchev's childish fit of banging his shoe on the table at the UN, the portable hog houses and chicken coops that usually were west of the dairy barn at the 4-H fair were replaced with fall-out shelters and panicky-looking men trying to sell survival kits. President Kennedy came on TV one night while my aunt and uncle were visiting. As my uncle blew clouds of smoke rings that choked the living-room air, Kennedy scared the bejesus out of me, talking about the Russians and Cubans attacking the United States with a nuclear weapon. Those were terrifying years.

Then Kennedy was shot. I was in English class, leaning over my beloved spotted, wrinkle-covered spelling book (my classmate Carolyn threw up on it the first day of class) when the principal came over the intercom at 1:05 and made the announcement. I was stunned and cried because I had a crush on President Kennedy and thought he was handsome and would protect us from nuclear annihilation. My English teacher Mrs. Siemers, my favorite teacher who always wore a black bra under her see-through red or white blouses and smelled like cigarettes and the night before's Scotch, broke from her militaristic teaching style to dismiss us.

The following Sunday, we went to church. During the sermon, the secretary ran to answer the phone. She came back into the sanctuary and whispered in the minister's ear. He turned back to the congregation and announced that Lee Harvey Oswald had been "shot in the basement at the Sheriff's complex." I had been leaning against my dad's shoulder, fiddling with his watch, and snapping the Spandex band to see how many hairs I could catch. Every time the band pulled a hair on his arm, he sucked air through his gritted teeth, which I got a big kick out of and smiled to myself. My dad leaned down and whispered, "Wow, I bet getting shot in the basement really hurts." Unfortunately, I got the giggles and snorted when he said that and couldn't compose myself. Then he got the giggles, and he started with a little chuckle that rippled into a full-blown laugh, and his throat sounded like un-oiled gears stripping, and it was all over for us. I think I startled our new safe minister with my snort because I noticed that his flat-top haircut stood up a little straighter, and I could smell sulfur and brimstone whipping through the room. We absolutely could not stop laughing and got the most-wicked glares imaginable from the old ladies in the congregation.

Shortly after that, the Methodists gobbled up our little Evangelical Church. It got plowed under and turned into a park after selling off some of the stained glass windows and the pews to a bar-b-que joint.

* * *

My mom had been a high school basketball player and an intelligent student. My dad, although a brilliant man, was such a brat that one day, a teacher took him out into the hallway and slammed his head against every one of the metal lockers from one end of the hallway to the other. Mom said it made a terrible racket. He was expelled from high school and could only return if he got involved in an extra-curricular activity. To spite them, he became a cheerleader and took up the tuba.

I discovered basketball when I was in about fourth grade. I lived to play and played to live. The first game I played in was in seventh grade with four 5-minute quarters, and I scored 28 points and was benched during the last half of the fourth quarter so that we wouldn't run up the score. At the end of the game, the score was 32-4.

I had finally found my niche. I played basketball with the high school boys and crawled through the boys' locker room window on Saturdays and Sunday afternoons so that I could play. In the evenings, I shoveled the snow off the driveway and shot baskets with the brick-solid basketball even when the temperature was below freezing. My neighbor didn't appreciate the constant banging of the ball and often stuck her head out the door and asked me to stop. As a sophomore, my name was on the All-Conference and All-County teams. By the time I was a junior and senior, I was also on the All-state teams.

My brother was the oldest, so he had dibs on being the smartest in the Sciences. My sister was popular with the boys and excelled at secretarial. I was the youngest and the athlete. The best part of being a basketball player was that my name and picture were always in the newspaper. My valedictorian brother's name or picture wasn't, unless he won grand or reserve champion for a pig or a cow, nor was my sister's, for being popular or typing 120 words a minute on the old manual Royal typewriters that sat like sentries with a cob up their butt on the typing-room desks.

I loved theater, acted in the school plays, and wrote and set up skits for the pep rallies. I enjoyed those skits until we did one where I was holding a pitchfork, which made sense in an Iowa farming community. I based the skit on Grant Woods' American Gothic painting, and I made the point at the end of the performance with a big exclamation mark by abruptly slamming the pitchfork down on the floor, straight up and down, tines first. Unfortunately, my classmate Susan's foot was a little too close to me, and I rammed the pitchfork tine right through her foot. After I pried the pitchfork out of the beige floor tile and slid it back up through her foot, we mopped up the blood. I tried to convince someone to get a fresh cow pie so she could stand with her foot stuck in the sweating, fly-infested crap so she wouldn't get tetanus. Evidently, few others knew about that farmer's remedy, and they looked at me like I was daft. After that, I didn't enjoy the skits as much and never again wrote one using a pitchfork as a prop. Three months later, I accidentally ran over Susan's cat when it was crossing the road and smashed it flat. Gosh, poor Susan.

* * *

One October night, my dad, my brother, his girlfriend, his best friend, and I decided that it would be a good idea to steal the outhouse from behind the neighbor's abandoned house. (Word was the mother who used to live there was one of the two town prostitutes.) We carried it while we laughed uncontrollably across the street, over the railroad tracks, and parked it right in the middle of the main intersection of downtown. The following morning when people woke up and drove to their stores to open them and the shoppers came into town, they were shocked to see the old outhouse leaning windward precariously in the middle of the street. My dad parked his van in front of the post office most of the day to watch people's expressions. I wandered back and forth downtown and hid in the shadows to watch people. There seemed to be mixed reviews about our plan that went from uproarious laughter to disgust. The thing sat there all day until the constable tipped it into the back of his old green pickup and hauled it back to its foundation. We really appreciated the genius of it, and evidently, so did the veterinarian. He simply quipped, "Good, now we have public restrooms."

That would be the last fun thing we would do together.

* * *

My best friend in high school was the preacher's son, who was so goofy looking that I couldn't help but wonder. He was unbelievably smart and musically talented. He and his older sister and brother had long hair, round, wire-rim glasses, peace sign necklaces, or a bell around their neck that hung from a leather or hemp cord. They were the first family of hippies I ever knew, plus they had an Ouija board, so I wondered if they were the anti-Christ family-in-hiding that the previous ministers harped on and on about. They sometimes snuck out to their car and smoked pot, and the first-hand word was that the preacher often joined them. It was the first time I ever heard the word marijuana or pot; all I could think of was the white toilet bucket we used as a child. At that time, I had no compunction about using marijuana or drinking alcohol. It scared me too much, and I knew I would go straight to hell.

On Friday and Saturday nights, we sat around their living room until one or two in the morning while his sister played the piano and the boys played guitars. We sang folk songs and talked about the Viet Nam War, whatever that was. Then Larry would either walk home with me or illegally drive me home in their old orange Volkswagen bug that chugged, knocked, and tapped as we went down the street. (He was too young to have a driver's license.) Those were the happiest times of my high school days.

Larry's dad, the preacher, eventually got fired from our then narrow-minded Methodist church for going to Washington, D.C., and marching in a protest against the Viet Nam War. Five years later, the church would do a turnabout against the war. That war, or any war, made no sense to me. If I had been older, I would have marched with the reverend.

I knew by then that I would be gone when I got out of high school. My brother and sister had married two weeks apart, which set up a feud between them as my sister up-staged our older brother by setting her wedding two weeks ahead of his. After they moved out, friends were no longer invited to our house, and the cut-glass plates and punch bowl were put away. My parents' pretense of staying married no longer kept them civil with each other. I learned to tip-toe around the house and test the waters with my big toe before I even considered going into the house. The chasm between them spread wider as if a massive earthquake had come through our home and sped up an earthly geographical shift. My dad's chuckle was gone, and his blood boiled to geyser degrees just under his skin. My mom tip-toed around and just got quieter than she had ever been before.

* * *

I tried college. And even being on the college basketball team that, for the first time, actually traveled to other colleges to play did not hold my interest anymore. Several of my classmates were attending college so they wouldn't be drafted. My brother already planned to escape to Canada if he got drafted. He didn't need to worry. He was both flat-footed and color-blind and failed his physical. The only color he could see was green, so that's the color of the car he bought.

The itch had gotten to me. I quit school and moved to Vermont. Perhaps I would have stayed in college if Billie Jean King and others had gotten Congress to pass the Equality for Women in Sports bill a year sooner. We had to drive our personal cars to the opponents' town to play in games and had no uniforms except for the jerry-rigged matching shorts and University t-shirts. When we met at the gym to go to the games, we enviously looked up at the charter bus that the boys' basketball team was boarding and realized, once again, that women were second-class citizens.

I drove the old 1955 two-ton Buick with the "Dagmars" on the front bumper and three Venti-ports on the front fenders to the games. I could get eight girls in that three-colored green Buick, but every time I hit a railroad track, the trunk lid popped open and banged up and down until it settled half open in the wind current. The car was actually kind of an embarrassment. It did have a Variable Pitch Dynaflow transmission, turn signals front and rear, and a factory-installed air conditioner. It was one of the first cars with a light that came on automatically in the glove compartment! My mom backed into it one day, and the Dagmars put two perfectly inverted nipples in the rear bumper of the Chevy.

I quit college after one semester and worked at ISU for a while. Then my friend Sue and I decided to go to Chicago to apply for jobs at United Airlines. They said we were too young to apply, and to return the following year. We stayed at Sue's uncle's house, a pilot for United. He told us that his pilot friend was looking for help for the winter at his inn in Vermont.

So off to Vermont, we went. Sue took the job at the inn. I worked as a nanny for a family that ran an inn in the mountains. They had extraordinarily fuzzy math, and I had to work about thirty hours a week to pay off the un-indentured bedroom I was staying in and for my meals. At the end of the first month, I got a check for around $17 for about 180 hours of work. The paterfamilias decided he was going to teach me how to drink while we listened to the wretchedly depressed music of Leonard Cohen. My drinking lessons did not turn out well. Unbeknownst to me, each drink he gave me was added to my paycheck tab at $4 a pop at the time of consumption. Unfortunately, not gulping and "only one" was not in my vocabulary.

I quit the job after two months and went to work at a ski area. It was the perfect job for me, and I loved it. I took a few hours off to ski in the afternoon until some out-of-control kid flew past in front of me, knocked me flat, and wrecked my knee. Ironically, most of my new east coast friends were Italian, Jewish, Polish, or some other concoction. I couldn't figure out why my dad had included them in his prejudice catalog. Except for their weird accents, they looked just like anyone else.

I made a vat of hot gluhwein in the late afternoon for the Austrian ski instructors' presentation. They danced around clapping their hands, feet, and thighs and singing in unintelligible, throat-clearing guttural words to the moan of a huffing, puffing exuberant accordion. All of us in the kitchen sampled the gluhwein until we couldn't walk straight anymore and were banging into stuff. I thought it was such a waste to put the oranges, lemons, cinnamon, and cloves in it and ruin the wine.

After the people in the entertainment room of the lodge emptied, a group of us borrowed the fiberglass cafeteria trays. We trudged up the mountain, sat on the trays with our legs wrapped around the person in front of us, and let her rip! We got to going so fast that my eyes watered, and if we didn't break away from the chain of "trayers" and flip end over end and slide about a hundred yards freestyle, we almost slammed into the ski lodge before we got stopped. It was sort of like the first extreme sport in our country. However, we always did get caught by the big rigid Austrian security guard Hans, who wore his soldierly bumpy wool hat cocked to one side. The SS logo and soldier ranking was the only thing missing on his long wool coat. Hans could barely hold on to his German shepherd dog that reared up on his hind legs as it pawed at the air, pulled its tether taut, growled, and snapped at us as we scattered like trespassers. The ones who weren't fast enough to bolt away from Hans and his dog were ordered in a thick Austrian accent to gather up and return the trays to the kitchen.

Hans scared the crap out of us, and we always did what he said. Those of us with overly-vivid imaginations thought he had a SS uniform under his coat and was in hiding and posing as a security guard to avoid being arrested for his heinous WWII acts.

* * *

I lived in a chalet nestled in a forest of tall pine trees with five other women who drove Volkswagen "bugs," except for one. We had many parties at that chalet where the most prominent party sport was to do back flips off the balcony into snow drifts until Harvey, the assistant manager where I worked, missed the snow drift and landed flat on his back in the driveway. We all decided after that that backflips were not a good idea.

I am pretty sure I discovered the shag haircut when I cut my hair one night when stoned. Within a year, it became the trend. I discovered hashish when one of my roommates, Betsy Ramsbottom, brought it back from Boston. I left the comfortable sounds of Peter, Paul and Mary and Simon and Garfunkel and started listening to Jimi Hendricks and "Blue Haze."

On Monday nights, we all piled into lone Artemus, an old, faded-blue, unheated Toyota Land Cruiser whose top speed on the speedometer jiggled somewhere between thirty-four and thirty-six miles per hour. In the vehicle's back end were two bench seats facing each other. When Artemus hit her top speed, and the transmission started to howl, I noticed that the passengers on the driver's side leaned to their left toward the front. The passengers on the other side leaned to their right and forward. Sue and the other passenger in the front seat, usually Carolyn, leaned forward as if our poses could help the girl go faster. We were not allowed to talk or breathe through our mouths because the windshield would ice over even more, and Sue was already peeking through a scratched-out hole in the ice on the glass. No matter the weather, we drove thirty miles to New Hampshire every Monday to watch *Laugh-in* at Sue's dad's house, which strangely had the barn attached right to it in true New England style.

After the ski area closed for the summer, I worked in a root beer stand in New Hampshire where, to the dismay of my cooking partner, I tap-danced in my saddle shoes, even though I had clearly never had a dance lesson, and sang "On the Good Ship Lolly-pop!" while cooking burgers. The unfortunate thing about that old building was that a mighty shock would zap you when you touched the ice cream freezer unless you turned off the power first.

When there weren't any customers, we played basketball out back with the boss Moe, my boss at the ski area, and we water skied after work. Sometimes we hopped in Moe's convertible and sped off to Boston for seafood and a Red Sox game. (I can't stand seafood.)

I worked at a napkin packaging factory for a day and a half (the napkins flew all over the place, and I saw several people smirking). I worked half a day in a blistering hot jewelry foundry in Providence, Rhode Island, where we weren't allowed to talk to anyone while working, which was impossible for me. I tried working for four days in the kitchen at the University of Rhode Island for two days and as a cook at Howard Johnson's, where I got engaged to the manager until he got fired and took up moping. I guess I wasn't cut out for factory work, but the jobs were scarce, and the choices were few.

During the summer, I didn't have a ski area to work at and had to find lodging closer to town. I had a terrible time finding a place to live as a single girl, yet they were okay when we pulled into their yard with a carload of boys and girls, and they would rent a place to us—how odd. Those New Englanders back then did not like that I put "r's" in the words where they belonged and didn't put an "r" after a word ending in "a" or call a car a caw.

I just wanted to have fun, and fun I had even though it had a secret edge to it. My best friend Diane and I traveled and lived all over New England. Unable to find jobs, as there weren't any, we moved to Fort Lauderdale, Florida. I returned to school, got my CNA certification, started classes at Broward Community College in Physician's Assisting, and started an EMT class I didn't finish. I spent days on the beaches swimming and building sand castles while dodging oil clots that had washed up on the beach from the back-to-back tankers lined up with nowhere to dump their oil. After sitting in hour-long lines to get my gas fill quota and wondering why the lined-up oil tankers couldn't empty, I worked in the evenings.

My roommate and I worked such exciting jobs as salad preparers at a restaurant where people had to have a reservation to park their yachts. We hated the job in the sauna-like kitchen so much that we took our shoes out back on the last night of the job and set them on fire. We stood there and watched them melt and burn while we listened to the ropes on the sailboats clang and ding against the boats' staffs in the breeze. Someone saw the fire and called the fire department, and we had to fake stupid so we wouldn't be arrested even though we were standing there shoeless.

Many nights after work, we went to a swanky hotel where our neighbor was a bartender. He stuttered so badly that sometimes his face turned red to get the words out. We begged him to sing for us, and when he sang, the words flowed out as smoothly as silky Mel Tillis.

Often we saw the bar's customers' brows furrow in surprise and their heads cocked back when Frank's smooth baritone voice blasted out an aria from Paganini.

I started smoking pot again and rarely drew a breath when I wasn't stoned. I met one of my quickly-balding roommates, Peter, at the door each afternoon with a lit bong in hand, especially on Fridays. He was a hairdresser and especially hated Fridays because that is when all the old ladies came out. He called it "Blue Hair Day" and, with his Massachusetts slightly-lisping accent converted to a Lon-gislander's slightly-lisping accent, mimicking the 'oh, my Gots' and the 'my Rachels' of the Blue Haired ladies while flopping his limp-wristed hand. Peter and I giggled uncontrollably and had more fun than I thought was possible. He taught me how to cut hair, and my curly shag haircut became more controlled.

College went right down the toilet from the excessive THC highs. Diane moved back to New Hampshire, and I moved in with my friend Russell and his roommate Chuck. Chuck was a musician and played for a dinner theater group. I got involved with the group, and we went dancing many nights after the show. When the bars closed, we walked on the beach in the moonlight and waited for sunrise. Occasionally someone got bonked on the head by a coconut or slapped silly by a falling palm frond.

I kept postponing my wedding and couldn't quite bring myself to marry the man I was supposedly engaged to. I kept forgetting to return to Vermont, and he never found the time to track me down in Florida. The signs were already on the post, and I knew better than to "go there." It seemed there was another direction I was supposed to take.

CHAPTER 3
Firebombing

I went to Iowa to visit my family for Christmas in 1972. Our neighbor Muriel lived across the street from where I had lived from fifth grade through high school and invited me to Saudi Arabia with her and thirty-two others, who had family and friends working for ARAMCO (the Arabian American Oil Company) the following Christmas. I said yes. That decision would change my life.

I got my passport and visa and all of the required vaccines. Muriel's son-in-law in Saudi Arabia purchased the tickets for our group *in* Saudi Arabia. As we would later learn, this was a very crucial point. A currier handed what I thought were the tickets to us at JFK Airport in New York.

I received information about the "don'ts" of Saudi Arabia, which consisted mainly of no alcohol and no Star of David. Drugs were prohibited, and life in prison was the punishment meted out. Pork was taboo because Islam believed that eating pork contributed to a lack of morality and shame, greed for wealth, dirtiness, and gluttony. Anything related to pork, including pig skins, was taboo. I couldn't figure out how a pig could cause such things. They forbade possession of the Holy Bible, pornographic material, and preaching any religion other than Islam.

* * *

When I returned to Florida after Christmas, I started having nightmares, hearing explosions, and seeing fire and people burning alive. I couldn't figure out what the dreams meant and wondered if this trip would be my last. The year rolled on as if nothing had changed, but I had changed. The nightmares sent me into a weird state: one minute, I felt like I was spinning in a circle, and the next, I felt I was moving toward something more significant than I had ever experienced.

I rode from Fort Lauderdale to Philadelphia with my neighbor Larry with the top down on his big green Pontiac Bonneville convertible until it got too cold. We had enough pot to last until we got where we were going, so everything was peachy. We stayed at his friend's house in Philadelphia overnight and went out dancing. I didn't enjoy myself that night like I usually did when I was dancing. Something was niggling at the back of my mind. I felt out of place and disjointed, like the life I had led before no longer made sense.

The next day, Larry and his friends Rick and Claire drove me to JFK airport, where I met Muriel and her niece Barb, with whom I had played basketball through middle and high school. Muriel introduced me to a 12-year-old boy named Russell Turner, who was visiting his parents in Saudi Arabia. We were his chaperones. Russell just cracked me up. He was wearing an adult-style trench coat buttoned up to the wide lapels and had the belt cinched up, with the buckle resting securely in the exact center. Russell acted like he was forty instead of twelve. I thought that at any moment, he might whip out a pipe.

I met two cousins named Robyn Haggard and Bonnie Presnell. Robyn was just 16, Bonnie 20. They were from Walland and Greenback, Tennessee. Robyn's dad was a dentist and was working in Saudi Arabia in the ARAMCO community. Robyn was a little hellion. During the trip, she told me stories about her life-sentence incarceration at fourteen in a Saudi dungeon with dripping water and a dirt floor because of her conviction for marijuana possession. She said her parents had to pay off the Saudis to free her. Bonnie was a direct-opposite cousin of

Robyn. She attended a Christian College and had just received her pilot's license. Bonnie and I hit it off immediately because she was also a basketball player.

Patricia Julavitis was from Franklin, Indiana, and Frank and Dorothy Fraser were from New Jersey. Clarence and Thelma "Toni" Hildebrand were from Marshalltown, Iowa, and I knew them from their drugstore where Clarence was the pharmacist, and Toni worked the floor. I met the Wilsons, the cutest little woman named Mary Martin from Denver, and Mary Wamp, the Manions, Henrietta Echmenn, Robert Ghormley, and Emily Kempf, among others. I met another nineteen-year-old named Charles Walker Heywood, a college student at Stanford, California. He had grown up in Saudi Arabia before moving to California for school. He wore wire-rim glasses, had longish, wavy hair, a blazer with patches on the elbows, hated his first name, and insisted that we call him Walker. Janie Kirby, 19, and her brother Randy, who had turned 21 two days before, whom I would meet later, were students at Harding College in Searcy, Arkansas.

I met the other people in our group who were also traveling to Saudi Arabia via Rome, Italy, and a photographer took a picture of our group.

Just before I got on the plane, I called my mother and told her I had nightmares and felt the plane would blow up.

She said, "Then don't go."

I said, "But I'm supposed to."

Next, I called my actress friend, who I knew from the dinner theater in Fort Lauderdale. Bette had spent many evenings and days at our apartment because my roommate played piano for their plays. She was now back in New York City and doing acting work. I told her I felt that the plane would be blown up. She said the same thing as my mother, and I told her the same thing. "I'm supposed to go."

We boarded for a non-stop trip to Rome, leaving at 7:30 p.m. We landed the next day at around 8:55 a.m. and rode by bus from Fiumicino Airport to Rome. I was shocked to see red brick houses with doors and windows open in the cold, damp December air. Pigs, chickens, and goats wandered in and out of the homes without restraint.

We arrived at the Commodore Hotel and moved into our assigned rooms. Barb and I shared a room. We all met in the lobby an hour later and went on a walking tour and shopping. Muriel couldn't figure out the lire system, so I paid for her souvenirs, and she said she would pay me back later. Muriel, Russell, Barb, and I tossed coins over our shoulders into Trevi Fountain so that "someday we could return," as the adage goes.

Muriel Berka, Russell Turner, Me, Barbara McKinney

Our group visited the Coliseum and other monuments, ruins, and statues the following morning. That afternoon, we toured the Vatican, and I was intrigued that there were only a few spots left for pictures of the Popes. When we exited the church, Muriel said, "I have seen everything I've ever wanted to see. I could die now and be happy." We were standing at the top of the church's steps, and a flock of pigeons exploded in flight from the middle of the square seconds after she made her statement.

We returned to the hotel that night and had sour wine for dinner and spaghetti that I pushed several little white maggot-shaped objects out of—I just wasn't sure. Robyn, with her fake ID, Walker, a few others in our group, and I decided to go out dancing. Bonnie said she wanted to stay in and read her Bible. Barb wanted to sleep.

We went to the Piper Club. We drank and danced to old American tunes with Italian macho-thinking and acting men who wore outdated Italian renditions of American outfits with several unbuttoned buttons on their shirts. They had a peculiar smell—sweat, olive oil, and garlic. When the club closed, we went outside and looked for a cab. There weren't any.

Bless Walker's heart. He had a joint that he passed around. Walker had been quietly secretive clear through the trip until he whipped out that joint. With the production of the joint, a grin split his face. His voice and a laugh released from their cage. I asked him how he had pulled off slipping a joint on the plane, and he just said, "Oh, ye know...."

Most of our group decided to walk back to the hotel. I watched them as they wobbled down the street, shrieking with laughter. Robyn and I decided to stick it out and stayed perched on the edge of a fountain putting up with the macho men who kept nagging us to go home with them. We waited and waited for a taxi, and only a bicycle whizzed by with its bell jingling. Italy had a law saying no cars driven on weekends, only taxis and buses. The oil embargo was on, and Italy was rationing gas. We finally got a cab at 5:00 in the morning. By the time we got back to the hotel, we only had about an hour to sleep before we had to get up for our flight to Teheran via Beirut.

We left early for the airport since so many of us were in our group. We boarded the charter bus and rode through the mist of an overcast day toward the airport, past the pigs, chickens, and goats wandering in and out of the open-door houses. Someone led us under the terminal, where they did group check-ins, and we stood shivering and shaking in the cold, damp air. We went inside and found our gate and were dismayed to discover that connector Pan Am Flight 110, which was supposed to depart at 10:35 a.m. with a stop-over in Beirut, was delayed with a projected departure time of at least two hours. An ice storm in New York had grounded the 747 scheduled to arrive from JFK. They were trying to figure out whether to cancel our flight until that plane could get to Rome the next day or find another alternative.

We all wandered about the terminal, looking at kiosks and watching people. Russell walked over to a life insurance machine, bought a life insurance policy, and put his parents' names on the policy as benefactors.

Someone finally announced that a smaller eight-year-old Boeing 707-3218 called the "Clipper Celestial" was rerouted. We all went back to the gate area to await our flight. I watched the plane pull to its spot and found that suddenly I could barely breathe. Something didn't feel right. I glanced at the plane, then looked at the faces of the people in the group I was with. It was as if time stood still for them, and they were lost in their thoughts. Oddly, everyone was hushed and seemed pensive. Several people commented that they had a bad feeling about the flight.

A couple not in our group sat behind us, and I heard the woman say to the man that she didn't want to get on the airplane. I kept glancing out the window and watched as the workers scurried about—in and around and under the belly of the plane.

The gate attendant finally announced that the flight was going to board. We reluctantly stood up and went single file past the table where the check-in people were standing. Neither security personnel checked our purses or bags, and Russell turned to me and said, "They're not even checking our bags. Someone could get a bomb on the plane."

Two people still sat in their chairs. They kept looking at the plane, then talked and shook their heads. I knew that they had decided not to get on the plane.

We went out the door, walked through thick damp air down the ramp set at an angle to the building, and walked across the tarmac to the plane. Since all of us in our group were in the economy section, we went to the stairs at the back of the plane and climbed the steps to our seats.

From the window seat to the aisle, Russell, Barbara, and Muriel were in the back row to the left of the aisle and could see out the windows toward the terminal. I was in the aisle seat, then Robyn and Bonnie to the right. The Hildebrands were in front of us. Walker sat in front of Russell. We sat down, and I could have sworn that I would crawl out of my skin then and there. When everyone had boarded the plane, I noticed that more than half of the seats were empty. Almost everyone on the plane was seated on the right side, away from the terminal. I decided to move forward and asked my row and Walker if they wanted to move. They all declined.

I moved to the left, halfway forward and over the wing. I was carrying my powder blue White Stag ski jacket and wearing a thin navy blue windbreaker because I knew it would be hot in Dhahran. I could see the terminal from where I was sitting. Barb decided to move forward and sat directly opposite me next to the wing exit. The rest of the people in our group were on the right side, toward the back half. I also noticed that only a few people were sitting on the aircraft's left side. *That's odd*, I thought. *Almost everyone is on the right side.* I settled in for a longed-for nap.

Muriel came forward, sat in the aisle seat beside me, and said, "How much money do I owe you for the souvenirs?" I told her we could wait until we got to her daughter's for her to pay me.

She said, "No, I want to pay you now."

I did the math in my head and told her the amount. She gave the money to me, and I put it in my purse, leaving the flap open. We chatted for a few minutes, and she also thanked me for helping her get her luggage on the plane.

Suddenly, the captain came over the speakers and said, "Everyone! Get down on the floor! There's a commotion in the terminal! Get on the floor!"

I heard a voice I learned later was a flight attendant named Lari Hamel, shakily, hurriedly, translating in Italian what the Captain said.

I dropped to my knees and peeked out the window. *Is this a joke*? I could see a commotion inside the terminal and people scrambling around where we had been waiting. Then I saw men dressed in white with black belts that cut their uniforms in half and black berets and shoes. Some had guns strapped over their shoulders and were carrying boxes in their hands. Others had guns aimed at people with raised hands. They were coming down the ramp.

In the meantime, Walker shot up the aisle, leaped between the seats in several rows, and snapped pictures through the windows. He disappeared through the first-class curtain.

I looked to my right and saw Muriel had laid down on the floor in the aisle. Barb was crouched out of her seat on one knee and lowered her head to look across the aisle through the windows. I could see that people in the immediate rows behind her didn't even unfasten their seat belts.

The captain returned to the intercom and ordered us to "Get down! Get down! Lay down flat! Get away from the windows! They're coming to our plane."

Someone shut the doors! I thought.

I glanced out the window and saw Walker on the platform of the first-class stairs snapping pictures. He suddenly turned and ran back inside. Two terrorists ran up the front steps and tossed something through the front door. Suddenly, there was a loud explosion. The plane rocked and shimmied from the percussion.

People in the front screamed. Someone behind me and to the right shouted, "What was that?"

I yelled back, "It was a bomb!"

Another explosion rocked the airplane in the front and there was an explosion behind us. Muriel had started to get up and run when the grenade in the back of the aircraft went off, but the impact knocked her down on her hands and knees. I looked to the back of the plane and saw bits of airplane seats, and things blasted into the air.

A stewardess yelled, "Go to the front! Go to the front!"

I grabbed my purse, slung it over my shoulder, straddled Muriel, picked her up under the arms, my bag between us, and waddled as fast as I could toward the front of the plane. I knew we couldn't go backward. That is where the grenade had gone off, and the back of the plane was filling alarmingly quickly with smoke and poisonous gases. The smoke enveloped the fuselage, and I was pushing, pushing, pushing, carrying the faltering Muriel toward the front of the plane. At the same time, I could hear pop, pop, pop sounds in the plane's first-class section.

I yelled for Barb to follow me. I looked back, and Barb wasn't coming up the aisle behind me. I thought about turning around to ensure Barb was moving, but I couldn't let go of Muriel, and the stewardess yelled again, "Go to the front of the plane!" I called her name again but heard no response. As I moved past seat rows, to my right, I could see people lying on the floor, some with hands over their heads, others clutching their purses. At the first row from the first class curtain, I saw movement to my right. A couple crouched in the corner—on their honeymoon, the woman cowering against the man, his arms wrapped protectively around her, her fists clenched under her chin.

Suddenly, an arm threw the curtain back as an explosion ripped through the air. Hair, skin-riddled smoke, and aircraft chunks exploded through the opening. I looked directly into the man's dark, dark eyes and saw blankness in them. The couple in the corner moved. The terrorist glanced to his left and saw the couple crouched in the corner.

Muriel fell to our left, and as her weight pulled us down, the terrorist most assuredly thought we were dead, stepped over us, and ran down the aisle. The last thing I remember before the landscape changed was drifting chunks I dared not consider floating lazily like autumn leaves dancing in a disturbed breeze through the gray haze—floating this way, then that, then this way, then that. And then, the couple jumped up, leaped over the top of us, and ran down the aisle.

Suddenly another explosion split the air and blasted me into another realm.

* * *

A Being, shimmering brightly with iridescent colors that cast off little spark-like light fields stood before me. I could see the cord that attached me to my body, but it tethered outward only a little way. It was cool, clean, and clear in this realm, and I felt surrounded by loving arms that were part of a Power greater than myself. I felt no fear, angst, or shame in this new place. I felt nothing but peace and love, and acceptance.

* * *

I don't know how much time passed—it could have been seconds, or it could have been minutes—but then I was pushed back into my body like a hand stuffed into a glove. I was on my knees, patting the floor with my hands, inch by inch, attempting to find Muriel. I could not see two inches before my face because the smoke had turned from light gray to black. My vision was completely gone. *Where the heck am I? This space is bigger than the space we were in.* The spot fires were rapidly engulfing the front of the plane. The seats' burning material and the plane's plastic sides and ceiling panels had become a toxic, poisonous holocaust. Although I didn't realize it then, I was nowhere near where Muriel fell. Had I been catapulted through space by the blast?

My lungs were closing down. I could taste the acrid poison in the smoke. I gasped, then gasped again, then realized the air was killing me, but I was not about to leave that plane without Muriel! I had to find her! *Don't give up*. I was searching, searching, but Muriel was nowhere to be found. *Where did she go*? I kept asking. *Where did she go*? It's like she fell into Alice's hole.

I was quickly melting downward. My head was spinning. My vision blurred.

I felt a tap three times on my shoulder, and then in a blast, I heard a soft commanding voice whisper, "It's time to go now." My eyes blinked. I looked over my shoulder and saw no other living person there—just the essence of a huge, powerful, opalescent masculine filmy being and realized it was the same man who stood in the corner at the top of the stairs as a child. This time, however, I wasn't afraid of it.

I stood up and started walking toward the back of the now eerily quiet plane to where I had started. I bumped into a wall, tried to figure out where I was. *Feel the seat backs*. I reached out my right hand. After several steps, I found the first seat back. I tried to breathe, and the poisoned air seared my throat and lungs. I was strangling, and then I heard a soft voice say, "Hold your breath."

I held my breath. I felt the next seat back—hand over hand, hand over hand…one, two, three, four, I silently counted—just like when I was young and pretended I was blind. When I had gone several rows, I felt a breeze brush in front of me. *I can't hold my breath much longer*. It had to be more than twenty seconds. *Oh God, Oh God, I've got to take a breath*. My lungs felt like they were exploding. My head was pounding. And then I noticed the emergency doors on both sides of the aircraft were now open. The wind sucked a trail in the choking smoky path, pulling the smoke toward it. I suddenly could see Barb was no longer in her seat, but Mary Martin, Mrs. Wilson, Mrs. Wamsutter, and Janie were still sitting in their seats, not moving—just waiting, waiting, not moving anymore. Behind them, as far as I could see through the thick smoke, were people still seat-belted, just sitting there, waiting. "When are we moving? When are we moving?" their confused sealed expressions silently seemed to ask.

There was no feeling in me about what I was seeing. It was as if I no longer had a physical vehicle through which to feel. I could only file this image away to deal with another day.

Suddenly, a man wearing a Pan Am flight attendant uniform shot up the aisle toward me. He burst through the cloud of smoke, turned to his right, and leaped out the emergency exit door onto the plane's wing. *How,* I wondered, *did he have so much oxygen in his lungs and so much energy?*

I peeked out the emergency door to my right. I could see people outside the plane on the wing. *When and how did they get out there,* I wondered? *Not that much time has passed.* I crawled out the emergency door next to the seat I had been sitting in and fell onto my knees. I tried to stand up but felt too disoriented to move for several seconds. My lungs and throat screamed with pain. I coughed and gasped for air. I was light-headed and dizzy from lack of oxygen and the sudden realization I was alive.

I looked up and blinked, startled by my new surroundings. Chaos, earthly manifestations, and the sounds of the turned-up volume replaced the ethereal, slow realm I had been in. Mr. Wilson was frantic, bumping into and shoving aside the zombie-like people standing on the wing to escape the horror or perhaps to find help for what I knew was his now-dead wife. His shirttail hung half out of his trousers. Somehow his white hair had become tousled. His hands waved wildly in the air. Others stood frozen or moved in slow-motion, shocked by the bombs and the horror.

I remembered my coat, put one foot back into the plane, and reached down but couldn't feel or see it through the dense, gray smoke.

A woman was moving toward the wingtip, telling people, "Jump, jump! Get off the wing! The plane is going to blow up." Her words had no effect. Mr. Wilson just became more frantic.

This plane has a full tank of gas! If I jump down here, I'll break my legs.

"Move, move, move," something urged me. *"These people need help... get moving."*

I jumped off the lowest part of the wing next to the belly, landed on my feet, and fell on my knees. I felt a sharp pain in my back and neck. The flap of my purse was wide open. Several items fell out onto the tarmac. My inner self was urging me, *"Don't lose your passport and visa. Don't lose your passport and visa."* I stooped back down and stuffed the dropped items back in my purse.

I stood up and saw that one of the terrorists who had been shooting at people as they poked their heads out the back door of the plane had turned and was now pointing his pistol at me from ten feet away. He calmly pulled the trigger. I heard nothing. His eyes grew wide. His eyebrows furrowed; a surprised expression crossed his face. His mouth fell slightly open. He looked at the gun, amazed, amazed, and smacked the gun against the deceiving palm of his unworthy left hand. The terrorist again leveled his gun at me and pulled the trigger. Nothing happened. We stared at each other for a few seconds. He looked over his shoulder at the Lufthansa plane, then looked back at me and dropped the gun to his side. His mouth fell ajar. I kept my eyes on him. "What happened to you?" my eyes asked him. "What happened to you?"

His eyes darted from side to side. He lifted the gun slightly and looked down at it, confused, confused. He silently accused it of betrayal—perhaps wondering why he'd picked it up in the first place, then suddenly turned and ran to the Lufthansa plane the other hijackers had commandeered.

I turned back to the wing, yelled for people to come over to where I was standing, and told them to jump, that I would catch them. At the same time, the woman on the wing was still urging them "Jump! Jump! The plane is going to blow up!"

...I just hoped that they believed that I would...God, I hoped that I could.

Over-weight Mr. Wilson was the first down, grazed me, and knocked me to the tarmac. I got back up. A woman jumped, and I merely broke her fall.

I saw men climb out the cockpit window and slide down the nose of the plane. They immediately ran toward the terminal. One dark-haired man, wearing blue pants and a white shirt with a determined look, ran up the first-class stairs, looked in the door, and immediately ran back down. He ran to where I was urging people to jump off the wing. He seemed to give people the confidence to jump. A woman jumped; her skirt slid up her thighs. *Hm. A garter belt holding up her nylons. Why not pantyhose*? We grabbed an arm. We grabbed a leg. After a few people, I stepped back. I told them to "Run, run to the terminal!" We urged another terrified jumper and then another. Then, the helping man disappeared.

* * *

Suddenly, it was quiet. Yards ahead, a few people still straggled, some clutching their chests, some with arms a-flail, running, tripping, stumbling to God knows where. The plane was smoking dangerously with white and black, billowing, roiling, pouring out of the holes in the roof and the open doors. I thought about running behind the others to safety but knew I had to check again to see if anyone else was still alive. I started toward the back steps of the plane to see if I could get back on the plane that way. I still had not seen Barb, and I couldn't leave there without her. Nor could I leave without finding Muriel, Russell, Bonnie, or Robyn.

Perhaps Muriel crawled out the first-class door. There might still be people alive. Just one more look. I'll look one more time. Take a deep breath. Get up the courage. Run or check? I head for the stairs.

And then the strangest thing happened—there were Bonnie and Robyn. They peeked around the side of the back door just as I started up the stairs—Robyn's head below Bonnie's. I looked around and saw no terrorists hanging from the Lufthansa plane's door or on the tarmac. I could see people hanging over the edge of the terminal's roof and, since they weren't shooting at us, decided they were policemen and photographers. I told Bonnie and Robyn the guy with the gun was gone, and they came down the steps.

I have never in my life and hope never to see what I saw coming down those steps that day. Robyn's skin had melted right off the end of her arms and hung off her hands like drooping clear plastic gloves. Her rings cut into the flesh on her now sausage-sized fingers. Her polyester blend clothes were melted into her skin, as were her necklaces. Her beautiful wavy raven hair was scorched, chunks of it were missing, and there were silver-dollar-sized burns all over her body that were still smoking. Bonnie was right behind her, and her clothes also melted into her body, the edges of the burns curled up to a crisp. She also had patches of burns, was missing most of her hair, and had silver-dollar-sized holes that were also smoking. The phosphorous acid from the grenade was eating right into their skin, melting their tissues, devouring their hopes, heading right to their bones, killing all of their dreams.

Oh, and the unforgettable smell....

I wanted to hug them, I was so amazed they were alive, but I knew I would hurt them, so I just cried inside.

They said they had checked for survivors and were the only ones left. Yes, they were sure; they nodded to each other—the only ones left. Yea, we're the only ones left. They were sure—that were, or could still be, alive. The rest were dead, including little Russell, and they hadn't seen Barb, Muriel, or Walker.

(But were they? Were they the only ones left?)

Bonnie told me they had crawled under the seats next to where the white phosphorous grenade got tossed.

My God, that's the seat I was supposed to be sitting on, wide-eyed, I said to myself. *I should have stayed in that seat. I would have taken the brunt of the bomb. They wouldn't look like they did if I'd stayed behind.*

They said the terrorist was shooting at people who tried to go out the back door, so they had hidden in the bathroom and locked the door. "Where were the Pan Am flight attendants?" I asked them. "Why didn't they help?" Robyn said two of them locked themselves in the other lavatory. *Holy crap*! I thought. *That's why the man I saw running up the aisle and jumping out the emergency door over the wing looked unburned and unblemished*! *Where did the other one go*?

The three of us spoke as quietly as we could because our throats were scorched, amazed, in shock, hardly moving. *What the hell had just happened*? We shook our heads, but it didn't help. It didn't stop the pain that burrowed into our nervous system and into our hearts.

While they were talking, I saw movement over the wing. Below the wing, I saw the same man who ran up the aisle and jumped out the emergency door on the right side peeking from behind the wheels, with a distressed look on his face.

A blond-haired woman poked her head outside the emergency door. Her hair was dripping down her face, partially torn from its clip. Soot covered her face and her disheveled, tissue-stained Pan Am uniform. She was blind with terror, completely distressed. She looked right, left, then disappeared. Suddenly, she bolted out the door. She jumped off the wing, the man behind the wheel dashing out to catch her. They took off in a tear. I shook my head, amazed at what I had seen, and turned back to Bonnie and averted my gaze. I looked at the ground. *I couldn't look at them again. I knew my heart would burst. I couldn't look at them again. I had guilty hurt.* I don't know how she did it, but while she talked, Robyn kept watching what was happening on the wing and beyond.

Just then, two terrorists leaned out of the door of the Lufthansa plane and started shooting again. Someone from the terminal yelled, "Run! Run! Get to safety! Get to safety!" Bonnie, Robyn, and I jolted back into time.

I gauged the distance between the terminal ramp and a truck and decided to run to the truck parked between the Lufthansa plane and the terminal because it was closer. "Come on! Come on!" I coaxed Bonnie and Robyn. Bullets pounded the pavement and glanced around us as we ran. We crawled under the truck, where we thought it was safe. Another policeman lay flat on his stomach, holding his hat, hiding and shaking, cowering. I said, "Pull your gun. Shoot! Do something!"

He shook his head adamantly, wide-eyed, and said, "No, I don't want to get involved."

We've been had, I thought. *This is a setup. We've been had. What's going to happen next? Who can we trust? Who do we trust?* "Trust no one," my internal voice said.

A woman yelled from a small door in the terminal, "You're under a gas truck! Get out from under there!"

"*Move, move, move...*" a tiny voice said.

"We have to go," I told the girls. The policeman averted his eyes and offered no help.

Bonnie, Robyn, and I crawled from under the truck and ran, crouching and wheezing toward the exposed ramp, back up to the door we had come out of, hoping no bullets would find us. We had to stop several times because we could not breathe. "We've got to keep moving.

Come on! Come on!" I urged them. We finally got to the door, and I found it locked.

We ran back down the ramp and got to the downstairs door. I grabbed at the handles and pulled and pulled. They would not open. They were also locked. A woman crouched down as she ran through the hail of bullets and splintering glass, pushed the lever on the door, held it slightly ajar, and we squeezed inside. Two carabinieri stood inside the door, not helping but also not trying to stop us. Glass was flying, and bullets were smacking into the concrete and the walls.

The Frasers were lying on the floor just inside the door, a pained, shocked look on their soot-blackened faces. They had burns on their hands and holes burned into their clothes. Their eyes spoke volumes and looked hollow and bereft, empty for the loss of their senses. George held his burned hands in the air, keeping them from touching the floor. A crouching reporter jumped in front of the Frasers and snapped their picture. *You've got to be nuts*, I thought. *You've got to be nuts*!

Several other people were lying on the floor, covering their heads with their arms, attempting to protect themselves from the flying shards, chipped concrete and bullets, and a reality check. Some of the people tried to scramble to safety. Others just lay where they were. Others were just too stunned to move and possibly couldn't. I asked the woman where the First Aid station was, and she pointed to the middle of the room and said, "It's behind that green wall—right over there."

I knew that Bonnie and Robyn needed to get first aid as soon as possible. I knew that my lungs wouldn't last much longer. We had to move—bullets or not. "Come on! come on!" I told them. *We can't just quit.*

The Frasers, Bonnie, Robyn, and I crawled about fifty feet to the block wall built halfway down a portion of the room. At one point, we had to stop as a burst from several machine guns fired, simultaneously riddling the remaining terminal windows.

...Keep moving...keep moving, come on, keep moving. We've got to get to the safe green wall. We ducked our heads from another hail of fire and kept pushing and crawling—ten more feet to safety.

Finally, finally, we reached the green wall. We stood up and plastered ourselves against the cool, cool bricks. For the first time in what seemed an eternity, we were away from the bombs, flying bullets, the horror, the smoke, and the shattering, flying glass. And, just like that, the shooting stopped.

We went into the first aid station, and to my amazement, a few people from our group were sitting or lying on tables. Where had all those other people come from? How and why were they in there? They weren't on the plane or the wing. Most were sitting on the edge of the tables. Some were lying down, stricken looks on their faces, deathly silent, their bodies still with shock. Those not from the plane looked at us in wide-eyed horror. Some simply turned their heads away—too much to handle. *What do we look like*? I wondered. *Why this look of horror*?

I just had to ensure that I did everything I could before I fell apart—*don't fall apart*—and could do nothing more. I went from person to person I knew and asked how they were and if they had seen Muriel or Barb. No one had seen them, even though I had hoped that Muriel would miraculously be in that safe, cool room. But she was absent, and so was Barb. *How could I face their families and friends and tell them I'd failed*? *How would I ever get over the guilt, and how could I ever look in the mirror at myself again*?

Bonnie and Robyn's skin was starting to dry. The pain on their faces was choking me up. My lungs and throat continued to swell. My airway was closing down. I was gasping for air.

...just a little bit longer, I told myself...*just a little bit longer...stay with Bonnie and Robyn just until...*

One by one, with Bonnie, Robyn, and I in the first ambulances, we were shuttled away—some going to one hospital, some to others, while those on the plane waited, still strapped in their seats, just waiting, just waiting for the plane to take off.

CHAPTER 4
More Trauma

I was strapped onto a gurney and rolled inside a cold ambulance. Heat would have done no good anyway. Within miles, I went into shock. My teeth chattered from the trembling; my hands shook uncontrollably, and I could no longer breathe. The driver pulled the hee-haw-wailing ambulance over to the side of the road. The next thing I remembered was one of the attendants propping me up, his hand on my back, and the driver returning to his seat. Obviously, the silver cord tethering my soul to my body stretched but did not break again. What the heck? Dead, but not dead? Is that what a "near-death experience" really is?

The attendant reached into a cooler, pulled out a thermos then gave me a drink that tasted like milk and brandy. I was surprised at being given alcohol, but I choked down what I could. I was shaking too much to hold the glass steady and swallow past the swelling in my throat. I don't know how it worked, but it did. I could finally take a breath without shaking. The attendant gently eased me back down.

Oh, God, oh, God, what happened today? *Where are Muriel and Barb, and Walker? Where are they taking Bonnie and Robyn*? "*Could I have done anything else, anything else*?" The questions plagued me like a festering, man-eating sore.

It seemed like it took a long time to get to the hospital, but it probably didn't—the roads were closed to all except emergency vehicles. As we zipped along, I thought about the animals and wondered if they were still wandering in and out, in and out of the houses.

Finally, we pulled into a brick-paved drive, and I saw a large, red brick building, several nurses and a doctor standing outside waiting for the attendants to roll me from the back of the now non-wailing ambulance.

Oh, God, oh, God, I'm scared. What if no one knows where I am? Where are the rest of the people from the group? What if the terrorists find me here? Who are they really after? What if they figure out I'm not really dead?

Still outside, they covered me with a blanket and undressed me. They strapped oxygen to me. Soon I was given a shot that knocked me out.

* * *

When I woke up, it was dark outside. I couldn't figure out where I was and couldn't figure out what day it was. I looked around and saw that I was in a ward with about twelve beds. The screen-less windows were open, and I saw cats perched on the sills.

Sweet Jesus, I chattered. *It's cold in here! What the hell? Where am I? This can't be a hospital. Look at the cats.* Then I noticed there were only three other patients in the ward. My throat hurt so much that I could not swallow without intense pain. Every bump and every sound I heard scared me so badly that I just wanted to run. A nurse wearing a goofy-looking hat came in and checked on me. I couldn't answer her questions because my throat was too swollen, and my lungs hurt so much it was horribly painful to get enough air to form words. All I could do was move my mouth like a beached fish. She gave me another shot, and I fell back to sleep.

A kind-faced older man stood next to my bed the next time I woke. He said he was from the United States Embassy and was there checking my condition. He asked if I needed a new passport. He told me they had been in contact with my mother and told her I had been moved to a ward because I was now in stable condition. I had no idea where I had been before this—only that I had been "unconscious." I got up the courage and croakily asked him who was dead. O*h, don't let this answer be what I think it is.* He looked away and said they did not have a list yet. *Good*, I thought, *a reprieve from the truth.*

I dozed again, and when I awoke, the man was gone, but a lady was sitting in the metal chair she had pulled up next to the bed. She introduced herself and said she was a reporter for the *London Times.* I asked her what time it was, and she said it was around 1:00 a.m. She said she had been sitting there for several hours.

She asked me if there was anyone she could contact for me and told me that she had spoken with my mother. I asked her about the other plane passengers, specifically Barb, Muriel, Robyn, and Bonnie. She had a paper with the survivors' and missing passengers' names. She told me that Bonnie and Robyn were in the same hospital as me but in another wing. Other survivors were at other hospitals. Barb and several other people were okay and at a hotel. She read the names of the survivors, and I had hope, but the short list of survivors stopped abruptly. She read the names of those still missing, and I felt a shredding of grief, but the tears were not yet coming. I was confused and wondered what "still missing" meant. Muriel and Russell were on the list as still missing, and I had also been on the list. I felt, quite frankly, like a failure and thought, *if I could have done more...if I could have done more.*

The reporter asked me questions, and I slowly, croakily told her what had happened in those terrifying minutes. I asked her if they knew who the terrorists were after on the plane, and as she shook her head in disdain, she said no one knew for sure. No one knew. I told her that I was afraid that the terrorists would come to the hospital and kill me and Robyn, and Bonnie.

She assured me they wouldn't, that we were well-guarded, and said the terrorists had hijacked another plane and, were gone, had flown into Athens making outrageous demands.

I asked her why the windows were open in the room because it was so cold in the ward, and she told me they left the windows open so the cats could take care of any mice in the building. I was surprised by her answer. I knew my mother's mouth would drop open if she heard and would get that crazed look on her face and in her eyes.

The horror of what had occurred in those few minutes of rampage was sinking in, and I knew I believed I would never feel joy again. I knew I would never know the serenity of building sandcastles, swimming in hurricane waves, riding a lift to the top of a snow-encrusted mountain, learning and singing Broadway shows with my actor friends, or experiencing the foliage of a New England autumn. I would never fly down the mountainside on a cafeteria tray or feel the experience of a new state and friends. My heart, very simply put, was just too broken.

When it became apparent I was in too much pain to answer any more of her questions, she asked if I wanted her to stay longer. She said she would be happy to sit with me even while I was sleeping, but I didn't feel I deserved kindness then or in the future. The reporter said she would stop by in the morning to see how I was doing. She left. I was alone—alone with my terror. Guilt and grief were ravaging my mind and seeping down to the end of my toes. I would never be the same, and I knew it, just knew it. The lump in my throat grew and grew and finally blew up in my chest and crushed what was left of my heart.

Once again, a nurse came in and gave me a shot. I slept like the dead the rest of the night.

* * *

A nurse woke me the following morning and gave me food I could not swallow. The reporter from the night before came by to see how I was doing. She showed me her paper with her terrorist article. It said I was one of the heroes. Nothing could have been further from the truth. If this is what being a hero feels like, I want no part of it.

The nurse returned. I asked her if I could see Bonnie and Robyn. In an accent, she looked at the floor and whispered, "No," she told me, "Robyn's in intensive care, and Bonnie died during the night of respiratory arrest from smoke inhalation." I was devastated. A cry ripped through my swollen throat.

Tuck it away, tuck it away…you can't take in one more thing today. The impact the news had on me had to be postponed.

She told me I could take a shower and I would be leaving within the hour. She told me men from the State Department were there to get me. She led me to a large shower room wide open to the world. It had one-inch frigid-cold creamy-white tiles on the floor and walls. She handed me my freshly laundered burn-holey clothes, pivoted on her heel, and left me alone.

I looked in the mirror. I still had thick soot between my nose and lips and was surprised that no one had bothered to wash it completely off. My hair had frayed tips from being singed, and patches of hair were shorter or missing. The eyes that looked back at me were empty and hollow. Any light there had been was now wholly extinguished.

After the shower, the nurse led me to an office where a doctor told me they were releasing me. I was startled. I still could barely swallow. Two somber-looking men wearing black suits, ties, and overcoats and holding black Nixon-era hats were in the office. They said they were from the U. S. State Department and showed me their credentials. I wondered if they were there to arrest me for a reason I had no clue about. One told me they were immediately getting me and the other Americans out of Rome. When I asked him why, he said because they didn't know who the terrorists were after. Then he asked if there was anything I needed. I told him I wanted to talk to my parents and didn't have a coat. He said they couldn't help me with the coat, but I had ten minutes for the call, and then we were leaving.

The doctor pointed toward a big black European rotary phone with a receiver that weighed several pounds and was attached to it by a string cord. Then, he left the room. One of the men dialed the phone number for me. I learned that my parents had spoken to Barb's parents, and her parents had spoken to Barb, who was in a hotel with a few other survivors. They had also talked to Muriel's son. Muriel was still missing and presumed to be among the dead. I still wasn't sure what those hopeless words meant. *Presumed,* I thought, *Perhaps there was still a chance.* I couldn't take that in right then. I didn't have the time. *Stuff it down deeper, don't let it come out.*

The unsmiling men and I exited the hospital through a side door, each man holding one of my arms as they hustled me outside. We got into the back seat of a black car and sped out onto the street. The driver drove like a maniac, weaving in and out of traffic and making numerous turns that didn't seem necessary to me. One of the men on either side of me kept looking out the back window, the other out the side windows, worried expressions glued to their faces.

The silence of the night had burst open with honks. Screeching tires and bellowing arms thrust out of open car windows blasted other drivers with foreign words and upraised fists and middle fingers.

Suddenly we stopped. The men pulled me out of the car and onto the sidewalk. We jumped into a cab, and one of the men ordered the driver to drive as fast as he could to the place he gave him in a foreign tongue. We screeched to a stop in the middle of a block. One man said something in Italian to the driver. He nodded. They exchanged no money. The other man threw the door open. They took my arms, one on each side, pulled and pushed me out of the car, and we took off running. They looked behind us numerous times as we raced through a tunnel with me wheezing like a high note on a bagpipe with a hole in its skin. They finally shoved my arms to my side, cocked them at ninety degrees, picked me up by my elbows, and carried me through the last half of the tunnel.

We jumped into a waiting bulky black car and sped back into the traffic. Again, the driver took numerous turns and wove in and out of jammed lines of vehicles, with the two men beside me watching anxiously out the back and side windows. I asked them who the terrorists were after on that plane, and they told me, once again, that they still didn't know. He said they were trying to get the Americans out of Italy as quickly as possible, just in case, just in case a sentence unfinished.

We raced down the highway to the airport with the goats, pigs, and chickens wandering in and out of the houses flying by in a blur. The only sound in the car now was the whine of the tires sucking the moisture off the damp road.

I wondered, *Will my stomach muscles ever relax again? Don't think. Don't think until you get out of here.*

We arrived at Fiumicino Airport. The car abruptly halted at the curb. The men took my arms and hustled me into the terminal, the last place I ever wanted to see again. They took me into the First Class waiting room for the jinxed, vulnerable Pam American Airways. They led me to a chair in a row of four along the wall perpendicular to the door. One man spoke to the lady at the desk. She looked at me and nodded; then he left; the other man stood beside me, scanning the room but never spoke a word; his lips closed—checking, watching, his eyes flitting around. *This can't be happening. What am I thinking*?

Ten minutes later, the missing man reentered the waiting room and handed me a boarding pass for a Pan Am flight. I felt light-headed and thought I was going to vomit. I asked if there was any way I could fly on another airline. He said no. Pan Am was paying for my escaping flight home. I wasn't even sure if Pan Am paid for it—perhaps the State Department did.

Realization hit me. I snorted. This pass was the replacement ticket for the return ticket home from Saudi Arabia.

I asked him where I was supposed to go, what I was supposed to do when I got to New York. He said someone from the State Department would meet me at the plane and tell me where I was supposed to go next. I asked if anyone from our ARAMCO group would be flying back, and he said no, I was the only one going.

The men in black waited around for a short time, and after telling me to help myself to the food and drink, they abruptly left. Oddly, I didn't want them to go. They had surprisingly made me feel safe. I didn't want to be left alone. I looked around to see if I had lost my mind and wondered if what I had experienced had happened or if I was seeing a movie or having a horrible nightmare.

I must have been an eye-averting, disturbing sight. Even though the nurses had washed my clothes, they had burn holes, and patches of my hair were missing. I was embarrassed by my appearance and wondered if someone would drop some money in my lap or kick me out of the first-class lounge. Yes, people did avert their eyes. They seemed to know. The Pan Am attendant wandered over to where I sat several times and asked me if I was okay. No one sat near me, and I really can't blame them. No matter how hard I scrubbed, the smell of smoke and disaster would cling of my clothing, body, and psyche for a long, long time.

I had no appetite but took a little quartered sandwich with the crust trimmed off—just like those goofy sandwiches mom felt compelled to make to show how cultured we'd become after moving from the farm. I took one bite of the food and found it scratched my throat like a Brillo pad, and the liquid burned all the way down. I just gave up on trying to eat or drink.

I sat alone in the row against the wall, bowed my head, and stared at the greyish-blue carpet. I was speechless by that time. How was I supposed to talk to anyone, especially strangers, about what had happened? My brain was numb. I couldn't imagine ever speaking or thinking again. I wished I had never thrown that damn nickel into Trevi Fountain.

* * *

I was in that room for what seemed like hours before two carabinieri came directly to me.

I looked up, startled. *Where had I been*?

They led me and the other first-class passengers out of a door that opened directly onto the tarmac. The sounds of jet engines and the smell of jet exhaust assailed my senses. My heart started to hammer from the memory of the event. They took us and my leaden feet to a waiting armored, open-topped military vehicle with soldiers armed with rifles standing guard surrounding it. The vehicle looked like it could land on the beach or float in the ocean. The other first-class passengers and I sat on the benches inside the craft while armed guards stood inside with their rifles loaded at the ready. I anxiously rode in the vehicle to the airplane, waiting for a sniper to pop out and blow my head off. My vision became distorted. I couldn't tell if the armed men by the plane were policemen, soldiers, or terrorists.

When I looked up and saw that plane, I froze and almost threw up. There was no way I was going to be able to get on that plane and especially with that blue "meatball" logo on the tail that screamed out, "PAN AM"!

Someone asked me if I was alright, and as I sat trembling, I told them I was on the plane the terrorists blew up. They looked stricken and acted like they didn't want to get on the plane with me, but they were sweet to me anyway and told me that it would be okay—obviously, we were well-guarded—at least these men had their guns pulled, at least now I was seated in an armored track-tank.

Once I exited the rubber-tracked vehicle, it didn't take long to race up the steps because I didn't want to be caught unguarded, unarmed, or un-dressed in the middle of that tarmac. I looked over to my left at where our plane had sat, and it looked as mundane as the sun rising every morning, even though there was a big splotch on the concrete. *Perhaps it didn't happen...perhaps it was just a dream.*

I was the last on the plane and escorted to my seat by two very kind flight attendants—one in front of me and one in back of me. Once I sat down, I kept anxiously thinking, *Close the doors. Close the doors so they can't come in.* The doors on flight 110 were left yawning open, and the terrorists had marched right up, tossed their grenades and bombs inside, and then blasted away at innocent people.

It seemed like an interminably long time before the doors clunked closed, even though it only took seconds. I thought about the statement about getting back on the horse, but this was like no horse that I ever knew. It took every nerve I had not to jump up and run and order them to let me back out.

My seat was about a third of the way back on the plane's left side, looking out at the terminal. Fortunately for my sanity, the airplane was parked at the other end of the airport from where we had tried to leave the day before. The other end was closed. The windows were missing.

* * *

I couldn't believe it. Pan Am seated me in the tourist section of the plane. You would think they would have put me in first class.

However, they did give me the aisle seat in the emergency exit row. A couple sat next to me. Shortly after takeoff, the man opened an Italian newspaper. He was looking at the pictures and commenting to his wife about how horrible the pictures were and what a disturbing, disgusting thing the attack had been.

I lost it then; I just broke down and wept. Somewhere in my mind, perhaps I had thought it was all a dream and didn't happen. But, there it was, in black and white on thin muslin-colored paper for the whole world to see.

The man asked me if I was alright, and I told him I'd been on that plane. I am sure that flight was the most uncomfortable flight they had ever been on. They looked like they wanted to crawl out of their seats, move as far away from me as possible, or get off the plane completely. By then, I was sobbing and blubbering and had snot dripping off my lip and figured that they would soon take me away in an arm-binding straight jacket.

A short time into the flight, one of the stewardesses kneeled beside me and asked if I would come to the first-class section as someone there wanted to see me. I followed her, and she led me to a large, plush seat. Sitting there was the stewardess, who (I thought) was the last off of the plane.

She introduced herself as Lari Hamel, and we hugged each other and cried like lost sisters. She told me that she had been in first class, and when the terrorist tossed the bomb inside the plane, the passengers started running. When the bomb went off, she was knocked down, and several people fell on top of her. The terrorist shot into the pile of people and killed all of them but Lari, who was at the bottom of the heap. She told me she played dead.

I told her I remembered the pop, pop, pop sounds—so that was the terrorist I ran into at the first-class curtain. She said when she was sure the terrorists were gone, she crawled out from under the bodies and ran to the exit over the wing.

I stared at her and told her I remembered her soot-blackened face and disheveled head peeking out of the emergency door, then stepping out onto the wing. I told her that when I saw her that I couldn't believe my eyes. By then, I was at the foot of the stairs, telling Robyn and Bonnie that it was safe for them to come down. She came out of that door a full four minutes after I did. I saw her jump off the tall side of the wing and run to the terminal. All I could think was that that girl must have had a set of lungs on her.

Then I wondered, "*What happened to the pilots and the rest of the flight crew? Why was there only one man who helped me catch people jumping off the wing of the plane? Why were the passengers still on the plane left to fend for themselves, and why was no one there to tell us what direction to go? Surely they wouldn't have just abandoned us in the middle of that tarmac!* I shoved those thoughts away, just glad that Lari was alive.

For some reason, talking to Lari helped ease my anxiety. We exchanged addresses and phone numbers, and both got very quiet. I felt safe sitting with Lari, but the stewardess told me I couldn't stay in first class despite several empty seats. Lari and I were both survivors and now had an inexplicable bond.

I returned to my seat and saw the frightened looks of my seatmates, who'd been reading their newspapers. I sat down quietly with an apologetic smile that probably looked like a grimace if someone played the reel in slow motion. The man handed the two newspapers to me and told me to keep them. I wondered what else they would give me to keep me from crying. I tucked the papers in the seat pocket before me and fell into a deep, unhearing, unmoving sleep.

* * *

The Captain instructed passengers to stay seated when we landed in New York at JFK. Amazingly, everyone complied. An airline employee entered the cabin and came directly to me. He said to follow him and immediately led me, Lari, and a dark-haired woman to the front of the plane. It was freezing in New York, and I didn't have a coat, so I started to shiver when I stepped off the plane. The jet engine exhaust fumes were intense and harsh on my sensitized nose, but I couldn't help myself. I actually smiled. State Department officials were waiting at the walkway for us. They hustled us past customs, which surprised me. Well, we didn't have anything to claim. I just had my purse and newspapers. Lari and the woman with her also had nothing to declare. As soon as we left customs, two men latched onto me, and two stayed with Lari and the woman with her. I was taken in a half run in the opposite direction of Lari, through the airport, with reporters behind a black rope yelling questions at me and flashbulbs popping. I would later see that it was Lari's disheveled soot-covered, tear-streaked, distraught face that was on the front of almost every newspaper in the free world. I found out later that mine was on the front page of newspapers in my home state.

Once again, the men pushed me into the back seat of a behemoth black car that sped away from the terminal. I was taken a short distance to, of all things possible—there it was, the Pan Am Hotel. *Sweet Jesus, what the hell*! I was tired beyond words and aching and hurting inside and out, from the top of my head to the bottom of my feet. One of the men flashed his badge at the desk in the lobby. The clerk immediately handed him the room key. The other man and I stood behind a pillar—his eyes darting all over the room. They walked me to the door of my room, gave me a food voucher, and said they would be at my door at 5:00 a.m. but would not tell me where they would be taking me. By then, I was a nervous wreck. *Why*, I wondered, *why the Pan Am Hotel*? *Was it another one of their generous gifts*?

I wanted to go outside and kiss the ground but had strict orders not to leave the hotel. The men in black had told me not to talk to anyone about what had happened, not to tell anyone who I was, and not to leave the hotel with anyone. They still didn't know who the terrorists were after. And besides, I looked like a crazed person with my holey clothing, singed, patchy hair, and the new blank look in my eyes.

I bathed, climbed back into my smoky, peculiar-smelling clothing, sucked in my scratchy breath, peered into the hallway to see if anyone awaited me, raced to the elevator, and entered the dining area. I had a choice between the dining room and the cafe. I chose the cafe and shimmied up to the counter. I had a food voucher and could have had a steak in the dining room with white linen napkins, but I chose to go to the cafe so that I could have, of all things available, a cheeseburger, fries, and a Coke. What could be more American than that? And so I sat there and choked down some of my food while grinning like a

Cheshire cat, a Cheshire cat with a dual-edged secret that no one in that restaurant could possibly know.

I slept fitfully that night; every time a door slammed, I jumped up and almost ran. Whenever I heard the banging, I thought a terrorist had entered the room.

At 4:52 a.m., there was a knock on the door. Through the peephole, I saw two new black-suited, black hat-wearing, silent G-men waiting for me. The men last night said they would be at the door. I asked where the other men were, and they told me they were off duty. Once again, they hustled me out the door into a black, hulking sedan.

We raced to the helipad in Manhattan, where the men pushed me onto a helicopter. It took off instantly, and the next thing I knew, I was at the airport in Newark, New Jersey, where another man met me. The man-in-black handed me a ticket for a plane flying to Chicago. There were no reporters this time.—perhaps it was too early. I kept asking each man from the State Department who the terrorists were after. The pat answer was always, "We don't know who they are after. They could be after any of the passengers." *Jesus. Can't anyone answer*?

By the time I landed in Chicago, I was on my own. The terrorists had been caught—the nightmare was over. Every time I got on a plane, I did not take a deep breath until the doors were closed. I felt more relief at every mile put between me and the hijacking. I wished again that I had never thrown that damn nickel into Trevi Fountain.

No more State Department guys raced me to gates, into and out of cars, through tunnels, and in and out of cabs. I was stunned. Had I stepped into a time warp?

When I landed in Des Moines, my parents, sister, and her family were waiting at the gate, as were numerous TV and newspaper cameras and loud, pushy reporters.

My dad hugged me and started to cry. I had never seen him cry, except at his mother's funeral, or hug me like he did, for that matter. It was quite disturbing because, by that time, I think my brain had ceased to make sense of anything anymore, and my fear and exhaustion were loud and palpable. The reporters shot numerous questions, and I answered what they asked while trying to sound like I wasn't wholly frazzled and insane. We finally left the airport and started the hour drive home.

My parents didn't talk to me or each other. The silence was worse than the questions. I wanted to talk and talk and talk about what had happened in the last forty-eight hours…forty minutes to take over an entire airport, to destroy and kill seventeen people I knew and commandeer another airliner. The silence from the front seat just fed my guilt. I wondered if they blamed me for Muriel's death. Of course, I didn't know the story of what was behind the silence until later. What my dad told me stunned me, yet it didn't surprise me. He told me he had been in Omaha when the attack happened. He saw it on the news. He called my mom, who refused to tell him if I was alive or dead. She just said I was among the missing. He got in his van and drove pell-mell through a snowstorm toward home. He hit the interstate and came to a dead stop. The truckers were on strike, and the trucks were blocking the road. He frantically spoke to a truck driver who radioed ahead to the truckers along I-80. Each one of those truckers pulled their rigs aside to let my dad through. Even when he got home, my mom wouldn't give him an answer. He wouldn't find out the truth until he was on the phone extension when I called from the hospital.

The following morning after I got up and got dressed in some borrowed clothes to go clothes shopping, I reached into my purse. I pulled out my stocking hat, and a dried hunk of someone's body fell into my hand. Standing there watching, my mom's eyes widened; she turned her head, then looked at the floor.

Deceased

(Information in brackets is who the "ARAMCO employee" was visiting in Saudi Arabia.)

Abdelatif, Inani, Moroccan state secretary for economic planning.
Berka, Muriel, 53, Iowa, ARAMCO employee, [mother-in-law to Wally Stoelzel].
DeAngelo, Giuliano, 35, Teheran, Iran, Alitalia clerk.
DeAngelo, Mrs. Emma Zanghi, 34, his wife.
DeAngelo, Monica, 9, his daughter.
Erbeck, Bonnie, wife of the pilot.
Echmenn, Henrietta, ARAMCO employee, [mother of Margaret Echmenn].
Filipe, Miss, Portugal.
Ghormley, Robert, ARAMCO employee, [student son of employee R. E. Ghormley].
Heywood, Charles Walker, ARAMCO employee, [student son of C. P. Haywood].
Hildebrand, Clarence, Marshalltown, Iowa, ARAMCO employee, [brother of Mrs. Alex Szostel].
Hildebrand, Thelma, Marshalltown, Iowa, ARAMCO employee, [wife of Clarence].

Julavitis, Miss Pamela [should be Miss Patricia], Franklin, IN, ARAMCO employee, [niece of Mrs. Robert Oertley].
Kempf, Miss Emily, Denver, ARAMCO employee, [mother of J. Leadbeater].
Kirby, Jane, 19, student at Harding College, Searcy, AR., ARAMCO employee, [daughter of D. R. Kirby].
Kirby, Randy, 21, student at Harding College, Searcy, AR., ARAMCO employee, [son of D. R. Kirby].
Lazrak, Mohammad, general secretary at the Moroccan Ministry of Commerce and Industry.
Martin, Mary, Denver, CO, ARAMCO employee, [sister of Julia Hunt].
Narcisco, Raffaele, 41, an Italian mining expert.
Perez, Diana, Pan Am purser.
Presnell, Bonnie, 20, Greenback, TN, died of severe burns in the hospital, ARAMCO employee, [niece of Dr. Barton Haggard].
Rodrigues, Miss, Portugal.
Rountree, Mrs. Bruce, Columbus, OH, ARAMCO employee.
Tuninga, Lambert, 47, Rome, Pan American catering.
Turner, Russell, 12, ARAMCO employee, [son of W. B. Turner].
Wamp, Mary, Dansville, NY, ARAMCO employee, [mother of Schlumberger employee Wamp].
Wilson, Margaret, Houston, ARAMCO employee. [mother-in-law of Al Dowell]
Wouters, Miss, Belgium, ARAMCO employee.
Zailacpii, Mekki, Attache to Moroccan Premier's Office.
Zietteman, A., Johannesburg, South Africa

Survivors

Anderson, M.E., [visiting M. C. Anderson].
Blythe, Elsie, [visiting LaFlammes].
DiGioia, William, [DiGioia family visiting the Huddlestons].
DiGioia, D.
DiGioia, G.
DiGioia, J.
Elkins, Lloyd, [visiting son Lloyd].
Elkins, Virginia, [" " "].
Fraser, George, [visiting the De St. Croix].
Fraser, Dorothy, [" " "].
Geisler, Bonnie (hospitalized), 24, [visiting the Stoelzels].
Gulpiruck, Miss S. (hospitalized).
Haggard, Robyn (hospitalized), 16, student, [daughter of Dr. Haggard].
January, Mildred, [visiting the Lowmans].
Kowsarmada, Mrs. N.
Manion, Agnes, [mother-in-law of P. J. Halpin].
Manion, Francis V., [father-in-law of P. J. Halpin].
McKinney, Barbara, 22, [niece of Rosemary Stoelzel].
Noguchi, Mr. R.
Penaherrera, Mr.
Pizzinelli.

Stoessel, E.
Tabor, Adoph.C., [visiting the Tabors].
Tabor, N., [" " "].
Wakitojar, Mr. S.
Wilson, Travis, [father-in-law of Al Dowell].

Pan Am Employees who survived:

Erbeck, Capt. Andrew C., Las Vegas.
Davison, First Officer Robert C., Stamford, CT.
Pfrang, Kenneth M., engineer, Plymouth, WI.
Franco, Dominic K., purser, Commack, NY.
Jacobson, Linda C., stewardess, Milton, MA.
Marnock, Barbara R., stewardess, Winter Park, FL.
Dyer, Sharon G., stewardess, Albany, NY.
Hamil, Laurette R., stewardess, Bedford, MA.
Parrott, First Officer John D., off-duty pilot riding with passengers, Kew Gardens, Queens.[1]

(For a video of the aftermath of Pan Am 110, go to youtube.com/ SYND 17 12 73 SCENE AFTER ATTACK BY PALESTINIAN GUERILLAS ON PAN AM PLANE.)

How accurate was Pan Am's list versus the U. S. Embassy? The following is an "Un-classified" document from the U. S. Embassy. Notice how many errors they made. Somehow they married me off, lost me, then found me in the hospital. At first, they told my mother that I was among the "missing." She, of course, didn't tell my father I wasn't "missing." Also, they had Mrs. in front of names that should have been Miss and Miss in front of names that should have been Mrs. Some said to be in the hospital were deceased. They also misspelled many names. They

1 Pan Am World Airways, New York, and "Terrorist Attack in Rome Airport, December-1973," *Aramco Ex Pats*. https://www.aramcoexpats.com/obituaries/terrorist-attack-in-the-rome-airport-december-1973/.

got one survivor's name right versus Pan Am's version, but I would not learn that for almost fifty years. Unfortunately, this is the list that got sent to the families in Saudi Arabia awaiting our group's arrival.

PANAM PASSENGER LIST

Date:	Canonical ID:
1973 December 17, 19:00 (Monday)	1973ROME14015_b
Original Classification:	Current Classification:
LIMITED OFFICIAL USE	UNCLASSIFIED
Handling Restrictions	Character Count:
-- N/A or Blank --	2546
Executive Order:	Locator:
-- N/A or Blank --	TEXT ONLINE
TAGS:	Concepts:
CASC - Consular Affairs--Assistance to Citizens | IT - Italy | PAN AM - Pan American World Airways | PFIN | PINS - Political Affairs--Internal Security | US - United States	AIRCRAFT HIJACKING | DISASTER VICTIMS | PARAMILITARY FORCES | PASSENGER LIST | UNCONVENTIONAL WARFARE
Enclosure:	Type:
-- N/A or Blank --	TE – Telegram (cable)
Office Origin:	Archive Status:
-- N/A OR BLANK –	Electronic Telegrams
Office Action:	
ACTION SCS – SPECIAL CONSULAR SERVICES	

From: Markings:

ITALY ROME

Declassified/Released US Department of State EO

Systematic Review 30 JUN 2005

To:

STATE DHAHRAN |
SAUDI ARABIA DHAHRAN
| SAUDI ARABIA JEDDAH |
SECRETARY OF STATE

7. PANAM REP ROME HAS PROVIDED EMBASSY, IN STRICT CONFIDENCE, WITH LIST OF PASSENGERS WHO SHOULD HAVE, REPEAT SHOULD HAVE, BOARDED PANAM FLIGHT 110 AT ROME. FOLLOWING IS BREAKDOWN OF PANAM LIST SHOWING THOSE HOSPITALIZED, THOSE WHO HAVE REPORTED TO HOTELS,AND THOSE NOT YET ACCOUNTED FOR.

2. PASSENGERS HOSPITALIZED (TOTAL 8):

MISS GULPIRUCK
MR. S. WAKITOVAR
MRS. KOWSARMADA
MR. RANDALL KIRBY
R.T. HAGGARD
MRS. BONNIE PRESNELL
MR. GEORGE FRASER
D. FRASER
LIMITED OFFICIAL USE
LIMITED OFFICIAL USE

PAGE 02 ROME 14015 171932Z

3. PASSENGERS RELEASED FROM HOSPITAL AND/OR IN HOTEL (TOTAL 12):

MR. R. NOGUCHI
M. JANUARY LLOYD ELKINS

MRS. VIRGINIA ELKINS
A.C. TABOR
N. TABOR (CHILD)
D. DI GIOIA
G. DI GIOIA
J. DI GIOIA
W. DI GIOIA
M.E. ANDERSON
E. BLYTHE

4. PASSENGERS NOT YET ACCOUNTED FOR (TOTAL 45):

MISS F. RODRIQUEZ
MISS FILIPE
MISS W. WOUTERS
MR. M. ZAILACHI
MR. IMANI ABDELLATIF
MR. LAZRAK
MR. MOUNIR DOUKKALI
MR. PECO MR. NARCISO
MR. E. STOESSEL
MR. A. ZIETSMAN
MR. PENA HERRERA
H. ECKMAN
N. WAMP
MISS P. JULAVITIS
MR. HEYWOOD WALKER
T. HILDEBRAND
C. HILDEBRAND
MISS A. MANION
F. MANION
R. GHORNCEY
MRS.E. KEMPF
T. WILSON
M. WILSON
MISS KIRBY
LIMITED OFFICIAL USE LIMITED OFFICIAL USE

PAGE 03 ROME 14015 171932Z

MRS. MARY MARTIN
MRS. BONNIE GEISLER
MR. RUSSELL TURNER
MISS MURIEL DERKA
MRS. ROUNTREE
MRS. BARBARA MCKINNEY
MR. L. TUNINGA
DE ANGELIS
DE ANGELIS
DE ANGELIS
PAN AM CREW:
PAN AM CREW:
CAPT. W.H. ERBECK
FIRST OFFICER R. DAVIDSON
D.H.D.PARROT
K. ELRANG S. [I assume this is Pfrang]
FRANCO D.
PEREZ
JACOBSON
B. MARNOCK
S. DYER
L. HAMEL

5. TOTAL LISTED IN PARAS 2, 3 AND 4 ABOVE IS 65 RPT 65 PERSONS.

6. AFTER ABOVE WAS DRAFTED EMBASSY LEARNED FROM PANAM THAT ALL OF PANAM CREW LISTED ABOVE HAS REPORTED INTO HOTEL EXCEPT ONE. MISS- ING CREW MEMBER IS PRESUMED TO BE DEAD PERSON FOUND ABOARD PLANE IN PANAM WOMAN'S UNIFORM. MISSING CREW MEMBER IS D. PEREZ.

7. EMBASSY NOW LEARNS MRS. BONNIE GEISLER IS IN HOSPITAL AND NOT REPEAT NOT UNACCOUNTED FOR. VOLPE

IMITED OFFICIAL USE

NNN

* * *

Half the people in the following image would die that day. Randy and Jane Kirby are not in the photo because their connector flight to New York was late. Shortly after this photo was taken, we met them hurrying down the hallway.

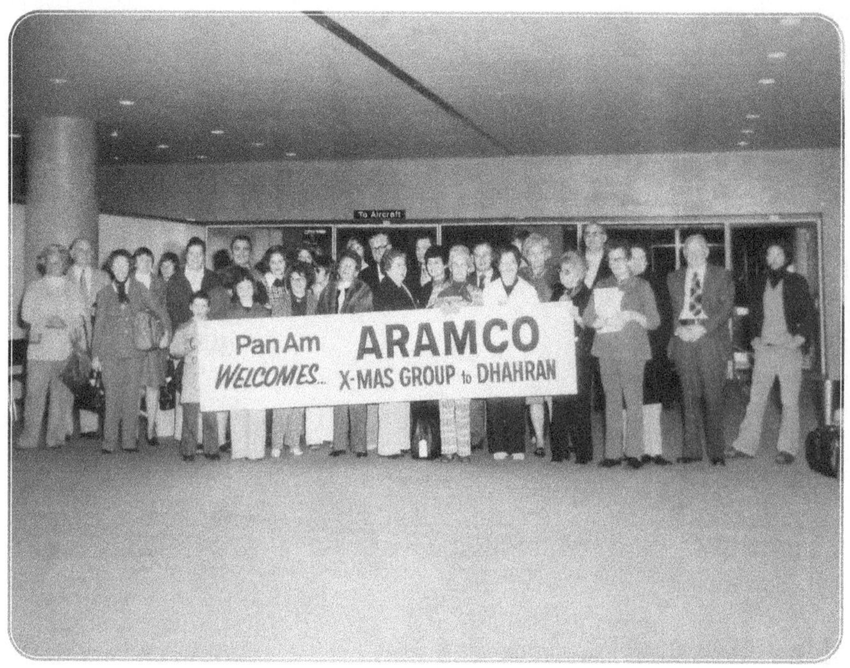

Astrological Chart 1

December 17, 1973, at 1:05 pm

The most dangerous aspect is the first house Mars at 28-Aries in opposition to 7th house Uranus at 26-Libra. This indicates sudden wounds, gunfire, and explosions to the body. This volatile aspect also falls in the author's 1st and 7th house. The first house represents your body, and because Mars is in Aries, your head is going to get hurt [even psychologically]. The 7th house represents the attacker, your open enemies, which will be odd, irrational, unpredictable, erratic, or sudden (lightning strike). The 1st and 7th house are in opposition which means that someone else was going to push her around and she will push back. Uranus was sextile the sun, so males would help her. Uranus [terrorists/ outlaws] was trine Saturn (old men/ authority), so people in authority stepped up to the challenge and saved people by helping her [State Department officials]. Mars (young men) is sextile Saturn, which is old men, and they worked together to save lives (EMT's, doctors, State Department Officials). The next dangerous aspect is the 3rd house Saturn 1-Cancer is square to the 6th house conjunction of the Moon 5-Libra and Pluto 6-Libra. Moon square Saturn is danger to women. Saturn square Pluto means that women will die. Pluto was exactly conjunct the author's Natal Sun which means that the author died that day or almost did. The heroes of that day were often women because the besieged Moon/Pluto was also trine Venus/Jupiter in the 10th house. The fact that anyone survived this tragedy is a miracle. The chart also shows that she was divinely guided that day. –Joy Archer

(This chart also showed almost every planet lined up in an absolute horizontal line. The astrological chart for Rome that day shows disaster.)

CHAPTER 5

More Mistakes Were Yet To Come

We're not done with the errors because Pan Am's "World Wings International, Inc." report states the following conflicting reports about December 17, 1973:

World Wings International, Inc.
dSnseoptor00b3llu8m3e0c8cu5i2h Dmrc41m1c
746904u,6e8h90g1he5

> On December 16, 1973, a Pan Am JFK based 707 cabin crew was on a layover in Rome. That night they had champagne and caviar at the Metropole Hotel before heading to the ballet.
>
> The next morning they headed to Fiumicino Airport to work PA110 to Beirut and Tehran. While they were boarding the Captain came over the PA. He told the passengers and FAs [Flight Attendants] there was trouble in the terminal and to stay away from the windows. Stewardess Lari Hamel began translating the Captain's

warning in Italian. Purser Diana Perez screamed to Lari, "Oh my God, Lari, they're coming on the airplane!."

Terrorists threw a grenade into the 1L [First Class left side] door killing Diana. The terrorists also came into the cabin from the 2L[Second Class left side] door. They started throwing grenades, white phosphorus bombs, and shooting passengers. A terrorist went to shoot the Aft Purser Dominic Franco, but he was out of bullets. The terrorists then ran to a Lufthansa 737 parked nearby and hijacked it.

Flight Attendant Barbara Marnock and Flight Engineer Ken Pfrang opened the overwing exits and lead passengers to safety. Flight Attendants Sharon Dyer and Linda Jacobson armed the 2R [Economy right side] door and deployed the slide. Lari Hamel was knocked unconscious and came to under a pile of dead First Class passengers. She crawled to the overwing exits and was the last person to leave the plane alive. Purser Diana Perez and 28 passengers died in the terrorist attack on Pan Am 110 in Rome on December 17, 1973. Among the dead passengers was Bonnie Erbeck, the wife of Captain Andrew Erbeck. She was sitting in First Class tagging along on her husband's trip. They had planned to explore Tehran together.

On December 16, 1973, a Pan Am JFK based 707 cabin crew was on a layover in Rome. That night they had champagne and caviar at the Metropole Hotel before heading to the ballet.

The next morning they headed to Fiumicino Airport to work PA110 to Beirut and Tehran. While they were boarding the Captain came over the PA. He told the passengers and FAs that there was trouble in the terminal and to stay away from the windows. Stewardess Lari Hamel began translating the Captain's warning in Italian. Purser Diana Perez screamed to Lari, "Oh my God, Lari, they're coming on the airplane!."

Terrorists threw a grenade into the 1L door killing Diana. The terrorists also came into the cabin from the 2L door. They started throwing grenades, white phosphorus bombs, and shooting passengers. A terrorist went to shoot the Aft Purser Dominic Franco, but he was out of bullets. The terrorists then ran to a Lufthansa 737 parked nearby and hijacked it.

Flight Attendant Barbara Marnock and Flight Engineer Ken Pfrang opened the overwing exits and lead passengers to safety. Flight Attendants Sharon Dyer and Linda Jacobson armed the 2R door and deployed the slide. Lari Hamel was knocked unconscious and came to under a pile of dead First Class passengers. She crawled to the overwing exits and was the last person to leave the plane alive. Purser Diana Perez and 28 passengers died in the terrorist attack on Pan Am 110 in Rome on December 17, 1973. Among the dead passengers was Bonnie Erbeck, the wife of Captain Andrew Erbeck. She was sitting in First Class tagging along on her husband's trip. They had planned to explore Tehran together.

Return to the Pan Am record and count how many people they listed as "Deceased." There are 30 listed, not 28. That is incorrect because one on the list did not die on the plane, but one died later, still making the total dead 30. That still is inaccurate because the final tally would be 31. The terrorists killed one on the tarmac for a total of 32. If you compare the U. S. Embassy list to the Pan-Am list, you will still find 29 dead, not counting Bonnie Presnell, who died that night. Add the body killed on the tarmac in Rome and the body dropped on the runway in Athens, Greece, and the total murdered by the terrorists is 33, the correct number.

In one report, Aft Purser Dominic Franco states he tried to hide in the server cart but couldn't get under it. Bonnie and Robyn said two Pan Am employees hid in the other lavatory. Was it Dominic, or was another Pan Am employee in the back of the plane? Would I be able to solve this mystery?

Who was the man who said he "lead people to safety" in the World Wings report? He was the aft purser Dominic Franco who the Embassy listed as being hospitalized. When Dominic was running up the aisle, he was leading no one to safety, nor did he grab or direct me to follow him as he ran for his life. He most assuredly did not slow down enough to check and see if any of the people in the seats or lying in between the seats were still alive. But one caveat exists: He was coherent enough to notice Lari's underwear brand. But is this the end of the Dominic story? Did Dominic end up leading people to safety? I would find the answer to that question forty-nine years later.

According to an article in the book, "Pan Am Personal Tribute to A Global Aviation Pioneer," Lari (Laurette) Hamel wrote, in her story entitled "Fury at Fiumicino,"

> December 17, 1973, Our crew had been together all month and we had worked well as a team and become good friends. The night before we had seen Giselle with ballerina Natalie Makarova. The next day we boarded Clipper Celestial for Beirut and Tehran but were delayed due to a late inbound flight from New York.
>
> Purser Diana Perez and I were working the first class cabin when Captain Andrew Erbek made an announcement telling us there was trouble in the terminal and ordered us to get on the floor and stay away from the windows. I was the language-qualified flight attendant so I grabbed the PA and threw myself on the floor translating his announcement. Diana was perched on a seat looking

out of a window and screamed, "Oh my God, Lari, they're coming to the airplane!"

From her tone I knew that 'they' were not good. Running into the galley I tried to hook up the slide but my hands were shaking so badly that I could not slip the hook into the floor D-ring. There was a huge explosion as two terrorists threw a hand grenade. We were in a 707, a large aluminum tube, and the blast was so great that I flew through the air, landing by the first row of seats in first class. First Officer Bob Davison later told me that as I flew through the air I shouted, "I've been hit." Several passengers fell on top of me when the terrorists threw another grenade, then threw a white phosphorous bomb and began shooting anyone who moved.

I was on the bottom of the pile and passed out. When I came to, it was deadly silent except for the sound of a fire. I began screaming at the passenger on top of me to move but everyone was dead. Reaching up to dislodge them I would grab pieces of bodies, a foot in a shoe or someone's hand. I finally managed to get out but everything in the airplane was on fire and the air was black. My contact lenses had burned in my eyes. I tried to reach the forward door but it was blocked by several burning objects. Coughing, I tried to go to the wing exits but still could not see. At one point I stood up to feel for the bump on the hat rack that would indicate the wing exit but an oxygen bottle exploded. When I fell to the floor I ended up back in first class.

Despondent, I turned around and crawled toward the wing exits again. I saw a light gray through the blackness, crawled toward it, and escaped.

After exiting the airplane, I stood on the wing and began retching black material. The surviving crew stood near the wing and shouted, "Jump, jump!" The airplane's going to explode." They had been told that explosive plastique had been attached to our full fuel tanks. I jumped and Dominic, the aft section purser caught me in mid-air. "Why, Lari, what beautiful Pucci underwear you have," he commented. "Why, thank you, Dominic." To which he responded, "Let's get the hell out of here."

We began to run and hid behind a large barrel. Already hiding there was a carabineri (Italy's military police). I screamed at him to go after the terrorists that I had just seen boarding a Lufthansa 737 and he replied, "They're crazy. I'm not going to get killed!"

A little girl around four years old was running, crying, "Mommy, Mommy!" I ran to hug her then grabbed her hand and told Dominic I was taking her to safety and would meet up with him later. The terminal entrance was blocked by another carabineri with a machine gun. He asked for my passport. I told him I did not have one, that I had been on Pan Am 110 that was still on fire. He was adamant. No passport, no entry.

Irate, I stormed past him yelling, "So shoot me, everyone else is." We found the Alitalia VIP lounge, and the attendant agreed to take the little girl. She begged me not to leave her and then she began to cry. When I started to leave the lounge to return to help our passengers, everyone surrounded me, crying and hugging me in the Italian fashion, telling me that it was not safe. I returned to the area near our airplane where there were ambulances.

> Dominic and I started translating who needed to be in the first ambulances. Most passengers died of burns at the hospital. [Only one person died in the hospital of burns—Bonnie Presnell. Most were treated for their burns, smoke inhalation, broken ear drums, and shock and released that night or the next day.] We then went to Pan Am Operations and made lists of where passengers were sitting, who was with whom, and who was missing. I finally found the parent of the little girl, hysterical with happiness knowing that she was safe. We stayed at Operations until dusk.
>
> Exhausted, we finally took taxis to our hotel. We were all crying, telling and retelling our horrific experiences. Even our taxi driver cried. This incident by Palestinian terrorists proved to be my most life-changing event.
>
> The company subsequently told me that I had been on the airplane, not for hours as I had thought, but merely 22 minutes. Diana died in the first explosion; we buried only her gold wings.[2]

At least now I know where the two Pan Am flight attendants, one of whom was Dominic Franco, who shot past me in the plane and out the emergency door ended up. Notice how Lari said she couldn't reach the 1L door because "several burning objects blocked it"?

According to the Italian newspaper *Il Messaggero*, December 18, 2017, which I translated,

> **12,50** [12:50 p.m.] At the transit hall of the international airport Fiumicino, a group of people shows up: They

[2] Jeff Kriendler and James Patrick Baldwin, "Pan Am Personal Tribute to A Global Aviation Pioneer," compiled by (Pan Am Historical Foundation celebrating the 90th anniversary of Pan Am 1927–2017).

have a distinct look, they are all young: some have moustaches, their lineage Middle Eastern. At the gates of the metal detector there is no passenger. There are, however, six agents on duty who chat among themselves.

12,51 Suddenly from the briefcases they take out pistols and short machine guns. Strangers don't say a word, they take up arms and shoot wildly into the ground and into air, sowing panic. The windows shatter, the neon tubes that serve for lighting crumble, water rains from the pipes of the air condition pierced by bullets. The agents do not react, they are petrified by surprise. The passengers who are in the large hall flee screaming. There is great chaos, people are terrified. One of the guerrillas of medium height, corpulent, holds a machine gun and a bomb in his hands. From how it behaves, it seems to be the postal cap of the expedition.

12,54 Only four minutes have passed since the terrorists went into action, but now the transit room is in their hands. They are seven in all including a young woman. Some guerrillas continue to shoot without stopping, the others head towards the door that lead to the outside emplacement.

12,55 Two terrorists move towards parking lots 13, 14, 15 where there are a Pan Am plane, a second from Lufthansa and a third from Air France. In the first aircraft which is to take off for Beirut in a few minutes, there are about fifty people. It's a 707: a young man and a young woman approach each other, the first climbs the ladder, reaches the top, throws the bombs and runs away. He is wounded in the face, [Yay!] but still joins his companions who, meanwhile, guns in hand, had taken away the hostages. The girl disappears, no one can see her anymore.

12,56 All hell happens on board the Pan Am plane: first an explosion is heard, then shouts of start; finally smoke and fire. Tongues of fire rise from the aircraft, while the alarm goes off: dozens of policemen and agents take to the runway. [And do absolutely nothing but hide under trucks and behind barrels.]

13,00 While guerillas and hostages are reaching the Lufthansa jet, a 1100 van from Aza, the airport services company, passes by. There are two helpers on board: one is taken prisoner by the guerillas; the other manages to save himself by hiding. The same fate suffers a finance guard on duty near the big aircraft. His name is Antonio Zara. Also taken hostage.

13:05 After remaining a few minutes on board, the guerillas decide to make a sortie to check the hatches: the financier, the Aza employee and the jet engineer; a second terrorist remains on the ladder and shoots to keep the police away. Once the inspection is complete, the small group retraces its steps, but before getting back on the plane, the guerrilla shoots cold on the finance guard, killing him instantly.

13,10 Terrorists, hostages and crew are aboard the airplane. The police are on the runway in strength: the jet is surrounded, but the hostages are inside. Meanwhile, the Pan American aircraft burns, the firefighters intervene with fire engines, but the job is extremely difficult. On board people die. The dead are 28.

13,25 The Lufthansa twin-reactor taxies on the runway, gets rid of its scales, and is ready to take off.

> **13,32** While aboard the Pan American jet the tragedy assumes catastrophic proportions, the Lufthansa aircraft with the guerillas and the hostages rises from Fiumicino to Athens. The airport is closed, thousands of people are kept away from the police. We no longer left Rome by plane.

According to this timeline, this whole thing lasted 32 minutes, which means Lari was off the plane by 13:05 (1:05) when the terrorists shot Zara and began shooting at the police surrounding the Lufthansa plane. (Lari and Dominic ran and hid behind the barrel.) That means she was on the plane for less than 10 minutes—not 22 minutes. Of course, Pan Am could have been counting the minutes from the time she boarded because we boarded the plane quickly, and the plane was in the last stages of approval for departure.

The only thing that probably saved Lari is that she was on the floor, in an altered state, and barely breathing. Plus, the bodies on top of her acted as filters. Did she pass out from fear? She told me she played dead and only crawled out when she thought it was safe. But, as they say in those dopey T. V. programs to get you to not switch to another channel because of their perpetual ads, there's more to the story. You'll have to wait to discover what else was happening in that plane.

What else is wrong with the timeline article? They say a young man and woman approach each other, "the first climbs the ladder, reaches the top, throws the bombs and runs away." He did not run away. Could it be that after throwing in the first grenade that killed Diana and then the second bomb, he entered the cabin, shot into the pile of people, and ran past me after tossing another grenade into first class? Would he be stupid enough to throw the fire bomb before he shot into the people and left first class? I doubt it. He wasn't wearing a gas mask or fire-proof gear. It makes more sense that the third bomb in the first class went off while he ran down the aisle, and that's why he was in such a hurry to push past me and Muriel. It was this third bomb that caused Lari to pass out and me to see the beautiful beings. Let me show you why he was in such a hurry:

> Most grenades will detonate about 3-5 seconds after the trigger is released, giving you a few critical moments to react. The kill radius from a grenade's explosion is about 15 feet, and the casualty radius is about 50 feet, though pieces of shrapnel can still fly much farther than that.[3]

Well, shoot, I was trying to save Muriel's life, and she ended up saving mine when she fell to the floor, pulling me along with her. The grenade's blast radius is also probably why I had yuck all over me and found that hunk of body in my purse. If this is the terrorist who they said had burns on his face, is it because he was in the fire while shooting into the pile of people, or is it because Muriel and I impeded his progress as the third bomb went off? Not finished with his reign of terror, as the terrorist ran out the back door, he threw a bomb into the back of the plane.

While the first and second terrorists were at the first-class door throwing the first bomb in the front of the aircraft, another terrorist came up the back steps and threw a grenade into the back of the plane. Then the third terrorist, or a fourth terrorist, stood at the bottom steps shooting at people trying to leave. *Il Messaggero's* report does not mention that a third or fourth terrorist ran up the back stairs and simultaneously threw the bomb in the aft cabin.

In the meantime, the shooting at the police and the killing of the finance guard is when Bonnie, Robyn, and I hid under the truck, and Lari and Dominic hid behind the large barrel. I wanted to run out and pull the injured man lying on the tarmac to safety but knew I couldn't because of the shooting. The newspaper said this final spray of bullets occurred at 1:05. That is only 9 minutes from when they entered the Pan Am plane, blew it up, and took over the Lufthansa plane. Did the police align themselves without regard to where the terrorists' bullets would end up going? Because of the way the planes were parked, from

3 Patrick Hutchison, "How to Survive a Grenade Explosion," May 28, 2020, https://www.artofmanliness.com/skills/outdoor-survival/how-to-survive-a-grenade-explosion/#:~:text=Most%20grenades%20will%20detonate%20about,fly%20much%20farther%20than%20that..

the door of the Lufthansa plane, the shots went directly into the lower floor of the terminal. Also, remember this for later: fire engines were pulling up to the Pan Am plane as soon as the shooting stopped, and the Lufthansa plane was pulling away. Notice that *Il Messaggero*'s report of 29 dead onboard is incorrect.

(The 1973 bombing was the least of Pan Am's problems. There were three deadly crashes in the Pacific in nine months. The good news is it changed airliner's safety culture. The FAA faulted Pan Am for its inadequate training, and Pan Am [finally] made sweeping changes.[4] According to John Steele, from 1934 to 1991, more than 95 Pan-Am airplanes were "lost" to either accidents or terrorist attacks.[5])

According to reports, authorities captured only five men. Two disappeared immediately after the attack. The woman who ran up the first-class steps with the man and tossed in bombs is one of the two who disappeared.

(Update: Lari Hamel became a vocal advocate for airliner cabin safety. She also became right-down belligerent about carry-on baggage. Lari passed away from esophageal cancer in June 2016. (Her type of cancer is no surprise to me as I have battled throat and lung problems since the plane ordeal. I have also had three spine surgeries using rods and spacers and two throat surgeries sutured with metal clamps. TSA is not fond of me, as I set off the alarms every time I go through a checkpoint.)

The *Baptist Press* newsletter posted the following about Bonnie and Robyn. Notice that I placed corrections in brackets.

---

4 Adam Nebbs, 5 Apr, 2019, "How three deadly Pan Am crashes in three months changed airline's safety culture," *Traveller's Checks*, https://www.scmp.com/magazines/post-magazine/travel/article/3004503/how-bali-hotel-was-connected-pan-ams-three-fatal.

5 Wikipedia, s.v. "Pan Am," https://en.wikipedia.org/wiki/Pan_Am.

Baptist Coed Dies in Arab Bombing of jetliner in Rome 12/21/73

By Robert O'Brien
News Editor, Baptist Press

GREENBACK, Tenn. (BP)--A special kind of quiet joy--and what seemed to be a premonition of death--permeated the final few hours of life for Bonnie Presnell, one of 32 persons killed in an Arab fire bomb attack on a Pan American jetliner in Rome.

Bonnie, a 20 -year-old sophomore at Hiwassee College, Madisonville, Tenn., and her cousin, Robyn Haggard, a 16-year-old junior at Harrison-Chilhowee Baptist Academy, Seymour, Tenn., were enroute from East Tennessee to spend the Christmas holidays with Robyn's parents in Saudi Arabia.

Robyn, burns covering about 35 per cent of her body, lies in critical condition in Santa Eugenia Hospital in Rome. The prognosis is "guarded" but Robyn "is expected to recover, " reports indicate.

A Pan Am passenger, who escaped injury [no, I did not escape injury], talked with Bonnie at length before her unexpected death, according to Mrs. James H. Adams of Greenback, who worked with Bonnie for 12 years in Girl Scouts.

The passenger, a girl whose identity is not available, told Mrs. Adams in a phone call to the Presnells in Greenback, that Bonnie, in the hours before her death, appeared subdued and discussed the Bible and the fact that she had recently "rededicated her life to Jesus Christ and was happy to be alive." [That's not what I told her.

I told her that Robyn and a bunch of us went dancing the night before, and Bonnie said she wanted to stay in her room and read her Bible.]

But the passenger told Mrs. Adams: "Bonnie said more than once, 'If I had to die today I would be ready.' It was almost as if she had a premonition of death. This girl was ready to go and wanted everyone to know she had had a happy life." [I told her more than once that Bonnie said, "If I had to die today, I would be ready" because I heard the same thing from Muriel and was surprised at hearing this from people who ended up dying.]

"It struck me that the girl said Bonnie was subdued," Mrs. Adams commented. "The Bonnie I knew was anything but subdued. She was lively and outgoing. "

Bonnie, a member of Niles Ferry Baptist Church near Greenback, "never hesitated to give her Christian testimony in a down-to-earth natural sort of way," said Mrs. Adams, a Presbyterian. "She was a very unselfish person with so much to give. She always gave of herself. She was like my own daughter. "

Robyn's parents, Dr. and Mrs. Martin Haggard [incorrect—her father's name was Claude Barton Haggard, Jr.], both Knoxville natives, and their four other children live in Dhahran, Saudi Arabia, where he is a dentist with the Arab-American Oil Company.

She had attended school in India last year but enrolled at Harrison-Chilhowee Baptist Academy, a Southern Baptist institution, in September to be near her grandparents, Mr. and Mrs. C. B. Haggard of Seymour, both Southern Baptists. [Robyn told me she was at grandpa and grandma's because she had been busted for marijuana possession in Saudi Arabia and received a life sentence, for which her father paid a large sum of money to the police to get her out. Robyn described the cell they placed her in as a "dungeon with a dirt floor and dripping water." The Baptist Press version sounds better. Doesn't it?]

The grandparents and Bonnie's mother, Mrs. Houston Presnell, said in an interview with Baptist Press, Southern Baptist Convention news service, they had great difficulty getting exact details from Rome about what happened.

Baptist Press, working through its Richmond Bureau at the Southern Baptist Foreign Mission Board, alerted Missionary W. C. Ruchti in Rome. He contacted Dr. and Mrs. Haggard, who had flown there from Saudi Arabia.

"We hadn't been able to sleep for worrying about what was happening in Rome," said Mrs. Presnell, also a member of Niles Ferry Baptist Church." Mr. Ruchti's information about the arrival time of Bonnie's body and other details relayed to us by Baptist Press really relieved our minds. We appreciate him very much."

Ruchti, who serves as pastor of the English-language Baptist church in Rome, told the Foreign Mission Board he will continue to visit the Haggards and offer any assistance he can. Robyn is allowed no visitors because of the seriousness of her condition, he said. Mrs. Haggard, Mrs. Presnell's sister, accompanied Bonnie's body to the United States, Ruchti reported, but will return to Rome after the funeral.

Described as a "quiet and studious girl" by Harrison-Chilhowee Baptist Academy President Hubert Smothers, Robyn Haggard was excited about her visit to Saudi Arabia. [This paragraph cracks me up. President Smothers didn't know Robyn outside of the classroom.]

But she was even more excited about the "first snow fall she ever saw just before she left," says her grandfather. "Her eyes really glittered with excitement. " [Robyn also shared her first snow fall experience with me.]

Bonnie, a student pilot who soloed two weeks before her death, "showed the most elation about her plane trip," C. B. Haggard said.

Family and friends describe Bonnie as an active girl, full of personality, excitement and ambitions. An all-county player on the Greenback High School girls' basketball team, she received the first Bonnie Presnell Award from the school's athletic association, Mrs. Adams said.

Bonnie also earned the First Class rating in Girl Scouts (equivalent to Eagle rank in Boy Scouts) when many other candidates dropped out, her scout leader added. But what impressed those who knew her most, a friend said, "was the consistency of her testimony as a Christian--even to the end. "[6]

---

6 *Baptist Press*, Nashville, Tennessee, December 21, 1973, http://media.sbhla.org.s3.amazonaws.com/3708,21-Dec-1973.pdf.

CHAPTER 6
Life Undone

James Joyce wrote in his book *Ulysses*, "Mr. Duffy lived a short distance from his body." I, too, lived a short distance from my body after the attack. I couldn't and wouldn't get near myself. It was just too painful and terrifying.

For a week after the attack, I spent the days being interviewed by reporters who wandered in and out of our house. When I went shopping, friends, as well as strangers, stopped to talk to me. I robotically repeated what I had said fifty times prior. My mother seemed to enjoy the attention.

I talked with the parents and families of the deceased from our group via telephone and in person. The only thing they wanted to know was, what did you guys do while in Rome? Did their loved one have fun, and did they suffer? How was I to answer that? I told them where we had gone and what we had done, what we had for dinner the night before, leaving out the little white creatures in the spaghetti. I said their family member had enjoyed themselves on the trip. I told them where their child or loved one was sitting on the plane. I told them I was sure they hadn't suffered because the attack had happened lightning fast. I didn't tell them about people's confusion during the two minutes before the bombs went off. I didn't tell them what probably went through their loved one's mind if they happened to see the grenade or the bombs that got tossed into the fuselage and rattled around or landed on top of a seat at their eye level or that they probably couldn't move fast enough to get away from them. I didn't tell them how their loved one felt as they lay on the floor, stayed strapped in their seats, tried to escape out one of the doors, or had a gun leveled at them and felt the impact of the searing bullet as it stopped their life, or how they gasped for air that they didn't know was poisoned just like in a senseless Holocaust. How could I?

Sweet Jesus, I wasn't about to tell them that their loved one's last minutes were filled with terror and shock and that some sat stoically in their seats with their seat belts still on because they didn't believe what was happening. Many never got down on the floor when the captain told them to—not that it would have done any good for many of them.

Muriel's niece and my friend Barb was uninjured and remembered nothing about the attack. Someone had reached over her, pushed open the emergency door on her side of the plane, and shoved her out the door. She had no memory of who it was. She said several people also went out that door, jumped off the wing, and ran to a field.

Her rings identified Muriel. They lost her body on her trip back to Iowa. Someone placed her coffin on a shelf in a warehouse, and her son in the Air Force had to call friends to track it down. Her funeral was at the Catholic Church, where she played the organ. She was buried in a beautiful Italian casket in the Catholic cemetery on a bitterly cold, snowy Christmas Eve day. I cried like each tiny connector had ripped my heart out. Her Pan Am gold wings identified Purser Diana Perez. Walker's camera was under him. Only the under part of their bodies was left unburned. For three days before Christmas, laid to rest were the remains left of the people I knew.

As Italian newspaper *Il Tempo* highlighted under a horrifically gruesome image of three men carrying a hammock of remains from the aircraft, "Il corpo carbonizzato di una delle vittime viene estratto dall'aereo"—"The charred body of one of the victims is pulled from the plane." In another image, coffins, police, and soldiers line up at the foot of the steps of the aircraft. Under the picture are the words, "Un lunga fila di bare attende I corpi che vengono man mano estratti dal jet"—"A long line of coffins awaits the bodies as they are pulled from the jet." They even go so far as to show an image of the murdered Antonio Zara's corpse on the tarmac and "in the burial chamber of Ostia where it was composed." U. S. newspapers only printed the coffin picture, the burning plane, and our graduation or professional pictures—no charred bodies, no corpses with blood running out onto the tarmac, no unforgettable images of what's left of the remaining inside the aircraft.

What can be said now?

I was too numb and distraught to think straight or to sleep. I could relay to people what had happened, but I couldn't feel what had happened until I went to sleep. Then I would have nightmares. I never went to sleep that I was not on that plane listening to the screams of terror, smelling the burning flesh and hair, and running from the smoke and flames and running, running, running. I would wake up and sit upright in a panic.

Someone retrieved my suitcase from the belly of the plane and returned it to me. My clothes, although intact, smelled so disturbing, even after several washings, that I threw them away. My contact lenses were shrunk and bent out of shape, rendered useless by the heat of the fire. Years later, the smell would still be in the blue, hard-side Samsonite suitcase. I abandoned the idea the smell would leave and finally threw it away. My purse still sits, hidden in a box, and I recoil in shock every time I open the box and see it. It had a black smudge on the flap for years until I viciously rubbed it away. I wonder what story that smudge has to tell. I refuse to throw it away, as it was on loan from my old roommate Diane, and I give that purse credit for saving my life. She said she didn't want it back.

I became so apathetic that I could not stand to be alone, but I also did not want to socialize. I alternated between severe agitation and depression and jumped at the slightest sound. I wanted to run if I heard a siren or loud noise or saw a flash of light. I was listless in social situations and preferred not to get involved with anyone or anything. My survivor's guilt was so great that I had self-distrust and self-sabotage and hated the skin I was living in. I had lung damage from the poisonous gases and some hearing loss.

My doctor had me start taking Sinequan, an anti-depressant tranquilizer. They were not working. I still had nightmares. I went to a psychiatrist who hated Nixon, and for forty-five minutes of our fifty minutes together, he talked about Nixon and Watergate and ranted that Congress should impeach Nixon. He prescribed Vivactyl to elevate my mood and Tranxene to make me tranquil and told me to continue to take Sinequan, also. The combination worked for about a week, but gradually, they didn't work anymore. So I just took one more and then one more.

My fiancé's brother was a pharmacist, and he sent pharmacy-sized brown bottles of the drugs to me so that I could save money. Within a month, I took 5-6 of each drug every 6 hours or less. I knew I had to start socializing, so I started going to a bar in town and drinking heavily and smoking as much pot as I could get my hands on with old high school acquaintances. *I just need to step out of reality for a while,* I thought, *and then I'll wake up, and everything will be fine.*

Within four hours of each day, I was exhausted and would nap for an hour or two. I could sleep briefly on the living room couch, but going to a bedroom alone was torture. The psychiatrist said my prognosis for recovery could not be expected in the foreseeable future. He said he would give me a really extreme diagnosis so that Pan Am would have to divvy up more money—little did he know, his diagnosis was my actual reality.

In the meantime, my fiancé had been driving my new car and wrecked it. He got it fixed but forgot to inform me that the frame was bent and would need new tires every 5,000 miles. A friend of ours told me. When I confronted him, he said he didn't tell me because he didn't want me to know. My dad flew to Connecticut to retrieve the car. After a few months, my mom called the fiancé and told him the wedding would not happen. Maybe she figured it out when I removed the ring and stuck it in the kitchen cupboard.

I started making pacts with God and swore to Him that I would conform and settle down, get married, have 2.2 babies, and live in a 3-bedroom house with a white picket fence and own two cars.

One night I was at the bar, and a friend of mine named Ronnie, who was an alcoholic and eventually ran over himself with his own tractor—ironically, he had been sober for several months when he died—introduced me to a guy who was standing at the end of the bar by himself and seemed to have decided that he wanted to kill himself or someone else. Perfect!

I asked him if he wanted to dance. He said he didn't dance, and I kept badgering him. He finally wandered onto the floor, and I realized that he meant it. He really couldn't dance. Good grief. I loved to dance—more punishment if I hooked up with this guy—I deserved it. We started hanging out.

I was so disgusted with myself for surviving while the "good" people died that I started mingling with alcoholics and drug users. I re-established a friendship with a girl I knew from high school who lived with the ex-con I eventually believed had rabies, mad cow disease, or the disease people get from eating squirrel brains. After all, he was from Kentucky.

We were over at their house one night, and the guys were playing quick-draw and shooting at targets (at least it wasn't at each other). They both fancied themselves as hunters, cowboys, and marksmen. I told them I hated guns, and the next thing I knew, the idiot I was hanging out with shot himself in the knee because he pulled the trigger before he got the gun entirely out of his holster. We made a mad dash to the hospital at one o'clock in the morning with the ex-con driving the guy's car in low gear as fast as the souped-up car would go, where they performed surgery and removed the bullet. He would have a bum knee for the rest of his life. A few months later, a rod shot through the car's block as we drove down the road. No wonder. (About a year later, my friend would trip over a rug trying to bluff the extremely abusive ex-con she had stupidly married into not hitting her and "accidentally" pulled the trigger and shot him right between the eyes.)

While I was at the hospital visiting him, his mother showed up. She wanted to know about the airplane ordeal when he introduced us, so I told her. She hovered over her son like a mom with a newborn babe and clarified that I should leave. She even said I should go as "her

Ronnie" needed to rest. She was such a nasty, territorial woman that I decided then and there to marry him to spite her. I still wasn't thinking clearly—what a mess I was about to make. By then, I was shaking pills out into my hand, swallowing them, staying stoned on pot, and drinking prodigious quantities of alcohol.

So, we got married during a blizzard on Thanksgiving weekend of 1974, even though the night before, I told my best friend that I thought I was making a big mistake. In my mind, I still secretly felt I needed punishment for surviving. I figured the blizzard was an omen and vowed never to wear a dress again. I suddenly quit taking prescription and non-prescription drugs and alcohol right after the wedding. By then I had distanced myself from the rabble friends and established new healthier friendships.

The following summer, we went to the Cheyenne, Wyoming, rodeo—"the granddaddy of them all"—and one of the Blue Angel jets crashed into the bullpen. What the heck? Looking back, I think I must have had Forrest Gump Syndrome! But, of course, the calamities weren't over yet.

Our first daughter was born on November 9, 1975. I had a doctor who had just graduated from medical school. I was overdue and kept telling the doctor something was wrong with the baby. He did no tests or ultrasounds and decided to induce me when she stopped growing.

I went into the hospital, and he started a Ptosin drip. While he sat and read *Time* and *Newsweek* and then watched the University of Iowa football game, I lay there in hard labor. The hard labor continued all night long. The following morning the head nurse came in, examined me and the baby, and threw a fit. The baby's heartbeat dropped to 40 beats per minute on contraction. She took the doctor into the hallway, and I heard her rip him a new one. I didn't see him again that day.

The nurse took me off of the Ptosin drip. Just before noon, an ob-gyn flew into the room and said they were doing a C-section immediately. Nurses and O. R. techs threw me onto a gurney, and we made a mad dash down the hall.

I will never forget that weak little cry when the baby came out at 12:07 p.m. She had so many problems that they didn't expect her to live more than a year or two at the most. She had a defective heart, which occurs only in 1 of 200,000 births. They said she was too sick to have heart surgery, which would postpone the inevitable as the longest she could live was two years.

I got an infection, spiked a high temperature, and was too sick to see her.

The original doctor's wife had twins that afternoon. They put her in the room across the hall. I asked the nurses to move me or her because they had a parade of well-wishers flowing in and out of their room with balloons and gifts. Every time I saw that rotten doctor, I wished I had a bedpan I could throw at him instead of a catheter. The babies were in the room with the mom, and every time I heard the babies cry, my heart broke. I couldn't even see my baby. I thought my husband would choke that sawed-off little guy who was so short he had to stand on a Coke crate to do surgery.

During the night, my IV came out of my vein. My arm swelled, and my fever spiked again. To add insult to injury, the night nurse was a nasty old nun who couldn't find my vein to put a new IV line in. She stuck me about twenty times, finally said, "There!" and left the room. At about 3:00 in the morning, I woke up, and my arm was the size of Popeye's forearm. My fever was still up since most of the fluids went under the skin instead of in my vein.

That night there was a blizzard and a full Moon.

On the fifth night, I had a dream. I was walking through a field of golden waist-high grass. Ahead of me, I could see my daughter, who appeared to be about four years old. She was wearing a dress with a white apron with ruffled edges, and she had flowing, wavy blond hair. She was running toward me, and I was running toward her, and just as she reached me and threw her arms around me, she said, "Mommy, I can't stay."

I woke up and just lost it. I cried and cried, and the cry came from the very bottom of my soul.

My fever broke. I was finally moved to another room that morning and could finally see my baby for a few minutes. She was so weak but held on to my finger. My husband had spent almost every waking minute with her, holding her hand and stroking her hair. He had not held her yet, either.

On the sixth day, they said they had to transfer her to the University Hospital in Iowa City immediately. They said, "Now!" The doctor signed the release form. My parents arrived at the hospital and slowly drove us on snow-slickened highways to Iowa City. We were allowed to see her after the doctors stabilized her.

She was alone in that big, dimly-lit, rose-tinted room full of sick babies. My heart just absolutely broke again.

They wouldn't let us stay with her, and they said the only thing they could do was keep her comfortable. I asked if she was in pain, and the doctor said he didn't believe so. I told him to do whatever it took, not to let her be in pain.

We stayed at a motel that night and returned to see her in the morning. We spent a short time with her. The doctor said there was no hope for her. It was just a matter of hours or days at the most.

I was still fragile and still in a lot of pain. My parents decided it would be best if we went home, got some clothes, and returned the next day. I was torn. I did not want to leave her alone, but I knew I was too sick and weak to sit in a hospital waiting room where I would only see her for minutes every few hours. We made the two-and-a-half-hour drive home.

The phone rang around 1:05 a.m. (notice the time—the principal announced Kennedy's assassination to the school at 1:05 p. m. and terrorists attacked the plane at 1:05 p. m.). My heart was in my throat. My husband answered the phone. The person at the other end told him she had just died.

Whatever in the world could happen next? Was there a jinx on me? Was God still punishing me, and if so, for what? I'd gotten married and was trying to do what society expected.

We asked for an autopsy. The autopsy showed that the baby died of a cerebral hemorrhage that caused respiratory arrest—perhaps too many hours of ripping, hard labor?

The next day we bought a cemetery plot with space for four. We picked out a tiny casket and bought her a miniature yellow and white dress with a little white apron and a raggedy-Ann doll so she wouldn't be alone. At the funeral home, she also looked like a little doll lying there with a mini-me doll. My beloved Grandma said, "This is the saddest I've been since Grandpa died." More guilt fell onto my shoulders.

We buried her the week before our wedding anniversary. I was nowhere near my body and went about my day as if nothing had happened. I pushed everyone and everything away from me. I knew if I got close to anyone, they would die, too.

I just went deeper and deeper inside myself.

My husband sunk into a deep depression.

I took up denial with a vengeance. *None of this happened. It is just a newsreel.*

We picked out a tombstone with a lamb and the name Kim Ann, November 9, 1975–November 18, 1975, carved into it with the words *Our Little Lamb.*

A few years later, the original doctor became a professor of medicine.

* * *

Exactly two years later, on November 9, after doing amniocentesis tests and more stress than I wish to mention because of my fear that the new baby would die, our second daughter was born via C-section. She had jaundice because I was O-negative and she was B-positive. She was under the bilirubin lights for several days and got a clean health bill.

She was perfectly healthy until we took her home. She would break out in fevers and projectile vomiting. Food went in one end and out the other. I was in terror most of the time, watching the clock—waiting for the hands to reach the 1 and the 5.

Finally, on Christmas evening, she became lethargic and spiked a fever. I called the doctor, who told us to bring her the following morning. We took her to the doctor, who immediately admitted her to the hospital. They started IVs and antibiotics. Nothing changed. By then, her weight had dropped to what she weighed when she was born. She stayed seriously ill and continued to go downhill. Her fever went up and down. I got the flu and finally had to go home.

On the fifth day, the doctor discovered no one had done the ordered urine tests. Once completed, the tests showed she had a urinary tract infection. And they figured out that she was allergic to milk fats.

(Years later, a Vedic astrologer would tell me that from 1973 to 1977, I was in a time of enemies, explosions, near-death experiences, and death. No kidding!)

I started lightly drinking alcohol again. The world was just more than I could bear.

Astrological Chart 2

November 9, 1975

The Moon at 5-Aquarius in the 1st house is the Hyleg, "The Giver of Life" and it is most important for you as the native (client of that chart). It is opposed by Saturn at 2-Leo in the 7th house. The moon is also squared by Uranus at 3-Scorpio and Mercury at 5-Scorpio. The part of the body ruled by the sign which Saturn occupies is the weakest part of the body (heart). Saturn is also square Mercury and Uranus at 3-Scorpio. This is a heavy T-square with Moon, Mercury/Uranus and Saturn in cardinal houses. Most likely there was trouble with the rhythm of the heart of this child. –Joy Archer [She was born with one side of her heart missing.]

Astrological Chart 3

November 27, 1974

The classic rule for scheduling a wedding is from New Moon to Full Moon, and the rule was followed. You don't want squares to the moon, or there will be conflict. The Moon, ruler of the Ascendant, at 15-Taurus is in opposition to the conjunction of Mars and Mercury at 21/23 Scorpio. This aspect indicated lots of criticism and arguing from the groom. The groom would be critical of his bride. [He later told me it was my fault the baby died. His idiot sister convinced him it was because of poisonous gas I inhaled on the plane.] Since the Moon is sextile Saturn at 18-Cancer, the bride would believe it was her duty to obey the groom or the husband. The conjunction of Neptune to the Sun and Venus in the 5th house would lead to much deceit from the groom. He hid many things from the bride. He was not even aware of his own personality and goals in life at that time (not grown up). With Neptune square Jupiter you have the dreamer and schemer, not seeing reality with any clarity. The bride thought she was in the marriage for the long haul. –Joy Archer

CHAPTER 7
Injustice

The following summer, I was contacted by attorneys asking me if I would appear in court in New York City for Robyn. Robyn had been in and out of burn centers for months and had numerous skin grafts. She had been living in Tennessee and had gotten married. She and her husband Danny had a little girl. One night Robyn, Danny, the baby, Robyn's sister, her boyfriend, Danny's sister, and her husband went to Knoxville for pizza and a movie. On the way home, a drunk driver crossed the center line at a high rate of speed and hit them head-on. Robyn's husband died in the accident. Robyn sustained a broken neck and became a quadriplegic. She had total amnesia of even having had a daughter or a husband. She would spend the rest of her life in a wheelchair, now lived in a nursing home, and was only twenty years old.

How much can one person take?

My sister took care of our daughter, and we boarded the plane for, of all places, JFK airport. I had not flown since I stepped off the plane in Des Moines in 1973, but I felt I needed to be there for Robyn. I had taken some Valium to get on the plane and didn't take a deep breath until the doors were closed.

We landed in New York and took a cab to the hotel. That night, we went to a Broadway show named "Da," and I slept through most of it. The next day we went to some art museums and looked up my old friend Bette, the actress from the dinner theater when I lived in Florida. We visited the Statue of Liberty and the World Trade Center Twin Towers in the afternoon. We stood at the base of it and looked up. My husband said, "Do you want to go in and go up to the top?" The hair on my neck stood up. I saw blackness floating around the Towers and immediately said, "No. That building's going to get blown up and fall." He got the most frightened, confused look, didn't say one word, and we turned and walked away.

Robyn, her mother, and her sister were to arrive at the hotel late in the afternoon on the day after we arrived, but around 2:00, I said, "They're here."

I got up and started for the door, and my husband said, "But they're not due for another three hours."

I shook my head and told him, "They're downstairs."

We rode the elevator down to the lobby, and when the door opened, Robyn sat in her wheelchair, waiting for the elevator door to open. I thought my heart was going to explode. I was so happy, yet sad. We both started crying. She remembered me, and I could not believe how glad I was to see her. Burn scars still covered her body, but her emerald green eyes and wavy dark hair had not changed.

Her mother said they had caught an earlier flight.

We went up to their room and talked. Robyn had a terrible time forming words due to the effects of her head trauma and broken neck. We reminisced about what we did in Rome before the attack, and I asked her if she remembered going to that club dancing. I couldn't remember the name of it, but Robyn just piped up and slurred out, "The Piper Club!" Strangely, she could remember everything about Rome but not her husband or child, who her mom said just annoyed her.

We met with Robyn's attorneys at—of all places—the Pan Am building the next day. The Pan Am building was close to Rockefeller Center, and the courts were nearby. We discussed the questions Pan Am's attorneys would likely ask, and I wanted to get the answers right.

Unfortunately, during the trial, I was asked by a balding red-haired Pan Am attorney, who I imagined with the stub of a cigar hanging between his teeth, "Who delivered the tickets to your group at JFK?"—a question I somehow missed.

I gave the name of the man who [was supposed] to deliver the tickets.

The trial blew up. I was dumbfounded. I had given the wrong answer.

Pan Am's attorneys said that I had lied in every answer and that Robyn's attorneys had coached me on what to say. I was still sitting there wondering what had gone wrong. I could not for the life of me figure out what I had said that was wrong or a lie. I thought I had given the correct answer. And I certainly had not lied about what happened to us; they didn't ask what happened to us. They merely asked questions to exonerate Pan Am's culpability (ineptitude).

They put Robyn's attorney on the stand and asked if he had coached me to lie and to answer the question the way I did. The attorney, of course, denied having coached me. (Attorneys always discuss questions opposing counsel might ask.) He also denied telling me the wrong name of the contact. I was shocked when I later learned I had given the incorrect name. The whole thing was ridiculous because, in reality, my answer would have helped Pan Am. After all, it would have gone into the court record that we had received our tickets and had time to read them to buy additional insurance when the truth was that we had not received the tickets. We only received boarding passes in New York. We did not receive our tickets until we left Rome, so part of my answer was also wrong. Not one question pertained to whether Pan Am was libel because of the unclosed doors or that they should have hustled us out the right side of the plane when they knew the terrorists were coming to our plane instead of telling us to lie on the floor. The trial ended, and the Pan Am attorney requested the judge throw out my testimony. As I would learn years later, my testimony didn't matter anyway.

When I originally purchased my ticket, the people who bought the tickets told us we would not be flying through Beirut because of the war there and that our return flight would be through Athens, not London, but that is what the surprising final itinerary was. The rules on the ticket stated that the passengers must receive their tickets in "a timely manner" so that they could purchase insurance. We contended that we did not have time to buy insurance because we didn't receive our tickets in "a timely manner." Besides, we didn't know we needed to purchase insurance. They believed the key was in the name of the person who was supposed to hand us the tickets in New York but didn't arrive in time. See the flip-flop? My mistake would have been in Pan Am's favor. What the attorneys didn't press is that Robyn was only 16 years old and wouldn't have the maturity to understand that she needed to buy extra insurance.

Robyn received a ridiculously tiny amount considering her injuries and exorbitant hospital bills (attorneys got 32–33% plus expenses up to 50% of the settlement amount. Even more stunning is that in 1979 the average pay was around $15,000. Manhattan attorneys earned at least four times that amount and judges earned about eight times that amount). The most anyone could get for their injuries was $75,000, per Geneva Convention rules. What is the Geneva Convention? The parts vital to Robyn and the other cases are: It's

> a body of Public International Law, also known as the Humanitarian Law of Armed Conflicts, whose purpose is to provide minimum protections, standards of humane treatment, and fundamental guarantees of respect to individuals who become victims of armed conflicts. The Geneva Conventions are a series of treaties on the treatment of civilians, prisoners of war (POWs) and soldiers who are otherwise rendered *hors de combat* (French, literally "outside the fight"), or incapable of fighting.
>
> **Covention 1:**
>
> This Convention protects wounded and infirm soldiers and medical personnel who are not taking active part in hostility against a Party. It ensures humane treatment without discrimination founded on race, color, sex,

> religion or faith, birth or wealth, etc. To that end, the Convention prohibits torture, assaults upon personal dignity, and execution without judgment (Article 3). It also grants the right to proper medical treatment and care.[7]

Obviously, the terrorists broke the Convention 1 rules, as they tortured, assaulted, and executed people without judgment.

I received a copy of the ticket several months after the "accident." I did not read what was on the back until returning home after the trial. The Warsaw Pact, Geneva Convention, and Montreal Agreement rules were on the back cover in minuscule-sized writing. (You may not even know these rules and laws exist because, in today's world, you simply download an e-ticket with a map of black lines or get a flimsy one-page boarding pass that you now have to pay extra for. The laws and rules are not on these tickets, so how is one to know they need to buy additional insurance?)

Pam Am also claimed no responsibility for the "accident," which they termed a "hijacking" because they said our agent (Wally Stoelzel (Muriel's son-in-law)) purchased the tickets in Saudi Arabia. Thus they claimed they had no liability because Saudi Arabia was not a member of the Geneva Convention or the Warsaw Pact. More controversy arose when our attorneys discovered that Saudi Arabia *had* signed the Geneva Convention and the Warsaw Pact agreement. In essence, then we *were* insured. The question then became whether Pan Am was negligent or could have done anything to avoid the damage or that it was impossible for the pilot or them (Pan Am) to take such measures.

Of course, they could have. "They" could have deployed the chutes on the plane's right side and evacuated us when they knew the terrorists were coming to our plane! As earlier stated, the pilot even announced, "They're coming to our plane." These words were followed by these

---

7 Krystyna Blokhina, "Geneva Conventions and their additional protocols," Cornell Law School, June 10, 2019, https://www.law.cornell.edu/wex/geneva_conventions_and_their_additional_protocols.

crucial words: "They have a bomb." To this day, I wonder how Captain A. C. Erbeck knew which plane the terrorists were coming to and how did the Captain know they were carrying bombs?

Shortly after the attack, Erbeck sent the "WARNING!!!" letter on the next page to all of us, saying that everything was the terrorists' fault, security's fault, and the Italian police's fault and that he could have done nothing to stop the attack. Although what he said was true, we also believed he was trying to avoid a personal lawsuit. His wife Bonnie Erbeck was one of the casualties in first class. Here is what he said about his wife:

> "She died like everybody else in first class," said the shaken Captain Erbeck. "I thought, my God, Bonnie is in there and I've got to get her out. But it was impossible to get through. In the back one terrorist came up the stairs and actually grinned. He sneered, 'Pan American. Pan American.' They wanted us to burn alive and destroy the plane and everything in it."[8]

The question "Why?" comes up again. Why Pan American? Is it because Pan Am started using foreign oil, which is why, along with the many bombings, "lost" planes, and eventual lawsuits, they eventually went belly-up? You can see that the Captain also found it impossible to enter that fuselage—not that that makes me feel any better.

In the same *Newsweek* report are these words:

> "Some passengers managed to escape through the emergency doors, but many were trapped and howls of agony soon could be heard coming from inside the plane."[9]

---

8 Elliot Osborn, Ed., "The Mideast Talks Begin, 'Operation Hilton'," Vol. LXXXII, *Newsweek*, (Newsweek, Inc., Livingston, N. J., December 31, 1973), 16-18.

9 Osborn, "The Mideast Talks Begin, 'Operation Hilton," 18.

WARNING!!!

ꓘT TIME YOU ENPLANE ON A U.S. SCHEDULED AIRLINE, YOU MAY BE BURNED TO DEATH BEFORE THE AIRCRAFT EVER LEAVES THE RAMP

DEAR ________________________________ February 5, 1974

On December 17, 1973, Arab terrorists attacked my plane at Rome Fumicino Airport in a lightning commando type attack. The attack was a coordinated assault on the two main entrance doors of the aircraft. To describe briefly, first a fragmentation grenade was tossed from the ground through the front door, shortly followed by a white phosphorous grenade, also thrown from the ground. Thence a third grenade, or fire bomb was thrown directly into the rear of the first class section, presumably by a terrorist that had come up the forward stairs and had entered the aircraft. Simultaneously, at pistol point, an Arab at the rear main door prevented my crew and passengers from leaving the aircraft, or, in other words, he wanted to burn them alive with the grenades that he was about to throw. Subsequent information revealed that the gun was jammed. This terrorist than threw at least two bombs into the rear and center of the economy section of the aircraft. The purpose of this type of attack was not only to destroy the aircraft by bombs and fire, but to kill EVERYONE on the plane, or a 100% kill factor! To recap quickly, the Arabs wanted to seal up both ends of the aircraft with explosions at the two main doors and then throw more bombs into the interior of the aircraft to disable anyone from trying to escape through the overwing exits. Subsequent information revealed that they had attached a plastic bomb to the belly of the aircraft beneath the center fuel tanks, but this device failed to go off.

Why am I telling you all of this now? Because right at this moment every airport in the U.S. is vulnerable, or is wide open to this type of attack. All that we have now between our aircraft at the gate and a determined group of terrorists is one or two security guards carrying one small sidearm each and a couple of young ladies checking carry on luggage. Well, this is fine for stopping the occasional hijacker, but it is certainly not by any means a deterrent to prevent the type of attack these Arabs are being trained for. I predict that the Arabs will attack again soon and that it will be in this country. It seems to me that we have here in this country a state of emergency at our civil airports but no one has recognized it as such. The President and/or the Governors of the fifty states have the emergency authority vested in them to take whatever action they deem necessary to prevent a recurrance of the type of tragedy that I have described above from happening in the U.S.A. We must act immediately as this threat is very real and it is not going to go away until these Arabs are either eliminated or their demands satisfied, one or the other, and until then, we are going to lose more people and more aircraft. As one of our country's leaders, you must use all the influence you have to bring the pressure to bear on the right people to eliminate this emergency situation at our civil airports.

Very simply, this is what we should do and must do. You cannot expect an ordinary airport policeman/men to be able to cope with a commando type of attack such as that which occurred in Rome. If the Arabs are giving these terrorists commando training, then we must counter them with Army Ranger types or U.S. Marines. I'm sure that the old dollar sign must be ringing up in your minds by now, what is this going to cost to provide all of this protection? It seems to me rather than to organize a new security force of civilians that would cost billions, and that would also be ineffective, it would be very simple and economical to use our own armed forces that are already in uniform, trained and on the payroll. The President has the emergency authority to place federal troops at the airports. We have these men in uniform anyway, so why not use them during this emergency? As an added inducement to an all volunteer Army, why not put our soldiers on overseas flights to countrys that have a weak security defense against terrorists? In Rome, the Italians did not fire a shot. Beneath my aircraft there was an Italian policeman armed with a rifle who could have shot the two terrorists that attacked the front of the aircraft. They were right out in the open with no hostages in front of them and they could have been picked off easily.

As a last resort, we must allow the flight crews to arm themselves in the event we cannot implement some such program I have suggested above. This is already provided for in D.O.T./F.A.A. regulations since June 1972. At this time, airline managements will not allow flight crews to carry weapons of any kind. I guess they would rather take their chances and risk a law suit in the event one of us should accidentally shoot one of their passengers. Pressure must be brought to bear on all airlines to delete company regulations that prevent us from defending ourselves when no one else will.

Had I been properly armed and trained, I know beyond the shadow of a doubt that I could have stopped at least the two terrorists that attacked the front end of my 707 in Rome. This would have cut the death toll in half because the eleven people in first class would have thus been saved, and certainly some of those in the front of the economy section would have made it out of the front door.

In closing, I would like to suggest that you bring before the country's judicial system, legislation that would provide quick justice to skyjackers and terrorists. In the past, Arab terrorists have always attacked or skyjacked another aircraft in order to blackmail the country that is holding their colleagues in prison. Had these subject prisoners been tried and executed quickly, the threat of a future skyjack to free these men would have been immediately removed.

Time is running out and you are one of the country's leaders, do something now as the blood of those that are going to be killed will be on your hands. I'm sure that you can and will do it. Thank you.

Sincerely,
A. C. Erbeck
Captain, PAA

(To me, there was dead silence after the initial explosions and the pop-pop-popping of the gun. I would learn later that only one woman was screaming. Remember I said earlier that the people on the wing were "frozen." Only Mr. Wilson was physically animated; one woman was urging people to jump, and I had jumped, and was also urging people to jump. No one was screaming inside the plane. Of course, I don't know what was going on while my "lights" were out, but I do know no one in first class was making a sound nor was anyone in second class making a sound when I went down or when I got up. White phosphorus, smoke, fire, stun grenades and bullets will cause immediate disorientation and silence. I would not learn until forty-nine years later what happened later.)

The Montreal Agreement set an absolute liability of $75,000 per passenger regardless of fault, negligence, or degree of injury. The families of those who died got a check for the deceased person's "net worth." Most of the deceased's family received around $85,000 unless the person was just a "housewife," which I consider ridiculous because that amount was above and beyond what the injured survivors who had to live day after day with their injuries received. Robyn's hospital bills were several times over $75,000, and I can't begin to imagine her pain.

Furthermore, Pan Am v. Aetna Casualty and Surety Company in 1974 found that the following losses and damages were not covered in the hijacking near London and subsequent destruction of the Pan Am plane at Cairo: insurrection, rebellion, civil war, a taking by a military or usurped power, war or war-like operations, riot, or civil commotion. More or less, Pan Am told us that we were lucky to get anything because they had no liability in the first place. We were all basically—well, screwed.

The end findings of the attack were that from the ground, a fragmentation grenade was thrown into first class, followed by a white phosphorus grenade. One of the bombs blew a hole in the first-class section roof. The grenades (plural) were followed by a fire bomb that the terrorist, who had then come up the stairs, threw into the first-class section. A second terrorist went up the back stairs and threw two bombs into the economy section [one of which went off on the seat I was supposed to be sitting in] and held people at gunpoint before his gun jammed. This man is the same terrorist who tried to shoot me. Later reports by Purser Franco Dominic stated he "ran out of bullets." Erbeck's letter concurs with what I said and says the gun "jammed." A bomb in the second class section also blew a hole in the roof. One of the terrorists placed a plastic incendiary device on the belly of the aircraft, but that bomb did not go off. If you return to what Lari said and compare it to the official report, her sequence is off. The fragmentation grenade came first, followed by the white phosphorus grenade and the fire bomb. She had the fire bomb before the white phosphorus grenade. More than likely, it is the white phosphorus grenade that caused Muriel to fall, the reasoning which I will explain shortly.

One report said a rogue Palestinian terrorist group, not the Arafat PLO, had blown up our plane and hijacked the West German 737 Lufthansa plane. Black September, a group financially supported by Muammar al-Gaddafi, was also believed to be responsible for blowing up our aircraft, but Gaddafi denied supporting the group. (They were the same Gaddafi-financed group that blew Pan Am Flight 101 out of the sky above Lockerbie, Scotland, on December 21, 1988, killing 270 people. After protracted negotiations and UN sanctions, Gaddafi handed the two Libyan terrorists over to the Scottish court in the Netherlands. In August 2009, one bomber, Abdelbaset al-Megrahi, was released by the Scottish government on "compassionate grounds" because he was diagnosed with prostate cancer. Hm. He didn't have compassion when he blew up the plane. At that time, he was the only one convicted of the crime. (Update: In December 2022, the United States lawfully arrested the second bomber, Libyan national Abu Agila Mohammad Mas'ud Kheir Al-Marimi.)

Gaddafi said he never ordered the attack but paid compensation to the victims' families. Magrahi said Gaddafi did give the order. After paying compensation and admitting guilt, the UN lifted the sanctions. Disturbingly, an anonymous warning was given to the FAA on December 5 stating that a Pan Am Flight from Frankfurt to the United States would be blown up within two weeks by someone associated with the Abu Nidal Organization, the most common name of the Palestinian nationalist group Fatah—the Revolutionary Council (Black September). The U. S. government took the anonymous warning seriously, and the State Department cabled a bulletin to dozens of embassies. Unfortunately, the notice was not read. It was found under a pile of papers on a desk in Frankfurt the day after the bombing.

> One of the Frankfurt security screeners, whose job was to spot explosive devices under X-ray, told ABC News that she had first learned what Semtex (a plastic explosive) was during her ABC interview 11 months after the bombing.[10])
>
> What eventually happened to Ghaddafi?
>
> Muammar Gaddafi, the deposed leader of Libya, was captured and killed on 20 October 2011 after the Battle of Sirte. Gaddafi was found west of Sirte after his convoys were attacked by NATO aircraft. He was then captured by National Transitional Council (NTC) [First Libyan Civil War] forces and was killed shortly afterwards.[1]
>
> The NTC initially claimed Gaddafi died from injuries sustained in a firefight when loyalist forces attempted to free him, although a graphic video of his last moments shows rebel fighters beating him and one of them sodomizing him with a bayonet[2] [my favorite part] before he was shot several times.[11]
>
> Now let's hop aboard the hijacked Lufthansa plane.

---

10 Wikipedia, s.v. "Pan Am Flight 103," https://en.wikipedia.org/wiki/Pan_Am_Flight_103.

11 Wikipedia Online, s.v. "Killing of Muammar Ghaddafi," https://en.wikipedia.org/wiki/Killing_of_Muammar_Gaddafi#:~:text=The%20NTC%20initially%20claimed%20Gaddafi,he%20was%20shot%20several%20times.

CHAPTER 8
The Hijacked Lufthansa Plane

After hijacking the Lufthansa plane, the guerillas first forced the pilot Captain Joe Kroese to fly to Athens, Greece, for refueling and to demand the release of two Palestinians awaiting trial for their part in a hijacking that occurred the year before in Athens. The terrorists said they had already murdered four hostages and would order the pilot to crash the plane in the heart of Athens if officials did not meet their demands. However, they lied. They had killed only one hostage and wounded another. The murdered hostage was Italian airport worker Domenico Ippolito. After doing so, they staged a grizzly series of fake executions, complete with shots and screams, and said they would kill a hostage every half hour until their demands were met. They bluffed and bullied the Greek authorities for sixteen hours. As reported in *U. S. New & World Report*,

> It was a hoax. But it was almost a whole day later before that fact was known.
>
> In the meantime, the radio communication between the plane and Greek officials included these excerpts:

> **Pilot**: "For God's sake, tell Greece to give us the two prisoners and let us fly to some Arab country. . . . Please hurry. These people want to kill us all."
>
> **Tower**—"Be patient."
>
> **Hijacker**—"Can you hear? This woman will die."
>
> (A woman's scream was heard.)
>
> **Copilot**—"They are going to shoot me."
>
> (Silence, then the sound of a shot.)
>
> **Pilot**—"They just killed my copilot, a woman and three Italian soldiers."
>
> None of this happened, but it was dramatic enough to be believable. In the end, Greece did not give us its two prisoners, who reportedly didn't want to go anyway.[12]

And then the plane took off again. Lebanon and Cyprus refused to let them land, so they flew into Damascus. Even though negotiations occurred where officials tried to convince the terrorists to release the hostages, nothing happened. After being refueled, the plane took off again. This time it headed to Kuwait. After landing without permission, tanks were parked at the runway's end so the aircraft couldn't take off.

After much haggling, the terrorists surrendered, and when they exited the plane, they held up their hands with their fingers in a V for victory sign stating, "We are Palestinian Arabs, proud of what we did. We are not criminals. The criminals are those who bomb Palestinian refugee camps in Lebanon." The terrorists called their bloody attack "Operation Hilton."[13]

---

[12] Howard Flieger, Ed., *U.S. News and World Report*, (The Associated Press, Washington, D. C., December 31, 1973), 16. 28-33.

[13] Elliot Osborn, Ed., "The Mideast Talks Begin, 'Operation Hilton'," Vol. LXXXII, *Newsweek*, (Newsweek, Inc., Livingston, N. J., December 31, 1973), 16-18.

I tried to figure out the logic of blowing up a plane of non-terrorists to get back at people they called terrorists for blowing up Palestinian refugee camps. How are those people called criminals, but the bombers, in our case, were not criminals? The irony is that they only murdered one hostage and injured one on the Lufthansa plane. Why did they have a 100% kill factor on the Pan Am plane but not the Lufthansa plane?

Also interesting is officials retrieved a box of unused bombs, grenades, and bullets from the Lufthansa plane.

The Sheik of Kuwait decided to turn the terrorists over to the Palestinian Liberation Organization to bring them before a "revolutionary court." "Since 1963, thirty-three anti-Israeli terrorists have surrendered after killing eighty-one people. None of the terrorists served time for their crime except for three in Israel."[14]

Much hoopla occurred after the terrorists' arrest. The Arab countries were upset because they had recently garnered international sympathy for their situation, and general respectability for a new image was now tainted. Even the PLO was upset with the terrorists because they had stepped on their toes and called the attack "dirty action." The Arab states were now in a quandary. Before, they had not tried or convicted any terrorist for any action, and now the world was breathing down their necks to do something. Numerous media stated this was "the bloodiest skyjacking to date."[15] So, what happened to these characters? According to Wikipedia,

> **Aftermath[edit]**
>
> The terrorists negotiated their escape, but they were still captured shortly thereafter. The Kuwaiti authorities, after questioning the terrorists, decided not to put them on trial and considered the possibility of handing them over to the (PLO). The factors that came into play at this point were complex, and sparked a diplomatic case that saw the US and many Arab and European countries

---

14 Newsweek, 18.

15 Ibid.

clashing over the fate of the terrorists and which nation should have trialled them.

Italy, despite having made a formal request for extradition to the Arab emirates, did not appear really intentioned to trial and detain the terrorists on its own territory. It was indeed a mere formal act, and - when the Italian government was replied that, since there was no treaty that regulated extradition with Kuwait, it resulted impossible - no further pressure was applied. The most probable reason which dissuaded Italy from the desire to take over the command, was the danger that any detention in Italian prisons would have been a reason for retaliation by other Palestinian terrorists, who could have given rise to a new attack on Italian territory, eager to request the release of their companions. Subsequently, in fact, the last Palestinian terrorists detained in Italy, responsible for the failed attack in Ostia in 1972, were also released, probably for the same reason. Other European countries such as the Netherlands also followed this line. Those events were the genuine proof that the Italian government had decided to treat the tragic event of Fiumicino with the yardstick of "national interest", accepting compromises that were sometimes even humiliating.

After gruelling international events, in 1974 the Egyptian president Anwar Sadat agreed to their be[ing] taken to Cairo under the responsibility of the PLO and processed by the same for conducting an "unauthorized operation". They remained in prison until November 24, 1974, when following negotiations began during the hijacking of a British plane in Tunisia, carried out precisely to request their release, the five men of the commando were released in Tunisia with the complicity

> of many Arab, European governments and the US. From that moment there were no more certain news about their fate and they disappeared, probably hosted by some Arab country, remaining unpunished.[16]

Wow—accepting compromises that were "sometimes humiliating." (That's like releasing Jeffrey Dahmer because everyone fears he *might* cannibalize other prisoners or releasing Ted Kazynski because he *might* blow them up. (Oops! We don't have to worry about that anymore. Ted killed himself in his jail cell in June 2023. During his bombing spree, Ted killed three and wounded twenty-three others.) After all, they jailed them.)

The aftermath of what happened in Rome also tells me why the Italian policeman under the truck said, "No, I don't want to get involved," and why the policeman told Lari he was afraid to get involved. Obviously, neither of the Italian cops was like Paul Blart, the Mall Cop.

The Wikipedia article brings up another Geneva Convention rule.

> Every State bound by the treaties is under the legal obligation to search for and prosecute those in its territory suspected of committing such crimes, regardless of the nationality of the suspect or victim, or of the place where the act was allegedly committed. The State may hand the suspect over to another State or an international tribunal for trial. Where domestic law does not allow for the exercise of universal jurisdiction, a State must introduce the necessary domestic legislative provisions before it can do so, and must actually exercise the jurisdiction, unless it hands the suspect over to another country or international tribunal.

Woopsy Daisies! So this is how the countries mentioned above got away with handing the terrorists over to another country for prosecution. By

---

16 Wikipedia, s.v. "1973 Rome airport attacks and hijacking," https://en.wikipedia.org/wiki/1973_Rome_airport_attacks_and_hijacking.

rights, Italy should have prosecuted the criminals. Italy exercised that second sentence when they handed the men over to Egypt. It seems to me that someone needs to plug this hole in the dyke.

After the attack in Rome, the European nations decided to ramp up security in their airports. Italy was the only country not signing the agreement because they still feared terrorists would attack their airports.[17]

(Rather than dissuade terrorists by not signing, more attacks would be forthcoming in Italy. On December 27, 1985, terrorists hurled grenades and fired sub-machine guns at crowds of holiday travelers near Al El Israel Airlines ticket counter, killing 16 and wounding 99. Minutes later, three terrorists attacked passengers checking in for a flight to Tel Aviv in Vienna, Austria, killing two people instantly and wounding 39 others. A third victim died later. The outcome for the terrorists in this case was much different. El Al security killed three in the Rome attack, while the remaining one was wounded and captured. In the Vienna attack, the Austrian police and El Al security guards opened fire on the perpetrators who seized a Mercedes outside the terminal and fled. The guards gave chase, killed one terrorist, and captured the other two several miles from the airport after a short car chase and a gun battle.

Guess what happened to the surviving terrorist? He was given thirty years in prison but was released after twenty-two years for good behavior. He was living in Rome, was employed, and living with his girlfriend. He told a reporter from *Il Messaggero* that he condemned the terrorism, was remorseful for the attack, and prays for God's forgiveness.

I wonder what our attackers are doing.

Another attack occurred at Fiumicino on July 1, 1986, when a bomb exploded in the transit luggage section of the airport. Twelve people were injured.

In 1985 alone, 75 attacks in Western Europe resulted in 65 deaths and over 529 injuries. The hardest hit countries were Greece (14), Italy (13), and Cyprus (9). Notice that the Italian police did not stop the terrorists.)

---

17 Wikipedia, s.v. "1973 Rome airport attacks and hijacking," https://en.wikipedia.org/wiki/1973_Rome_airport_attacks_and_hijacking.

Something good did come out of all this death and destruction. I learned that our plane incident was the catalyst that forced the airline industry to change the fabric of seats. We learned that when the airplane seats caught on fire, it only took twenty seconds to kill everyone on board the plane because of the toxic, highly flammable material they were made out of. Since that time, hundreds of people have survived airplane crashes. The seats, which contained benzenes, formaldehyde, and other toxic foam rubber substances, killed most people in crashes or fires. The poison killed many people on our plane, not just the bombs and the fire. I knew I would not have made it off of the plane, especially without the "help" that I had and the whispery voice that said, "Hold your breath." Unfortunately, we also learned that airlines carry such toxic freight as swimming pool chemicals, fertilizers, oxygen, other flammable gas canisters, and even cows in the belly of planes. Why, then, did so many of us survive? Was it because we were on the floor and beneath the toxins? Was it also because the 1L, 2L, and over-wing exit doors were open, and the over-eager terrorists' bombs were too mighty and blasted holes in the roof, creating a chimney for the toxins to escape?

Almost nothing was written or spoken about in the U. S. after December 18, 1973, except in local newspapers. The big story in regional newspapers was the Watergate scandal. The call for Nixon's impeachment recaptured the nation's attention. The oil embargo was at a fever pitch, sometimes overtaking Nixon and other world headlines. One of the Arab emirates took out a full-page ad in every major newspaper in the United States denouncing the attack and swearing they had no responsibility for the attack. *U. S. News & World Report* [evidently] thought oil was a bigger story than the death of Americans at the hands of terrorists. Their December 31, 1973, front cover screams, "ARE BIG CARS DOOMED?, ENERGY MESS Groping for a Way Out, and WHY PEOPLE COMPLAIN ABOUT JURY DUTY. However, "Story of the Bloodiest Skyjacking" did land on page 16, but not until after stories about Alaskan oil and how much leverage the U. S. would have at Geneva on whether Israel would withdraw troops from both sides of the Suez Canal and other Arab lands.

Newsweek's cover was even chillier toward the attack; it simply asked, "The Coldest Winter?" They plopped the story like a block of ice on pages 17–18.

The December 31, 1973, *Time* issue wasn't much better. Their big front cover headline simply stated: THE BIG CAR: END OF THE AFFAIR. "Death in Rome Aboard Flight 110" faired even worse. It ended up on page 28.

The oil embargo in the U. S. consisted of long lines at gas pumps because of the fake fuel shortage. (In the early 1970s, oil tankers lined up along the Florida coast where I lived with nowhere to dump their oil. Clots of oil leaking from the tankers washed onto the beaches. The truth is: the supposed oil shortage was all about jacking up oil prices. If you want more information about the oil scam, read the book *The Energy Non-Crisis* by Lindsey Williams. He later stated a "higher-up" in the government visited him and told that if he didn't remove the book from the internet and stop talking about what he knew, "they" (the government) would go after him and his family. He backed down for a short time, then reposted the book.)

Perhaps if someone had listened to those of us who spoke at luncheons and on radio and TV about the impending terrorist attacks due to peoples' love for all things petroleum-based, including the walls and ceilings of airplanes, security would have been ramped up in the United States in 1973 instead of 2001. Perhaps the Twin Towers would still be standing; extremists would not have blown a big hole in the side of the U. S. S. Cole, and the U. S. Embassies in Tripoli, Libya; Beirut, Lebanon (63 killed); Nairobi, Kenya (213 killed); and Monrovia, Liberia (10 killed) would still be standing. There have been 54 attacks on embassies since 1974. (A woman who would become my physical therapist years later was at Fiumicino Airport when the 1985 terrorist attack occurred. She said there were still bullet holes in the green bricks from our attack.)

Time gave another version of what happened in the terminal. A travel editor of the St. Louis *Globe-Democrat* said he was waiting with friends to board a plane for New York when they saw a commotion farther down the concourse. "Must be some movie star," one of them remarked. After some nuns hurried past them, another quipped, "No, maybe it's the Pope." "Then some girls ran by, " [Robert] Suit recalled, "and they were yelling, 'It's a bomb, a bomb—everybody out!' We saw the bank slam down its window and heard some pops, which sounded like firecrackers. That's when we said, 'My God, it must be serious!'"

In fact, what the hundreds of unsuspecting travelers heard was the sound of gunfire. The fusillade signaled the start of a guerrilla attack in Rome last week that turned into the bloodiest rampage in the surreal five-year history of Arab skyjack terrorism. Before it ended 30 hours later—in the sand beyond a runway of the airport in Kuwait—31 people had been killed in Rome and one more in Athens.

The terrorists, who later identified themselves as Palestinian guerillas, first struck at the Rome airport's security checkpoint during the early afternoon rush hour. "I was heading toward the security check, and up front I saw a tall well-dressed young man," a British stewardess recalled. "As he approached the guards, he put his hand in his pocket and took out a pistol." Instantly, his companions—perhaps as many as seven—opened their overnight bags, took out submachine guns and began to spray gunfire in every direction.

Too Late. The gunmen then ran out onto the flight field. One group of the terrorists headed toward Pan American's Flight 110, which was preparing to depart for Beirut and Teheran with 59 passengers and ten crew members on board. At the first sign of trouble, Captain Andrew Erbeck told the passengers to crouch on the floor. Before he could order the 707's doors closed, a clean-shaven young man in a white sweater ran to the foot of the steps, a canister in his outstretched hand. "They're coming with grenades!" First Officer Robert Davison shouted. "Get these people out of here!" It was too late.

Flight Engineer Kenneth Pfrang was knocked to the galley floor by the first grenade. "I got hit by the concussion," he said later, "and I thought, 'Why aren't I dead?' Then I realized it was some sort of incendiary device and smoke was pouring out of the canister." Within seconds, there were more flashes as two phosphorus grenades went off inside the forward section. Two other grenades were thrown into the rear; suddenly the entire plane was filled with roiling black smoke.

Stewardess Lari Hamel was knocked to the floor in the first-class aisle and four or five bodies fell on top of her; she managed to crawl to a wing exit and escape. In the rear of the plane, one passenger saw a guerrilla appear, gun in hand, and stop passengers from escaping out the rear ramp.

"It was a miracle that so many people did get out," said First Officer Davison, "The whole thing took no more than 90 seconds." Added Flight Engineer Pfrang: "I flew C-123s in Viet Nam, but I've never experienced anything that happened so fast or in which you were so helpless."

...From the Pan Am plane, the terrorists ran down the tarmac to a West German Lufthansa 737 jet that had already been commandeered by the second group of

> guerrillas. On board, besides the pilot and three other Lufthansa crew members, were ten hostages who had been rounded up in the terminal and outside on the tarmac. An Italian customs guard had resisted the terrorists and been shot dead outside the Lufthansa jet. At 1:32 p.m., only 41 minutes after the first shot had been fired, the plane took off with the crew, hostages and five guerrillas aboard while other terrorists may have stayed behind.[18]

The Italian customs guard was 20-year-old Antonio Zara, who the guerillas ordered to pull away the auxiliary steps. After doing so, a terrorist shot him fatally in the back.[19]

A *New York Times* report stated:

> WASHINGTON, Dec. 17 (UPI) — The State Department described the Arab guerrilla assault in Rome yesterday as vicious and said it "underlines the urgent necessity to strengthen civil-aviation security measures throughout the world."
>
> A department spokesman, Paul J. Hare, said that the killings and hijacking by Arab guerrillas at Leonardo da Vinci International Airport was particularly reprehensible, coming at a time when the Arabs and Israel were preparing to hold face-to-face peace talks.[20]

---

18 Hedley Donovan, Ed.-in-Chief, "Death in Rome Aboard Flight 110," *Time*, (Time and Life, New York, NY), 33.

19 Elliot Osborn, Ed., "The Mideast Talks Begin, 'Operation Hilton'," Vol. LXXXII, *Newsweek*, (Newsweek, Inc., Livingston, N. J., December 31, 1973), 18.

20 "Arab Guerillas Kill 31 in Rome During Attack," *New York Times*, https://www.nytimes.com/1973/12/18/archives/arab-guerrillas-kill-31-in-rome-during-attack-on-us-airliner-take.html.

I ask again: Why did they attack our plane? Could it be because ARAMCO sponsored our group? Here is why I asked that question:

> **Saudi Aramco** (Arabic: أرامكو السعودية *ʼArāmkū as-Suʻūdiyyah*), officially the **Saudi Arabian Oil Group** or simply **Aramco**, is a Saudi Arabian public petroleum and natural gas company based in Dhahran.[6][7] As of 2022, it is one of the largest companies in the world by revenue[8] and has repeatedly achieved the largest annual profits in global corporate history. Saudi Aramco has both the world's second-largest proven crude oil reserves, at more than 270 billion barrels (43 billion cubic metres),[9] and largest daily oil production of all oil-producing companies.[10][11] It is the single greatest contributor to global carbon emissions of any company in the world since 1965.[12)
>
> Saudi Aramco operates the world's largest single hydrocarbon network, the Master Gas System. In 2013 crude oil production total was 3.4 billion barrels (540 million cubic metres), and it manages over one hundred oil and gas fields in Saudi Arabia, including 288.4 trillion standard cubic feet (scf) of natural gas reserves. Along the Eastern Province, Saudi Aramco most notably operates the Ghawar Field (the world's largest onshore oil field) and the Safaniya Field (the world's largest offshore oil field).[13]
>
> On 11 December 2019, the company's shares commenced trading on the Tadawul stock exchange. The shares rose to 35.2 Saudi riyals, giving it a market capitalisation of about US$1.88 trillion,[14] and surpassed the US$2 trillion mark on the second day of trading.[15] In the 2023 Forbes Global 2000, Saudi Aramco was ranked as the 2nd-largest public company in the world.[1]?[21]

[21] Wikipedia, s.v. "Saudi Aramco," https://en.wikipedia.org/wiki/Saudi_Aramco.

Do you think the world's wealthiest people want us to go electric, solar, or wind-powered? Solar was worth about $186.2 billion in 2022, and wind was about $71 billion in 2021. Oil is still more profitable to the wealthy than solar or wind.

* * *

Robyn's botched trial was one more thing to feel guilty about. After the court debacle, we went to Rose O'Grady's Pub. After all, it was St. Patrick's Day. We got to the pub early, and Robyn's mother asked the band if they knew any Merle Haggard tunes. Even though the band was an Irish band, they knew some of "Cousin Merle's" songs. Robyn was Merle's third cousin.

Robyn got snockered that night by sucking her drinks through a straw, as did the rest of us. By 11:00, the Irish packed the place, and the jig champions from Dublin and New York City performed. After the dancing, we drunkenly returned to the hotel, pushing Robyn's wheelchair around in circles and weaving her up and down the sidewalk. We scooped her up and poured her into bed.

Technically, Robyn "lost" her trial. I thought it was my fault and carried the guilt for almost 50 years. Here is what happened:

Robyn's dad decided to take Robyn out of the class action lawsuit (Manion v. Pan American) [the Manions were Frances and Agnes from our group] and sue for $1,000,000 because Robyn did not receive her ticket in New York, and her injuries were so significant. Here is a partial finding in Robyn's case:

> It is conceded that a ticket containing the notice required by the Warsaw Convention was delivered to Robyn in Rome several hours before departure. Certainly, under these circumstances, she was afforded a "reasonable opportunity to take * * * self-protective measures" *(Mertens v. Flying Tiger Line, supra*, p 856). . . .

> We cannot subscribe to the determination of the trial court that Robyn's trip from New York to Saudi Arabia was indivisible or to the court's reliance upon *Warren v. Flying Tiger Line* (352 F.2d 494, 498) as supporting a conclusion that the delivery of a ticket to Robyn in Rome did not cure the alleged failure to deliver a ticket to her in New York. . . .
>
> Interlocutory judgment, Supreme Court, New York County, entered on September 22, 1980, modified, on the law, to the extent of reinstating defendant's affirmative defense based on article 22 of the Warsaw Convention as modified by the Montreal Agreement, limiting the *ad damnum* clause to provide for damages not in excess of $75,000 and awarding plaintiff Robyn G. Haggard judgment in said sum, and otherwise affirmed, without costs and without disbursements.[22]

Of course, I left much of the Opinion out, but this was the general finding. My biggest question is, "Why would an attorney sue for $1,000,000 when he knew the rules in the Warsaw Pact and the Montreal and Geneva Conventions?" Furthermore, "Why didn't the attorney stress the fact that Robyn was only 16 and not mature enough to understand that she needed to buy insurance?"

[22] Birns, J.P., Manion v. Pan American, May 12, 1981, https://casetext.com/case/manion-v-pan-american.

CHAPTER 9

Cleaning Up My Act

I became clean and sober again when we returned home from New York.

I decided to take a class in the fall to complete the EMT training I had started in Florida. I was pregnant again. I had an amniocentesis done to ensure this baby was healthy, and the report said that the baby was a boy. The night before I was to go into the hospital for a C-section, I passed the final exam to be an EMT. However, that day, I also had the final exam with the ob-gyn. The doctor said, "Now you do know that it is a girl?" I almost fell off of the chair. We had planned for a boy. The doctor whipped out his report, and I told him our letter said it was a girl. He called the hospital that did the amnio- and double-checked; sure enough, it was a girl. I didn't care, however, whether it was a boy or a girl because she was one of the most beautiful babies I had ever seen. She also had jaundice like her sister and had to stay under the bilirubin lights for several days as she was O-positive, and I was O-negative. They were going to do a blood transfer at one point, but she pulled out of her calf-scour yellow color and was okay.

The oddest thing happened. As soon as the doctor cleared me for work, I got a job working as an EMT. In the eight years I did that work, not one patient died in the ambulance.

I started drinking again. I still could not cope with what had happened in Rome.

* * *

We moved to a little town south of Jackson Hole, Wyoming. I loved the people there. About half of them were alcoholics. Great! People I could relate to. I had a terrible time staying sober and could not face reality. I worked odd jobs, did volunteer EMT work, and started to distrust my husband, but I couldn't quite understand why I doubted him. Something was going on with him that he was hiding. What was his secret? Could I trust my instincts again, or was it the alcohol talking?

One night we went to one of the local bars with a couple who had just moved to the town we lived in. It was December 17, 1982, and I said, "Tonight is the nineteenth anniversary of the bombing of the plane I was on."

Kathy's mouth fell open. She looked at Bob, and wide-eyed Bob looked at Kathy. Kathy said, "Are you talking about the plane in Rome, Italy?"

I told her, "Yes."

She said, "You're not going to believe this, but we were supposed to be on that plane."

She continued her story and said that Bob was in the military and had received his orders to report to work at the Embassy in Iran. They had stayed with his uncle in New Jersey the night before they were to board Pan Am Flight 110, which was supposed to stop in Rome and pick us up. That night an ice storm hit. They did not realize that the airport had closed and slipped and slid to JFK. Bob's uncle dropped them off, and when they entered the airport, they realized no one else was there. When they looked at the departure sign, they saw all flights were canceled.

Because it was before the invention of cell phones, Bob's uncle was all the way home before they could reach him. He had to return and pick them up, and the car slipped and slid back to New Jersey. Kathy said she had always felt guilty about not being on that flight because so many people died, and she didn't. Many people said those words when a situation occurred and spared their life. A few years later, Khomeini seized the hostages at the Embassy. Ironically, because Bob missed the flight, he was stationed elsewhere. That ice storm perhaps saved Bob's life twice.

Fortunately, the 747 we would have boarded got iced in because it would have had about 374 passengers aboard, and the kill factor was 100% for that many people. Can you imagine 374 people stampeding to "the front of the plane," "to the center" of the plane, or lying on the plane's floor, as the flight attendant and Captain told people to do?

(Twenty years later, I was at some friends' house in an upscale neighborhood. We heard a loud bang. Randy almost dove onto the floor. I asked him if he was alright. He said he was always jittery when he heard a gunshot. I said, "Are you sure that was a gunshot?" Randy said he had been in the Marines and assured me it was a gunshot. I told him I would have been on the floor in a quivering mess if I had heard that gunshot thirty years prior. He asked me why. I told him the story, and his eyes widened in amazement. He said, "You're not going to believe this, but when I was in the Marines, my unit was packed and ready to go after the terrorists of that plane bombing. The assignment was cancelled just before boarding because the terrorists were captured." Talk about strange!)

* * *

My husband found a job in Salt Lake City, and the girls and I stayed in Wyoming—I, with my bottle and my demons, as far away from him as possible.

One day a woman named Shirley telephoned me. Several weeks before her call to me, we had gotten an ambulance call about Shirley. She was drunk, had a shotgun, and was going to kill herself and or her husband. I had met Shirley at a party several weeks before, and I had never seen anyone drink so much in such a short time. I was a lightweight compared to her. She, of course, got blubbery drunk like all of us who have a painful past. Deputy Sheriff Dan convinced Shirley to give up the gun, and they carted her off to the treatment center in

Evanston, Wyoming. She started an A. A. meeting in our town when she finished detox.

When she called, she told me someone had contacted her and thought I "might" have a drinking problem. I assured her I didn't have a drinking problem and could quit whenever I wanted to. She convinced me to go to a meeting with her. I went, and what I heard sounded great. The attendees' stories made me think I wasn't nearly as bad as they were, so I didn't have to quit yet. I just wasn't an alcoholic!

I went home from the meeting and celebrated having some newly acquired friends with a "few" drinks. I don't think that's the way it's supposed to work.

One night after a meeting, Shirley gave me an alcoholism questionnaire. I took it home and sat down at the table to answer it. First question: check—second one: hmm, third one: oh, oh. By the time I got to the tenth question, I was pleased. I had answered (lied) "no" to three questions. At the bottom, glaring right in my face, were the words, "If you answered yes to any of these questions, you have a problem with alcohol."

Holy crap! I needed to start hiding it better.

I just wasn't ready to quit drinking yet. I was not ready to face my past. Sometimes I went to the meetings and afterward stopped by the bar, bought a bottle, or sometimes saw the bar and just stopped in and never made it to the meetings.

Even though she was 35 years older than me, Shirley became the best friend I have ever had. She babysat my girls when I was at work, and they called her Grammy. We laughed so hard while talking on the phone that she said she had to have a dishtowel to wipe away her tears of laughter. That's one of the clues of alcoholism—you're a laugh a minute. Behind that hilarity is horrific pain. As Plato said in the *Republic* (388e), "laughter is an emotion that overrides rational self-control." Well, I was certainly lacking in self-control. How does one control the swirling, barb-pointed feelings that fester inside one whose been through such horror, helplessness, and grief? By this time, I had stuffed so many memories and abused my body chemically that my whole body hurt. I had trouble even dressing myself. I went to the University of Utah

Rheumatology Center and was diagnosed with secondary osteoarthritis. They gave me cortisone I was allergic to. They tried prednisone, and I couldn't figure out where I was half the time. I liked that drug, but I couldn't go in the Sun.

I was so desperate to die by that time I lay still some days, not wanting to move because it would mean I was still alive. I pictured myself lying in a casket with my arms folded across my abdomen like my Grandpa's. The casket was floating through space with the coffins of the people from the plane and my baby floating nearby. Sprinkling down around us were chunks of confetti-like sprinkles that floated down in slow, slow motion—similar to the chunks floating through the air in the plane. The caskets floated in lazy circles, the air was cool on my face, and I held the grief in my heart at bay.

* * *

During that time, I was helping the veterinarian, whose office was next door, do surgeries. He asked me if I wanted to try a painkiller that he had, so I took him up on it. The pills were for animals, and the size prescribed for a horse. I loved/hated how the pills made me feel, but I didn't drink as much. He said they were Talwins. I had never heard of them. All I knew was I didn't feel as much pain, and life looked pretty for a change. I found out later that they were synthetic opioids similar to heroin. (As I later found out, the veterinarian lost his license to practice because he was also supplying pain meds to other humans in the valley.)

When the girls went to sleep at night, I went across the highway and swam in the reservoir. The survivor's guilt was so great that I didn't care if I made it back to shore and set it up so I wouldn't. Something always stopped me, and I would return to the house even more depressed and discouraged than when I went to the water.

Finally, the husband demanded that the girls and I move to Salt Lake City. I dragged my feet for as long as I could—almost nine months. By then, I did not like him and thoroughly distrusted the man. He had told me years before that divorce was not in his book, and he was not kidding. He was manipulative, abusive, and deceptive; I also used that as an excuse to drink. He said he would come to Wyoming and take the girls if I didn't move, and I would never see them again.

Finally, I caved.

* * *

We moved to Salt Lake City on September 11, 1984. The date has a specific milestone memory for me. The day after I moved there, I knew something big was about to occur. I had been disappointed too many times, but I could feel a rumbling in my gut that felt like excitement. I didn't know what this excitement was, but I knew it would be life-altering.

On September 13, I got up and started unpacking around the house. By then, I was drinking nearly two bottles of rum, vodka, wine, or whatever, every day. I made sure that I never touched the bottles in the liquor cabinet. I had bottles hidden in the laundry basket (there were always a few dirty clothes), under the house, under paperwork in an antique secretary, and beneath the girls' bed. I had few morals by that time and didn't care. I wanted to die so damn bad but was too big of a coward to "just do it."

The first bottle I had was gone by one in the afternoon. I had drunk myself sober and was sitting on the deck at the new neighbor's house talking to her. (She later told me she didn't know I had been drinking!)

My husband came home early from work—at 1:05 p.m., and went into the house. I got up from my chair and started toward the house. He came back out. We met in the middle of the driveway. He said, "I just poured all the booze down the sink."

I thought *I'll bet you didn't find all of it.*

Then, a strange thing happened. I felt a tap three times on my shoulder and heard a voice say, "It's time to go now."

I glanced over my left shoulder. No physical person was there, of course, but I could "feel" a being standing there. I opened my mouth like a gaping fish and said, "It's time to go now."

My husband looked around, almost like he heard the voice too, then looked at me puzzled and said, "Go where?"

I said while looking around like a total idiot for the voice I had heard, "To the hospital."

He looked around like he was lost or trying to find a gnat buzzing around his ear and said, "Don't you want to get some clothes to take?"

I said, "Nope, let's just go."

I turned around, walked to the truck, and got in. The girls piled in, and I strapped them down. He got in, and we started driving, although I was unsure he could drive. He still looked too stunned to function, which did not surprise me because I had to drive to the hospital when the babies came because he became paralyzed. He asked what hospital, and I told him to go to the closest one.

A nurse told us to try Dayspring when we got to the hospital. Dayspring was booked for several weeks. We tried Highland Ridge Hospital. The lady told us the same. I told them I could not wait that long because I knew I would die if I took one more drink. They told us the only other option was to go to Salt Lake County Detox, but it wasn't a very nice place and that I would only be able to detox with no therapy. By that time, I was getting the shakes. I had not drunk for several hours, but I didn't care. I was on a mission. I was done, finished.

In the late afternoon, we found the detox center near downtown Salt Lake City, and I checked in. They took my blood pressure, and it was 180/86. The nurse, who I found out a couple of months later was the mother of a girl who would become one of my good friends, said my blood pressure was too low to be given Valium, Librium, or any other sedative. I told her that my average blood pressure was only about 90/50. She said the criteria stated no drugs for blood pressure that low (180/86).

I was about to detox cold turkey. My blood alcohol after several hours of no alcohol was .24% (.40% and above is pretty much dead. .02 is considered too impaired to drive). I hugged my daughters goodbye, and a lady took me to the showers. She handed me de-lousing soap, instructed me how to use it, and gave me a butt-show gown, a robe, and slippers. They took everything I was wearing when I got there away from me.

The nurse gave me the grand tour of the soon-to-be condemned, barred-windows building and showed me where the central meeting room was. Almost everyone in the room looked like street people, but those people would become my saviors within hours. I was introduced to each one and was grinning from ear to ear. They probably thought I was a moron, but I couldn't stop smiling.

She then took me to the room where I would be sleeping. It had two beds with World War II vintage brown metal round headboards, footboards, and frames with sagging plastic-covered mattresses that crinkled when I lay down. Right then, I was the only one in the room. I went to sleep with a determined smile, relieved I was doing something for myself.

Several hours later, I woke up when a nurse led a belligerent drunken woman to the other bed in the room. The woman's stomach was distended, she was blithering nonsensically, and she looked like she had been in a terrible windstorm or was somehow related to Medusa.

I went back to sleep, and when I awoke from the usual nightmare, I had a horrible infestation of snakes crawling on me and hanging from the ceiling. Somehow my head was at the foot of the bed, and I had the shakes so badly that my teeth rattled. I was drenched in sweat and thought I was going to die. There was no waiting drink to reach for. I had clearly entered the third dimension of hell on earth—the reptilian arena.

The following morning I had the hangover from hell. There was no Bloody Mary or Screwdriver to have for breakfast. I could no longer use the excuse of the juice-based drink being my fruit for the day and that it was healthy. My head throbbed, and the thought of food made me gag. I choked down a few bites of toast, returned to the room, and lay down.

The crazy lady that came in the middle of the night was snoring away in her bed. I prayed like a madman that I could pull this off. Since I was self-committed, I could leave any time, but I was more scared to go than to stay. I slept intermittently and was just as miserable as possible, but I had no desire to drink and felt like a rainbow had come up in the sky for me.

I started going to the central meeting room more often, talked with the other drunks, and watched TV on the grainy, flickering ancient set (at least, I think it was grainy and flickering). The drunks told me their stories; many said they had been at the detox center five or six times. I thought that drinking again could not happen to me. Every time I quit in the past, days or weeks later, I believed I could have just one drink. The next morning I would get up, and that one drink had turned into a whole bottle. It would scare me almost to death because I didn't remember drinking it. I always went into a blackout, where the following morning, I remembered nothing from the night before.

On the second day, the police checked in a fur-coated, bejeweled, handcuffed, beautiful young woman. Even though they took all her clothing and jewelry, I could tell she was dripping with money just by looking at her hair. She was pretty incoherent and ranting about her police-ordered detox. It was either detox or jail since the treatment centers were all at capacity. The third day she was there, she crawled out of a window in the second-floor bathroom in her butt-shine gown, ran across the roof, down a ladder, and to a bar across the street. There was much ado about the escapee, the first in detox's history. The drunks got a good laugh, and the nurses were embarrassed and angry and feared they would lose their jobs. Months later, I bumped into her, and she told me what had happened. She said she ran across the street, entered the bar, and shimmied up to it in her nightie. Many men were happy to buy her a drink. Of course, she was caught and had to go to court, where the judge ordered her to a treatment program, which she fulfilled. Fortunately, she stayed sober for a while. I don't know for how long.

On the third day, my withdrawals were so violent that I thought it couldn't get any worse than it was. I asked the nurse if I could have something to calm my shakes, and she told me no because my blood pressure wasn't high enough.

One of the men who had been at the center six times told me, "Wait until the fifth day. This is nothing." I thought he was nuts.

The fifth day came, and the Four Horsemen—"Terror, Bewilderment, Frustration, Despair,"[23] appeared with a vengeance. They had come daily, sometimes numerous times a day, but I could

---

23 *Alcoholics Anonymous*, (Alcoholics Anonymous World Services, New York City, 1976), 151.

hear the horses' hooves galloping through my throbbing head this time. My convulsions were so bad that I could not get a spoon of food to my mouth. I could not swallow because my gag reflex was in spasm. The other alcoholics helped me. One of the men spoon-fed me, and a woman held a glass of water with a straw to my lips.

By the sixth day, I started to feel like a human again. The seventh day was not half bad. I left on the eighth day, back to a marriage I never wanted to have.

The Four Horsemen would never appear again.

Astrological Chart 4

September 13, 1984

There is a Grand Trine between Jupiter 3-Capricorn, Moon at 0 degrees and 13 minutes-Taurus, and Mercury at 3-Virgo. This certainly helped the decision for sobriety to stick for years after the occasion. The need to protect her children was also a big factor. That the 3 planets are all earth signs also indicated practical common sense was involved. Neptune, at 28-Sagittarius is conjunct 5- Jupiter. Therefore Jupiter would also be part of this Grand Trine. Neptune is an indicator of alcohol and drugs (also pedophiles, ministers, and priests). The Moon being in a fixed sign also helped with her sobriety. Seven of the planets being on the eastern half of the chart indicated a strong free will that grasped the opportunity for a healthier life. –Joy Archer. [Perhaps churches should do astrological charts before allowing men (pedophiles) in their seminaries.]

CHAPTER 10
Finding the Ground

On my "belly button" birthday, I started therapy at Salt Lake County Drug and Alcohol Treatment Center. I went to my first A. A. meeting two days later. When they gave out the chips for thirty days of sobriety, I couldn't figure out how anyone could go without a drink for thirty days, including camels, and then they gave out chips for sixty days and ninety days. Someone got a chip for one year of sobriety, and someone else received one for two years. I was mesmerized. At the end of the meeting, they held hands when everyone got up to say the Serenity Prayer. I left. Hands hurt. I couldn't let anyone touch me. It was just too painful.

* * *

My beloved Grandma died three weeks later. I had seen her in the spring after she had suffered several debilitating strokes, and I said goodbye to her then. I knew when I walked out of the nursing home that she was in that I would never see her again on the physical plane. My grief over her death lasted for about six hours. I knew I could not wallow in self-pity this time, or I would drink again. I also knew she would be right there with me and help me stay sober.

After she died, I could see her spirit standing before me. I talked to her all the time as if she was right there. I understood why she had spoken to Grandpa's picture and acted like she heard what he was saying because I could hear Grandma as clear as a bell. She helped me get where I needed to be. It seemed that she could help me more from the "other side" than she could when she was on the Earth plane.

Shirley died of oral cancer from too many cigarettes and too much alcohol in December, the day before she was going to board a bus to visit us. After she died, she stood just behind me and to the right and was a vast, white-bright being. I wondered why I was able to see these "beings" as clearly as I could see you or anyone else. What was the phenomenon that was happening? Had these beings or others been there the whole time, and I anesthetized them away with alcohol so I wouldn't appear completely deranged?

I went to A. A. with a vengeance and met hundreds of other alcoholics, and we helped each other stay sober. I learned a new way of positive living, speaking, and thinking. One night after about two years of sobriety, I was sitting in the café in the basement of the Alano Club after a meeting. The Alanon meeting wasn't out yet, and I made a crack about how the Alanons always ran late. A friend looked at me and said, "It sounds like you need to attend an Alanon meeting."

The next night, I attended an Alanon meeting and discovered I was co-dependent. I was always trying to fix things and judgmental as hell. I was quite surprised because I thought fixing things was how it should be. After all, I was the one who always made sure my mom didn't commit suicide. When I was little and my dad hugged her, I always got between them because I knew what men did to girls. Then I had to ask myself a very grave question. Why was I always trying to fix others? It was because I didn't have the guts to look at myself, and fixing things outside me was much more manageable. I was always able to see the sliver in another's eye but unable to see the log in my eye. I discovered that alcoholism was merely a symptom of my co-dependency and inability to tell my secrets or the truth.

I got a rehabilitation grant and went back to college. I took the Drug and Alcohol Counseling course at the University of Utah and received my certification. I was rearing to go out and heal the world of alcoholics even though I had not yet healed myself.

I then wanted to learn more about the psychology of the way an individual thinks. I got grants and scholarships that paid for my tuition and had money left over. Then I realized that an individual is part of a bigger whole and took classes in sociology. I started volunteering at the Utah State Prison and helped create A. A. meetings. Then, I decided I also needed to know about criminology and the correction system.

I loved college and seemed not to be able to get enough. I had always avoided being around intelligent people because that was not my role in my family dynamic, and besides, I didn't want to look stupid next to them. Imagine my surprise when I discovered that I had a brain and that I was allowed to have a thought. These people were interested in what I had to say and, for some strange reason, thought my words had merit. This new-found venue was liberating to me, and I excelled. The only problem was that I could not take tests. I could write essays fluidly and, through writing, could zero in on the answer through some bizarre round-about logic. Speeches were a piece of cake because I felt I was on stage in a theater. Speeches gave me power. I knew I held the audience in my hands and could convince, corrupt, lose or win over the listeners. Besides, if I stepped out of my way, I discovered that I rarely remembered what I had said—it was as if someone else had been talking.

I knew that there were no absolutes in any multiple-choice questions. I had trouble resolving which answer was the most correct unless one of the answers was glaringly wrong. I studied test taking and discovered that if I looked to the left, I could find the answer, as that is where logic forms in the brain. If I looked to the right, I could not find the answer because that is the land of make-believe. Ah, but if you look past the land of make-believe, you will also find it is the land of intuition. I did hypnosis sessions to organize information in a logical sequence so that I could retrieve it when I took a test, and the next thing I knew, I could take tests.

Along with four other students in most of my classes, we tipped the scale and changed the bell curve for the whole class. Pretty soon, an academic sorority invited me to join. I had stepped out of my role as the class clown and the athlete, well, just the athlete part. During my senior year, I let my grades slide because I just didn't feel comfortable graduating summa cum laude. It was bad enough that I was consistently on the Dean's List—one step at a time.

One of the things I learned in A. A. was not to make any major decisions during my first year of sobriety and to not make any major changes. They also said to get rid of anything that gave me an excuse to drink.

My marriage was in the crapper. He was even more emotionally abusive after I got sober, and I had, quite frankly, outgrown his narrow fear-based way of thinking and controlling methods. I no longer believed I was supposed to behave in a certain way as a wife. It finally occurred to me that we were such bipolar opposites that we repelled each other rather than attracted each other. I did not believe in violence, including guns, hunting, and slaughtering animals for sport. He often said he felt like going out and killing something. What had happened to the man I had married? Was this behavior always there, and I ignored it through a drug and alcohol-induced haze in favor of conformity and an illusion? Was I starting to wake up from the deep, long sleep I had been in and seeing things around me for the first time? The truth is the behavior was always there. That's why he was standing alone at the end of the bar, his hands wrapped around a glass of Jack Daniels, glaring into the glass mirror, when I first saw him.

I did not want guns around me or in the house, and he often set up his bullet press on the dining room table to make bullets. He hated gays, blacks, Hispanics, Jews, and all minorities—huh, just like my dad. He ranted about these people constantly. I did not want my daughters to grow up learning such hateful thoughts. Good grief. I had to get out of there!

Before I got sober, I asked him if he would go to therapy with me if I got sober. He said he would. After I got sober, he informed me that he didn't need treatment and that I was the one with the problem and was nothing but a drunk and would end up in the gutter. While he said that, he pointed his finger at me. Then he laughed.

I just smiled. I had had it.

I asked him if he would go to an Alanon meeting. Of course, the answer was the same. He said he did not have a problem.

During other tirades, he told me that my education was costing money and was a waste of time because I was nothing but a drunk. I just informed him that, in case he hadn't noticed, I wasn't drinking anymore and that I had grants and scholarships, and it didn't cost us a penny for me to go to school.

He told me it was my fault that he kept losing his job (getting fired).

Wow, I didn't realize I had that much power. However, I did realize I chose him to continue manifesting my powerlessness role.

One day when he was ridiculing me, my Mars in Leo took over, and I picked up a chair and swung the chair at him while he was pointing at me and laughing. Unfortunately, I missed him. That sealed the deal for me. It was too bad that I hit the wall and broke the leg on the antique chair, but it was good because I made a decision that day. With the swing of that chair, it was almost like I had taken a sword and severed the bindings of our marriage. The shackles flew off with a clink and a clank of flying chain links as they rolled, tumbled, and bounced across the room. I filed for divorce, and the girls and I moved out because we couldn't afford to stay in the house. I received a second chance at life and felt like I had been reborn—that I had received a "new freedom and a new happiness."

Here is why he acted the way he did: When a person gets sober, the partner or family member often doesn't know how to control the person anymore, so they try to get them to drink again through an antic such as ridicule or drama. As a practicing alcoholic, someone is always controlling us. We pick those people because we can't control ourselves. When we stop drinking, we take our control back. When the controller's job is taken from them, they no longer know where they fit and will hang onto that role, kicking and screaming. Also, when a person gets sober, they begin to see people, their spouses, and their relatives in a new light, which is not always complimentary. I am grateful to him now for his codependent behavior because it pushed me forward in my recovery. This time, probably much to his bafflement and amazement, I didn't conform or try to fix it. Nor did I drink. The larger question was: Why did he want me to drink? Was he hiding something? If so, what was it? Was he leading a double life?

The divorce took two and a half years because he wouldn't turn in Discoveries and was found in contempt of court several times. Unfortunately, the judge never fined or jailed him, so he had no incentive to change. We bickered over ten-cent items and, as I found out later, had rented a storage unit and secretly moved things out of the house individually.

My attorney was afraid of him and refused to meet in a room with us without at least one other person besides the three of us and a cop outside the door. By that time, I was afraid of him, too. He was a tool and die maker and did tool work on a gun, the .454 magnum, that would put a hole through a bear. He owned one of the guns, and I would not put it past him to use it on me, the girls, and then on himself.

By then, I was under so much stress that my stomach twisted in knots. Finally, one night a friend rushed me to the hospital. The E. R. doctor shot me full of morphine, which I fought him doing like a madman. When they took x-rays, it showed that my large intestine had tied itself off in a knot in two sections, and my gut was the size of a football. The football had twisted around, and instead of being down in the area where the appendix should have been, it was up against my mid-spine. The doctor performed emergency surgery.

Before entering the operating room, I chatted with my "guides." I felt a calm come over me. My Grandpas and Grandmas, Shirley, Muriel, and others, showed up in the hallway for the occasion.

When they opened me up, my gut had untwisted and was lying exactly where it was supposed to be. They went ahead and removed my appendix and sutured my intestine to the abdominal wall. When they told me they removed my appendix, I was annoyed. I felt like the doctor had stolen part of me. After the surgery, I could feel my intestines pulling against my abdominal wall every time I got stressed. Several years later, it ripped free.

* * *

I took three of my psychology classes from a woman named Dee. She was black, a lesbian, and a female and said she filled all the requirements for hiring equality. She was also a concert pianist. How ridiculous that the University system treated her the way she was. The law may have made them hire her, but the University did not treat her equally. They gave her an "office" smaller than most people's closets. The office was on the top floor of what Dee referred to as the "symbolically penis-shaped" psychology building. The powers ensured that she never taught a class on campus.

One night in a class held at a community library that was eighty miles from her home, she told us that to resolve a dream, an issue, or a nightmare, to concentrate on finishing the dream. By doing so, we would find closure. That night I went home and focused on finishing my hijacking night terror. It didn't work that night because I woke up in a panic, the blood pounding in my ears and my heart exploding in my chest with the smells assaulting my senses and the sounds ringing in my ears.

The next night I was suddenly back on the airplane. I heard the people screaming. I was choking on the smoke, smelling the burning flesh, and feeling the heat from the flames. I woke up again. This same dream went on for several nights until finally, one night, suddenly, I popped out of the plane and stood on the tarmac, wholly surrounded by a bubble. I watched what was happening in the aircraft outside instead of experiencing it on the inside. I put my hands in my pockets and walked away from the plane whistling. I never looked back. I have not had a nightmare about the hijacking since. Several years later, I did dream that I was watching the dead people on the plane---only they weren't dead. Their happy, carefree soul-selves glided joyfully on a conveyor belt into the heavens.

* * *

While attending college, I went to the same therapist for about four years. She would tell me later that I had the biggest wall built around me that she had ever seen. We chipped away at the wall brick by brick and got maybe two bricks taken down. I couldn't tell the hidden truth to save my soul because I had spent my whole life talking in circles to figure out what the other person wanted to hear. By the time I came up with an answer, I had forgotten the question, but the therapist hadn't—how annoying. I had kept secrets for so long that I couldn't remember why I didn't tell them or what they were. Quite simply, I was a co-dependent people-pleaser who didn't have the time or the energy to please myself—after all, women didn't deserve to be happy. Besides, my dad had always told me that no one cared what I thought or felt and said I shouldn't let people "get the best of me." What was the "best of me"? I don't think I'd ever seen it.

I was surprised when I took an MMPI test (Minnesota Multi-Phasic Inventory), which showed I was too truthful. The cognitive therapist who gave the results to me said I would have a hard time getting along in society if I kept being so honest. I was shocked and asked her if I was supposed to start lying. She said I would need to if I wanted to get along. I thought that was the most ridiculous thing I'd ever heard. Good grief! If I was honest, how dishonest was the rest of society?

I sought unhealthy relationships with people I chose because they looked like a model that just stepped off the front cover of a magazine. There was no way someone would see me arm-linked with someone who wasn't candy-apple-perfect looking, and the sicker they were emotionally, the better for me because it made me feel more put-together and normal. My ego was entirely out of control, and the fact that I stayed sober can only be attributed to A. A. and my guides. I was warned about this pink cloud and told that I'd be in trouble when the air popped out of that pink cloud, like when air popped out of a pin-pricked balloon.

I kept myself on the pink cloud for two years after getting sober. My therapist kept telling me that I needed to cry. I couldn't allow myself to because, as I told her, "I'm afraid that if I start, I won't be able to stop."

She said, "No one has ever cried to death."

I wasn't so sure. Besides, Dad always hit us if we cried and threatened to hit us again if we didn't stop crying.

My therapist had me meet with the clinic psychiatrist, who walked me through some hypnosis sessions. After the first session, I started to cry, and of course, I couldn't stop. I cried over nothing and cried over something. The more I cried, the more depressed I felt. I cried for a year, and then, suddenly, it stopped. Now I was faced with depression and no box of tissues to reach for when I felt a memory or an issue come up. I knew my problems would not resolve this time by blowing my nose.

My inability to face my demons finally got me to the point that I couldn't get off the couch even to make it to my classes. I tried anti-depressants, which made it worse and postponed the inevitable. I felt like the big black blob that was weighing me down just got denser and denser. After six weeks of trying those nasty drugs that made me sleepy and fat, I realized that I had to get out a pry bar and pry out what was making me continue to be sick even in my sobriety.

* * *

By the third year of sobriety, I started having flashes from childhood while sitting in classrooms, driving down the street, or any other place I was. After the childhood flash, I would look around to see if I had gasped out loud or cried out. No one flinched or looked at me.

My secrets were still safe. By the fifth year, I again decided I wanted to kill myself rather than live in such intense, constant emotional pain and unknown-to-me-consciously secrets. I called my therapist and told her to come and get me and put me somewhere, or I was going to kill myself, but not really, and I didn't know why. It wasn't very clear. I felt like I was betraying my family because I chose not to be like them or how they expected me to be in the family dynamic. My mother spent much of her life either threatening suicide or attempting it. Had I picked up her behavior? Had I picked up her way of coping with her pain? Was I willing to die as a martyr to her misery? No. I was choosing to live. The problem was I didn't know how to. I had not had a daily example of how to live in the present or on life's terms.

My therapist found a residential treatment center where I could stay for just one night, and as we pulled up, she said, "Now, I'm going to warn you. These people are severely mentally ill, and you are not." I told her that I didn't care. I just needed a break from the world.

That night, I saw people walking around who had completely split away from logic and mind. I noticed that many had numerous entities walking around with them—all very dark. There was something else in them that I could not pinpoint at that time. It was almost as if they had some strange over-soul with them, that perhaps there was more than one of them. My curiosity peaked, but it would be years before I understood what I had seen.

Sometime in the middle of the night, a bright, white light came into that room, and I knew I would be all right. A calm feeling infused with pure love and serenity floated through me. I quickly realized those "crazy" people were helping me get sane. What was it in them that I could see on some level of my subconscious mind that I would not have understood in myself if I had not gone there? They also made me realize that I had a choice—that I could choose to be sane, or I could choose to be crazy. The line was so fine that it was as sharp as a razor. At exactly 1:05 a.m. (I looked at the clock), I knew I did not want to be crazy. I realized I didn't have to be depressed or crazy like my mother or angry like my father. I no longer wanted to have one foot in yesterday and one foot in tomorrow. I no longer wanted to "piss all over today." I also understood that I could not ride two horses with only one butt.

I went home the following morning, stirred with the possibilities of a different life than I had ever had in this incarnation. Still, on some nights, I woke up so afraid I couldn't move. These were not nightmares like I used to have about the airplane but about other events. Even so, I was still morbidly afraid. One night I decided to try another technique. I welcomed the fear, saying, "Welcome in…welcome in." I felt the fear flow right through my body. And, just like that, it was gone.

* * *

A few weeks later, and from some knowingness within me, I knew that I needed to expand my therapy. I could no longer simply schmooze with my therapist, or I would stay stuck right where I was in the "secrets" lockdown. I went to a psychic who told me to see a psychologist named Ralph Gant. Ralph is no longer on the Earth plane, nor is the psychic, but he taught me a technique called "integration." As we grow up, parts of our psyche disassociate from us when something happens. Those parts of us that disassociate hold our memories. I was willing to try anything. I was sick and tired of being sick and tired.

Ralph would completely change my life and show me how to put myself back together again. I was ready for and welcomed the change.

CHAPTER 11

Taking Back My Power

I started delving into childhood and found some startling things. I returned to those stored memories and retrieved what I call my "children," the parts of me that split off. The hole in my gut the wind blew through that I tried to fill with alcohol, sex, shopping, religion, drugs, food, or trying to control everything, and everybody in my life began to close up. When those parts of me returned, I felt like my stomach was huge, like some statues of the laughing, chubby Buddha. Within days the "psychological swelling" in the hole went down, and I could then integrate more "children."

Integrating the children is so easy that it is startling and holds no fear once the fear of possibility and success is gone. Unfortunately, I cannot tell you in this book how to integrate because sometimes the children come back with a memory one is not equipped to deal with alone. Sometimes the children come back "programmed" to self-destruct, and you must have someone who understands how to de-program these events until you have the tools to bypass the "essence" of the programmed words used to control and manipulate you. Good luck finding a therapist who knows how to do this technique because they are few and far between but search for a therapist who studied at the Menninger Institute as they are, in my opinion, tops in teaching therapists how to do integration work and how to work with all types of abuse victims. Unfortunately, some therapists are not adequately trained to do integration work, and they give integration work a bad name. Also, beware of therapists who might plant their unresolved seeds in you. Most therapists will look at you blankly when you even mention the word *integration*, especially psychiatrists, and most of them do not understand that it has to do with drawing, literally, thousands to billions of *children* back inside who have split off and away from the physical body. They are outside the body in the form of an "essence." I call it an "essence" because they have not left your energy field. They are outside the body and must be inside to feel whole.

Another reason I say it is essential to have someone help with this is someone might have programmed the disassociated part in some cult event. The cult event may be satanic cults, One World Order events, Nazi events/White Supremacy, television, schools, white noise in stores, etc. (One grocery store chain in the 1980s was notorious for white noise over the intercoms until sued by a man I knew who could hear the white noise urging him to buy certain products.) They can also be what religious cults and church rituals have programmed into people—you will go to hell if you do such and such. The leaders tell some people they will go to hell if they leave a particular cult/religion or don't tithe or have sex with them or another person in the cult/religion. Or, perhaps, you will go to hell if you're gay, or they tell you that psychics, tarot readers, astrologers, etc., are from the devil. Sounds pretty silly. Doesn't it? But those simple mantras not only program people to fear the past, present, and future but also cause self-denigration. When people buy into this programming, they give their power to others.

(Watch the documentary *Shiny Happy People* on Amazon to see how this programming works. As explained on Amazon.com, it's the story of

> the truth beneath the wholesome surface of reality tv's favorite mega-family, The Duggars, and the radical organization behind them: The Institute in Basic Life Principles IBLP. As details of the family and their

> scandal unfold, we realize they're part of an insidious, much larger threat already in motion, with democracy itself in peril.

Guess who was behind the overthrow of Roe v Wade? Would it surprise you that they also have people within the Supreme Court and the government? The terrifying thing is that numerous women of pedophilia accused the founder, Bill Gothard, of sexually abusing them when they were minors. Since the allegations came to light, Gothard resigned from his post, and Duggar took over as leader. Duggar's son Josh is serving time in prison for child pornography. While Josh was on trial, the father, Jim Bob Duggar, had the gall to run for Congress. Josh's sisters have also come forward and said Josh molested them. It is also alleged that IBLP teaches parents to beat their children into submission so they will do what leaders tell them to do. They can't very well say this is a lie because there is a video to prove it. A very disturbing docuseries, to say the least.)

This type of destructive programming reminds me of a joke I heard in Utah.

> A man died and went to heaven. St. Peter was showing him around. As they walked, Peter pointed to groups of people in fenced areas and said, "There's the Methodists. Over there are the Catholics. Over there are the Jews." This went on for quite some time until they came to a walled-off area. He leaned in close to the man and said, "Sh-h. The Mormons are over there. They think they're the only ones here."

Of course, you could change the name Mormon to the name Evangelical or any other religion, but the point is that no one is unique. One could even add the letters LGBTQ+ or alcoholics to any of the groups. As one lady said, "I'm an alcoholic; I have leukemia, and I believe I'm terminally unique. My belief that I'm terminally unique is the disease that will kill me."

Someone with a hidden agenda can easily implant superstitious beliefs in a person's mind. Superstitions are un-provable, and the *New College Dictionary* calls it "an unreasonable belief in or notion of the ominous significance of a particular thing, circumstance or the like."[24] Isn't that what these threats of hell are—ominous and unreasonable? When someone tells people such controlling words, they feel so unworthy upon death that they don't make it past the ethereal plane and stay stuck in what the Catholics call purgatory (from the word *purge*) or limbo. The Bible mentions neither word. The Catholic Church made up this belief to control their congregants through guilt and to make more money for the coffers. This belief is utter nonsense from a spiritual point of view. I know many people hang on to a cancer-riddled, disease-riddled, or age-rotting body because they fear going to hell.

The shows on TV about "ghosts," a German word for *spirit*, are misused and misunderstood. A spirit and a soul are two different things. A spirit can freely move anywhere, whereas a soul is within the body and is what animates the body. Some describe the difference between the spirit and the soul this way: the body is the glove, the soul is the hand in the glove, and the spirit moves the hand within the glove. When I was on the airplane floor and in the back of the ambulance, I could feel my soul leave my body and then feel it shoved back into my body. Oddly, it took a while for my spirit to reanimate my soul and body. Another way to describe this is: the body is the housing for gears, the soul is the gears, and the spirit is the electricity that makes the gears spin. Where does the spinning occur in the body? It occurs in 144,000 areas, thus the biblical 144,000 of Revelation 7:9, 14, which says the 144,000 will go to heaven. What does that mean? It means all energy centers in one's body turn on. Known as *nadichakras* in Sanskrit, Luke 12:32 calls them the "little flock," while John 10:16 calls them the "other sheep."

Those caught in limbo are souls that did not make it entirely to the other side when they left the physical body. The uncompleted sojourn might be because of fear of burning in hell, or they are unable to let go

---

[24] Stein, ed., *The Random House College Dictionary*, Revised Ed., (New York, 1975), 1325.

of their loved ones, their possessions, or their loved ones have not let go of them. The cord between their physical body and soul has broken, but the thread has only unraveled so far. It's like a balloon that has a string tied to it. When the helium evaporates, it begins to sink to the ground; at that point, the string begins to bounce along the ground. Sometimes these souls will borrow someone's body when they so wholly dissociate they are like an empty suit walking around town. It is like leaving your car in the parking lot with the keys in the ignition. Someone is going to steal it. These souls can cross to the light. Often, they kick and scream until they get to the actual light and are astonished at how wonderful and peaceful it is. In every re-entry I have witnessed, the person did not cross entirely to the other side for the above reasons, with the number one reason being their fear of going to hell. I have seen only one crossing where the person chose to go into the lower dimension. The person said he did not feel comfortable in the higher dimensions and thought he did not deserve the light (higher, lighter dimension) because he didn't think he had advanced far enough spiritually.

When I was in alcohol delirium, I was in hell, or what some call "the second reptilian dimension," where Adam went to in the allegorical story of the Garden of Eden when the snake tempted them. In my near-death experiences, I found no hell. My experience on the Earth plane was hell. On the "dead" side was utter peace and tranquility. I could see peaceful beings hovering and picture the upper dimensions. In this instance, I had no choice but to stay on the Earth or leave. The decision was not mine.

I see hell as the conflict within the psyche as it tries to traverse between the physical/Earth plane, the psyche's earthly programming, and the spiritual world/the ethers. There is no black and white on the other side. All are accepted back home. Unfortunately, some get stuck in that in-between space due to misunderstandings.

How did the Buddha describe the Garden of Eden story? Sometimes the Buddha is displayed under the Bodhi tree. The Bodhi tree is actually the same as the Tree of Good and Evil in the Eden story. Both trees consist of twelve branches. Those twelve branches are the hood of the cobra serpent and represent the twelve months of the year and the twelve constellations. When the Buddha sat under the Bodhi tree, Nagas/ Serpents protected him all night.

There is a reason why the Garden of Eden didn't occur first in the Genesis story. It came along third in the series of adventures of Adam and Eve. To understand this, in Indian mythology,

> Adishesha uncoils, and times moves forward. This means the remainder that is left from the previous creation stays and when it begins to uncoil, it is called as Adishesha because it is the first remainder. When it uncoils, it means that another creation begins to happen. This is a very profound aspect of life expressed in symbolic ways.[25]

In other words, the story of the Garden of Eden represents a time when humankind moved into a third phase of creation. Why does our life go in the crapper? We don't follow the way of the Naga/Serpent. We don't allow it to coil around us; we live life linearly.

Think about how your physical system works; it consists of cells, nerves, and blood vessels that flow like a serpent. While the first two phases of creation, known as swana (dog) and kaka (bird) in Buddhism, represent breathing/survival and wisdom/sensitivity, Naga/Snake represents perception beyond the five senses. As Isha says,

> There is intellect and then there is perception. If you empower the intellect, you will be very smart, but you need fools around you, otherwise, how will you be smart? In my understanding of life, accumulating a billion dollars is the dumbest thing you can do, because I know there is no banking services elsewhere other than this planet and I know my time is limited here. Why would I acquire billions of dollars? For what? But

---

25 Isha, Jan 11, 2022, https://isha.sadhguru.org/in/en/wisdom/article/naga-panchami-festival-snake-worship#point5.

> people think that is smart, so I said, "To feel smart, you need fools around you." But if you allow life to happen to you in its full glory, maybe you will not be considered smart in the society. If you close your eyes and sit here, you are neither smart nor stupid, you are just life and that is all that matters. How vibrant, exuberant, joyful, and wonderful a life you are is all that matters. In this pursuit, naga is very important.[26]

Isha's story brings up a dream I had several years after leaving Salt Lake City. I was walking down a gravel road near my childhood home. Suddenly, a giant snake crawled out of the ditch. My mother's programming of snake-fear kicked in. I jumped back; the snake lifted its head and looked directly into my eyes, forked tongue snapping. Rather than re-coiling, I looked into two stunningly beautiful diamond-shaped emerald green eyes. The serpent opened its mouth. I stepped inside, walked to the end of its tail, turned around, and walked back to its mouth. As I stepped out, the serpent became my spine; its head rose behind the back of my head, and its fins puffed out, forming a protective hood around me. I had stepped into my power, yet I was not a billionaire and realized I no longer needed to be surrounded by fools.

* * *

The disintegrative events that I experienced started before I was born. Does this happen to everyone? No. Some babies are wanted. In my case, I was not. I could hear my mother's voice and "feel" or "intuit" her thoughts. I was also unwanted by my brother and my sister. Somewhere in my psyche, I understood the perfect number was 3, and I was the number 3. I learned that my family and I set it up that way before I came to Earth so that I could experience what being unwanted felt like. I also needed a life where I would be alone to do the "work" I came here to do. Before I understood why I was unwanted, I always felt and

---

26 bid.

thought that I had no say-so over anything because I didn't belong in the family I chose to be born. My mother often told me I didn't belong in "this family." Let me repeat these powerful words: *I chose to be born into.* We are veiled when we come to Earth, so we can't remember our life contracts. Some of us, however, have a big tear in our veil, and, as many who have had near-death experiences will tell you, we can see into our life records and other peoples' records. What we must learn is how to control this.

Simply put, I came to Earth to learn lessons. How it felt to be unwanted was one of the lessons. Essentially my mother was a master teacher.

Perhaps the most valuable lesson she taught me was the difference between light and darkness. Now that she is old, she often "comes to me" psychically and asks for forgiveness. One must understand that you don't have to have physical or verbal contact with the person during the forgiving, nor do you ever have to see the person again. Forgiveness is for you, not for them. It is for them to understand that what they did is on them. To explain this further, my mother and I had a contract for her to manipulate, hurt, and abuse me that was to last for 42 years. She wanted it to last longer. I gave her many opportunities to stop what she had always done, but she wouldn't or couldn't. I completely severed ties with her. I did not sever the relationship through hatred or spite but through love and gratitude for her lessons. The irony is that she threatened to kill herself almost monthly when I was a child, which caused trauma to me and my brother and sister, and she lived to be over 100 years old. As the saying goes, "God works in mysterious ways."

When I started doing integration work, I found that doctors become a newborn's savior because they are the one who gets the baby out of a head-crushing birth canal experience, pulls the baby out with forceps or a vacuum, or is the one who untangles the cord from around a baby's neck, which can create a dissociative experience. Unfortunately, after birth, often the baby is removed from the mother—another dissociative experience; then the baby is stimulated in some form—disassociate; then they have a tube stuck up their nose to suck out the snot—disassociate. They are Apgar-ed, poked, prodded, and on and on, and each time they are, another part of them dissociates. Regardless of whether they disassociate during these experiences, this sets up a pattern for people to run to the doctor when they feel a twinge.

By the time the poor child is held by the mother, what she has is a child who is not quite "all there" in terms of a cohesive spirit-centered being and also has a being who has learned not to trust the mother—after all, she is the one who let them do this to them. Sticking the baby in an incubator in a room away from the mom, in a nursery, taken to another room for an inspection, thoughts being projected onto the child by a too-tired or too rough or mean nurse, causes the part of the child disrespected, mauled or emotionally abused to disassociate, disassociate, disassociate and on and on. If you do not think that a mother is not the most important thing on this Earth, please think again.

I worked on bringing the dissociated children back every chance I got. I integrated if I went to the beach, the forest, or the mountains. When I was showering, I integrated. I could not believe how much of me had split off.

After doing my integration work, I began to understand that I no longer needed alcohol to make me feel whole because I no longer used that outside stimulant to fill the hole in my gut that the wind blew through. However, after several years of intense work, the "essence" of the dysfunctional behavior was still a part of me. It took me a while to become conscious of the behaviors as I focused on staying sober. Just because I was doing the integration work, it did not mean that I would immediately stop the same behavior patterns, and letting go of some behaviors continues to be a process.

CHAPTER 12
Behavior Loops

In A. A. and Alanon, people talked about the tapes we have in our minds. I found that these tapes are the constant behaviors that I created to stay on the same mimicked behavior loop over and over, whether consciously or unconsciously. It didn't matter that the behavior stunk like a pile of shit. It mattered that it was warm, soft, and familiar.

I learned the dynamics of the spiral of defeat in our emotional and psychological makeup. For example, the only true feeling is fear. All other emotions are a by-product of fear—jealousy, self-esteem, pride, etc. The second by-product of fear is anger, rage, etc. Of course, anger has to do with powerlessness (fear). The third level is depression (feeling helpless over your fear), and the fourth is "self-defeating behavior" (I'm going to bypass my fear). These behaviors can be anything from alcoholism (sugar and carbohydrate addiction that turn into alcohol in the body), drug addiction (including food, pharmaceutical, and over-the-counter drugs), sex and religion and their enormous number of subsets, shopping sprees, gambling, crises or dramas, co-dependency, computer addiction, smoking, hoarding, pornography, "geographics" (constantly moving in the hope that the new place will make everything alright), or anything else that becomes a habit beyond what is sensible for the person financially, spiritually, emotionally, psychologically, and or physically. One grasps these things outside of oneself and makes one feel "high" and giddily happy, but then one crashes….

Everyone knows about alcoholics and drug addicts. They are the biggest bane in our society! They are the worst of the worst! Or are they? More often than not, people overlook the other addictions because they don't "appear" to have as big of an impact on society and are hidden more easily. This assumption is an enormous misjudgment as the other addictions have just as significant an impact. For example, over-eating, anorexia, and bulimia significantly impact our country's financial stability due to extreme grocery bills, medical problems, medical bills, and high insurance rates. Shopping sprees have caused the loss of homes and marriages and put people into debt they cannot possibly figure out how to solve. When they file bankruptcy, the cost of everyone's goods and services go up to absorb the financial loss to the companies, while clothes with tags still on them hang in their closets as a testament to the shopper's vulnerability to a little piece of plastic or fabric.

People go to church and wave their hands in the air to the pounding of repetitive music, and they praise Jesus ragged. They come out looking like they have just taken a hallucinatory drug and are ranting about how amazing Jesus is. Some days, however, like the gambler who loses, they may come out of church looking like they have lost everything because of feeling unworthy of the Jesus they hope will "rescue" them. Guilt seems to be the most prevalent by-product of religious addiction. Something as simple as having a thought or using a word or a sentence that is not part of the religion's mantra can cause guilt. These emotions are addiction by-products and run somewhere on the fear scale.

People who get caught up in religion and its constricting rules may exclude their family of origin members, including parents, from their life in exchange for acceptance into their religious cult (*cult*: "group or sect bound together by devotion"[27]), where they feel a false sense of acceptance, creating more guilt. They pray over everything before dinner until Grandma nods off and falls face-first into the gravy boat. They seem

27 Stein, *Dictionary.*

to bypass what Jesus said about prayer and hypocrisy—"And when you pray, you must not be like the hypocrites; for they love to stand and pray in the synagogues and at the street corners, that men may see them... But when you pray, go into your room [or closet or bathroom], shut the door and pray to your Father who is in secret...." (Matthew 6:5–6).[28] Jesus even had the courtesy to go off by himself to the Garden. The Bible does not say that you should spend five minutes praying over a bowl of gravy while it thickens to the sound of people's stomachs rumbling and their salivary glands kicking up noisy mouthsful of spit. Matthew 6:7 continues: "But when you are praying, do not use meaningless repetition [using the same catchphrases in each prayer], as the Gentiles [heathens] do; for they suppose that they will be heard for their many words."[29] So, I suggest "Keep It Simple, Stupid" or "KISS" and pass the gravy.

A person who has a sexual addiction plans and plans how to conquer their latest quest just like the alcoholic plans or schemes when and where to get the next drink. By the time the sexual act is over, they find they are still empty, still trying to fill up the void created when first molested as a child. Before they even get off the bed, couch, backseat of a car, or other surfaces, the offender thinks about their next conquest or what they will have for lunch. One person I know said, "I was a horn dog and jumped on everything I could find until I got out of my ego-based lower chakras."

There are no words in my vocabulary to express the disgust and powerlessness I feel for this most insidious of drugs. Some sex addicts get caught up in kiddy porn or adult porn. This drug runs the gamut from porn to strippers to snuff, and the addicts use **victims** for enjoyment. I can attest to how disturbing these victims and their voyeurs are as I have seen them in action. This drug seems to be the dirtiest of little secrets that society sweeps the furthest under the rug and is the one that unequivocally steals the victims' souls.

More than likely, sexual addicts got caught in the victim role as children, just like all other addicts and co-dependents. The victim

---

28 *The NASB Open Bible*, New American Standard, (Thomas Nelson Publishing, 1975).

29 Ibid.

role is where people go as adults when pushed into a corner through confrontation or when they don't want to take responsibility for anything, just like what happened to them when they were children (it's my fault this happened to me—again, the child's ego). Professional victims will make excuses (lie) to get out of anything that looks like responsibility for their actions.

People may go out dancing and bar hopping and are high on life until the next day. They wake up with a hangover, feel terrible physically, emotionally, and spiritually, and can't remember where they left their car or that they hit someone else's car. They might not remember who they fought with, had sex with, or woke next to someone they thought looked great the night before. (As many men said of Rita Hayworth, I went to bed with Gilda and woke up with the reality. Gilda was her most famous character (the dream).) They run away, hopping into their pants or tripping over their pantyhose that they desperately try to pull up to escape the sight before them. They swear they will never do it again, but they always do.

After their first hours of headache, shame and self-loathing, and a bloody Mary to bite the hair of the dog, they may spend the first part of the week at work reminiscing about what a great time they had because they want to cover up the horror of the reality.

In the second part of the week, they plan and look forward to making their next conquest (making a fool of themselves again), hoping there won't be the horror this time. (There will be). To keep the "high," the person must return over and over to the behavior that made them feel "high" rather than allowing themselves to feel the low. They must stop the behavior if they ever want to feel balanced.

Your average person sometimes decides to try just one hit of acid (LSD). That one hit of acid could make the person do something as bizarre as break into an aviary and rape an emu, thus killing it. This actually happened when I worked in the court system. After the rape, the police charged him with multiple counts, including bestiality on an animal resulting in death. We had a big argument at work the morning of his arraignment about who *got* to go to court that day—usually, we whined that we didn't want to go because it was so boring that we had to labor to stay awake. That day, three of us showed up to answer the judge's questions about whether the young man would be allowed out of jail on "bail," "supervised release," or his "own recognizance." (A couple of our co-workers also sat in the back like they were at a peep show.)

Finally, the moment arrived. The poor kid who raped the emu on Saturday night and looked like the wreck of the Hesperus in his mugshot walked in. Imagine our surprise when the manacled kid in the orange jumpsuit was a clean-cut, All-American-looking boy who looked nothing like his disheveled mug shot. He was clearly mortified about what he had done and slunk into the courtroom. I don't think I have ever seen anyone that embarrassed. We all watched and grinned at the judge, who we loved to work with because he was funny and kind. He tried to stifle the ripple of laughter, but the corners of his lips and the crinkles in the corner of his eyes gave him away. He only smiled once and quickly wiped it away with his hand while the poor kid found all kinds of things on the floor to look at.

PCP (angel dust) will cause a human to feel no pain and have no control over their sensibilities. People will think they can walk through a tree and continue to walk even after their bones break. I have seen numerous incidences where someone walked down the street punching in car windows with their fists. After ten policemen bring them down, they take the busted-up fellow to the hospital, where doctors attempt to rebuild their shattered hands. Do they retake PCP?—more than likely, yes, because they feel invincible and powerful when on the drug. Read that last sentence carefully. It should come as no surprise that people who use this drug felt powerless as a child.

Heroin addicts will steal from every member of their family. In New Mexico, which had the highest death rate per capita from 1993-1995 for heroin-related deaths (www.heroin-addiction.org), almost every window in every house has bars welded across them to keep relatives and non-relatives from breaking in and stealing money and things to pawn. Many places even have steel cages over swamp coolers and air conditioners to keep thieves from stealing the copper so they can pawn it. Heroin addicts will continue to shoot up even if they use tar heroin that causes an abscess that lands them in the hospital, where they sometimes lose that arm or that leg that was infected. And, of course, we all know about HIV/AIDS and Hepatitis C caused by using dirty needles and having unprotected sex, although most people, while "high," have no sexual desire whatsoever. Switzerland wisely set aside parks specifically for heroin addicts. There are vending machines containing needles so diseases aren't spread.

When a heroin addict stops using heroin and gets on methadone, they will go so far as to turn tricks to get the money for their methadone. If the addict gets off of heroin and methadone, there is a high chance that they will die of alcoholism. As you can see, the cycle of addiction changes its ugly face from one addiction to the next and includes all addictions.

Prisons are full of women who write bad checks rather than steal to get their "fix" and men who are more likely to steal. People shoplift to get "things" to steal back what was taken from them when they were little (their little bodies and innocence). One unknown perk of detoxing from heroin addiction is that it kills fewer people than detoxing from alcohol and barbiturates. Wow, what a bonus!

Methamphetamine use is possibly the most disturbing. Not only does it age a person irreversibly and causes brain damage with the first hit, but it also causes the most outrageous behavior imaginable. We lived across the street from a man who couldn't give it up. The police arrested him at least once a week, and the coup de grace was when he threw his four-year-old son through the picture window in their living room. The next day the man was back home. Imagine, if you can, what that four-year-old grew up to be.

What do these drugs mentioned above have in common? The people will repeat the use of the drug even when they know it will destroy them. Like any addiction, they do the same behavior repeatedly, hoping to have a different outcome—the definition of insanity. There is usually a different outcome, but it is often worse than the outcome before. The only saving grace is that the bottom keeps getting moved, and each use causes the person to devalue the impact of the behavior until they no longer feel or experience a moral regard or expectation for any of their behaviors. They fool themselves by thinking there is a light at the end of the tunnel. There is, but it is a train coming toward them.

Oh, and smokers. Why can smokers smoke in public, around their children, and so on, but a drug addict can't snort or shoot up during break time at work or on a street corner without being arrested, and if they use it in front of their kids, the kids get taken away? A drug is a drug is a drug.

Today's highly addictive nicotine-based tobacco is excused as a drug because tobacco is what our country based its economy on when founded. Approximately 600 chemicals are secretly added to cigarettes, including fungicides, pesticides, cadmium, benzene, formaldehyde, and nickel, all toxic to the human body.[30] Which and how many of those drugs did I list as being in the seats on the airplane that were culprits in killing the people? A friend of mine has a book written in 1922 that lists synthetic heroin and cocaine as additives in cigarette tobacco. If smoking were considered a drug that someone could be arrested for, they would have to completely re-vamp the U. S. Capitol and other buildings in our nation's Capitol that are decorated profusely with tobacco leaves and blooms. Ironically, tobacco and alcohol kill almost the same number of people annually—tobacco 4.1% and alcohol 4%. Oops! Tobacco kills more than alcohol! Cigarette smoking causes about one in every five deaths. That's right! One in five! Over 8 million die from tobacco use, while around 1.2 million die from second-hand smoke.[31] Tobacco is the second leading risk factor for death globally, causing more than $2 trillion in damage. "The amount of life expectancy lost for each pack of cigarettes smoked is 28 minutes, and the years of life expectancy a typical smoker loses is 25 years."[32] Why is it still legal? Alcohol-related causes are ranked the number four cause of death.

---

30 Lowell Kleinman, M.D. and Messina, Deborah Kleinman, MPH, drkoop.com Health Columnists, "Quit Smoking Support," 2010, www.quitsmokingsupport.com/whatsinit.html.

31 World Health Organization, s.v. "Tobacco," 2010, https://www.who.int/news-room/fact-sheets/detail/tobacco#:~:text=Tobacco%20kills%20more%20than%208,%2D%20and%20middle%2Dincome%20countries.

32 Medical News Today, "The effect of smoking on life span," *Healthline Media*,

What's the difference between the shopaholic, the food addict, the porno person, the sexaholic, and the co-dependent? (This is not a lead-in to a joke). Nothing. They are spiritually bankrupt.

The best way to describe co-dependency is anyone dependent on an outside influence to make them feel.

Wow, I know that sounds bizarre, but the best thing people can do for themselves is not to feel. Not feel? Well, how do you accomplish that? Feeling nothing includes the gamut from numb depression to giddy happiness. When anyone feels anything, they are out of sync with Force or God, whatever you want to call it. As pointed out in the last chapter, sit under the Bodhi Tree where you feel perfectly balanced.

I knew a woman who belonged to an altruistic group. I asked her about the group, and she explained that they help people without expecting payback, including a feeling that they did a good deed. She looked so neutral in the telling that I could not understand why anyone would want to do such acts if they didn't get some emotional payback for it. Many years later, I understood that when I did something with the expectation of retribution, whether positive or negative, I was not doing the deed without expectation. In other words, I was doing the deed co-dependently, as I was not doing the act unconditionally.

Addicts always have more than one addiction. They may shoot from religion to sex to some type of physical abuse (like the pedophile preachers do and those who also beat their children like is taught in the IBLP church), then move to shopping, or from one crisis to another. Anytime someone overdoses in one area, they will try to balance it out through another. For example, someone religious-to-the-extreme will often become a pedophile, a controller, or abusive in some other way, as they are very constricted people bound by "shalt nots." That constrictor makes their brain go, "Oh, yes, I can." They run in extremes just like the alcoholic or the drug addict; ironically, people trust their souls to the hands (literally) of these people.

If drugs were legal, would it take away the naughtiness of doing them? After all, a child will continue to repeat a behavior because it is

2023, https://www.medicalnewstoday.com/releases/9703#2.

naughty rather than choosing a not deviant course. When the adult no longer tells the child that it is naughty, the allure of the behavior quickly loses its power.

The crisis or drama-fixing addiction dynamic happens especially early in life within the family where there is always a family member with a problem the child thinks they can "fix," is told they can fix (come make mommy or daddy feel better/I'll feel better if you give me a hug or a kiss or touch me "there") or at least feels responsible for fixing because no one else seems to be able to step up to the plate to fix it. After all, who is more innocent, more intuitive, or has more of an ego state than a child? Children come from a place of love and could heal the adult with their love if the adult wasn't already so emotionally bankrupt because they couldn't fix their own life. Adults know they can manipulate (bully) these children just like a ball of clay. They are putty in the hands of a dysfunctional, co-dependent parent/person until one day, the child stands up, says enough is enough, and moves away from the bemoaning, wailing parent/person to heal themselves.

Often, the child feels responsible for the mother or father's emotional well-being. "It is your fault I feel this way." "Look what you made me do." Or, sometimes these are topped by a simple statement that crushes the child entirely and scares them into good behavior, such as, "I'll drop you off at an orphanage," "on an Indian reservation if you don't behave," "I'll feed you to the pigs," or "You don't love me. I'm going to go kill myself." Yep, these are all things my mother said to me.

After watching the false power that the parent obtains through their abusive, needy co-dependent behavior (like telling the child "I am proud of you" instead of saying "You did a good job," thus making the child feel pride instead of accomplishment), the child takes the cue from the parent and learns to expand their ego state and to set up their crises, dramas, and war of wills to see how far they can push the parent. Then when the parent explodes, the child enters the "victim" role and feels unloved, unlovable, and discouraged. Usually, by the age of two, the ego loop has been set in the child, and if not reversed by the age of three, the child will, if they have the propensity to alter their state, choose cocaine as their drug. Cocaine is considered the "ego" drug. Who's responsible for creating this behavior in the child? The parent is.

I knew as a child I could push my mother's boundaries beyond the breaking point. She would turn her frustration on herself and become self-deprecating. I then felt guilty for her misery, self-loathing, and self-harm. Then I would feel self-loathing and self-harm for myself because I caused that misery in my mother. My father's boundaries, however, were immovable and inflexible, and I was scared to death of him. He ruled his animal kingdom with a 2x4 across the head of an unruly cow that went into the wrong stanchion. Which was worse? Both were ways of controlling my mind and emotions, and the bipolar ends of the spectrum caused confusion and powerlessness in me.

The victim/dramatist sometimes sets up their dynamic by taking steps to make sure that the dynamics look different from their parents' dynamic and swears they are nothing like their parents when the reality is that the dynamic is the same but with varying stage props. When the drama maker or the fixer graduates from their family of origin, they set up their needy pods through marriage or other relationships to continue their addiction to constant drama or crisis and fixing, and the escalating dynamic continues generation after generation.

The co-dependent family members will continue to return to the family of origin if they can still get their fix from the family or if their new pod group figures out their "game" and dumps them from their lives or calls them on their game. Of course, this will set up a howl of denial in the dramatist. They might throw something across the room, into a sink, or at you, or stomp off indignantly sputtering epithets about how the person doesn't know what they are talking about and the "I'll show them(s)" or throw the "You don't love me!" at them. Dramatists will even go so far as to say, "I think she's going crazy" or "She doesn't know what she's talking about" when you call them on their dysfunction, thus dismissing your observation and a chance to change and get well.

The sick dynamics loop will continue when the parent allows the game-playing child dramatist and their acting-out behavior to return. Both parties get a charge out of the crisis, crash later, wondering what just happened, and swear they will never do it again—just like the alcoholic. And then the fear sets in, anger sets in, depression sets in, and then both move on to their self-defeating co-dependent loop behavior and find another scenario to re-enact it.

The co-dependent parent will continue the loop through a child who is constantly in crisis because it makes them feel momentarily wanted, needed, and essential (Fireman Syndrome—continually putting out fires or rescuing, and co-dependent love relationships are notorious for this). Or the co-dependent parent will continue their part in the drama because they don't have a life of their own and or are too afraid emotionally to have a healthy life of their own free from their "sick" child or their "clients" or "patients"—they might need me! I must be on call 24 hours a day!

Which one is sicker? After all, what would it feel like to be in a relationship where they are loved unconditionally and love unconditionally? Too scary!

If the parent's life is wholly invested co-dependently with their child's, they might refuse a life of love. They might even give up that love in favor of the child. Or they might push the person's patience to the point that the person who loves them gives up or sees that the codependent's brand of love might take away their soul just like they did their child's soul with their neediness to fix (control).

The irony is that the person watching these behaviors from the outside shakes their head and can't believe what they see. It looks like a little mouse dressed in a tiny fireman's suit with the hat falling over its eyes, running around in circles, squeaking, "Fire! Fire"! They can see that the co-dependent, belligerent child is wasting what little remains of the parent's life, and the parent is allowing it. The worst of these behaviors often come from a parent who knows they screwed up when the child was little and are trying to fix the brokenness that they helped create or allowed to manifest because they were too busy working, going to school, or avoiding a rotten marriage or relationship (guilt).

If you call the fixer on their apparent dysfunction, you will suddenly find yourself pushed out of their life with excuses such as I got too busy to return your call or "You know how it is." This excuse usually happens when you start calling the fixer on their dysfunction.

For the person who loves the co-dependent adult fixer, their love for them is like watching a branch rot and fall off of a tree. In a short time, their love for them is just gone. Their trust in the person has turned to cynicism, and their excuses (lies) are finally acknowledged for just what they are. Soon the relationship is over, leaving one broken-hearted and the fixer shaking their head, wondering what happened again. They will swear that they won't screw up another relationship but always do because the parent cannot detach from their children even after they become adults.

The spiral of defeat manifests, and the person gets sicker and angrier. And then, of course, the depression sets in, followed by another set of self-defeating behaviors. Sometimes the child has to detach entirely from the family to survive, and the parents howl in frustration (cry and feel sorry for themselves) because they can't get the kid to dance to their co-dependent music.

This type of co-dependent fixer will look like someone with boots stuck in the mud. Their feet are held down in the vacuum so tightly, waiting for their needy child to react to them, that they will step out of the boot when they hear something about the child or another family member they didn't know about and flail around trying to find their balance rather than stepping forward onto dry ground that they will jam their foot right back in the boot. The irony is that if they had taken that one step out of the life-draining predicament, they could have healed, and their child could have healed.

For the recovering alcoholic (or any other addiction), a co-dependent person is like manna for the starving. Even though every fiber in their being tells them that the person they are in love with will hurt them and that the relationship will never get off the ground, the alcoholic will continue to hope that something will manifest. Of course, the relationship looks very similar to when the alcoholic was in love with their bottle of alcohol, placing their intense love for their partner, spouse, or children on the back burner. After all, they can't make you feel better. No human ever has. They have always made you feel worse, but that glistening, shimmering, sentinel-standing, protecting bottle of "spirits" sure can. At least those spirits can make you forget, albeit for only a short time, how miserable your personal life really is.

The bottle, or other "crutch," becomes the alcoholic's/addict's best friend, lover, and confidante. Unfortunately, it is a friend, lover, and confidante that will turn around and stab you in the back—just like the new love you are waiting for and gambling for will do because they are incapable of stepping out of their role as the fixer and unable to pull their boot out of the mud. As one minister I heard said, "You can't be filled with the Holy Spirit if you're filled with spirits."

Your friends could see the train wreck coming. Your friends ask if you really want someone in your space who disregards your feelings and you.

"Of course I do!" you lie to yourself. "I love them!" you wail. Your friends told you it wouldn't work. "Then why couldn't I see it? Why did it take me so long to figure it out?" you ask. "Why was I so blind, and why did I ignore the obvious?"

People who build what they consider a safe wall around themselves cannot and will not consider another view, even when irrefutable evidence supports the opinion. These victims live in a world that is so tiny that they miss out on living and constantly criticize and judge others like a man with just a knife protecting himself from a pack of hungry wolves. They are in a constant panic state, which is the feeling they felt when backed into the corner as a child. They set up scenarios to repeat the feeling, hoping for a different outcome.

How do I know about these behaviors? Been there, done that.

So, the key is for the alcoholic or addict to be aware of their co-dependent behavior at the beginning of the relationship and not to think this time will be different or that they can win the person over just by loving them. It does not work. The result is the recovering addict feeling terrible about themselves and realizing they have failed again, both in not being loved like they hoped to be and being such a fool. And the cycle begins and repeats itself repeatedly until they finally get it. Of course, there is also the opposite: I will live alone and not risk a broken heart rather than stepping out of my safe (constricting) world of illusion where I might experience love and someone who loves me.

Often a spouse or partner will bash the other one's work ethic, ability to make a living, or one's personality. Those things that the spouse or partner points out become so magnified that they become a reality and make it so they cannot function no matter what. When this happens, the bashed partner freezes and becomes paralyzed. What does the basher get out of this?—self-loathing, then self-pity, and then self-defeating behaviors, and sometimes their hair falls out because their adrenal glands fail from constant stress mode. Of course, those feelings occur right after the brief exhilaration of triumph, or one-upsman-ship, that they dumped onto their [supposed] loved one. The next minute the basher will turn around and praise their partner and say how wonderful they are, leaving the partner so off-balance that they become indefensible. This dynamic is not love; it is the cruelty of co-dependency.

Or perhaps the person you hope loves you will call tonight, and when they don't, you sink into a deep sadness and feel unloved and unwanted and feel that the relationship must be over or they have moved on to someone else. Why else wouldn't they call, your panicked mind asks.

Co-dependency is ugly. It is powerful, and it is debilitating! The result is the same whether you are the addict or the co-dependent—the wind still blows through the hole in your gut. And why does that happen? It is because both parties look outside themselves for the answers rather than inside. Or the fixer is not allowing the person with the problem to find their solution, thus causing the addiction to continue manifesting. Why should they look for an answer? The fixer is fixing it for them again. If it is true that it is fixed, why does the dramatist still feel terrible and continue their dysfunctional behavior loop? Why are their self-worth and self-esteem still in the toilet? It is because they didn't fix their own problem. The fixer did not place the power in the victim's hands, thus leaving them powerless again.

The person in crisis and the co-dependent fixer is always searching for their drug of choice—to fix or to be fixed. This continuous cycle pushes both parties closer and closer to the abyss of helplessness, hopelessness, depression, and self-defeating behaviors that may eventually kill one or all of the parties involved through suicide, an "accident," popping too many prescription or over-the-counter anxiety and sleeping pills, high blood pressure, eating their feelings and developing diabetes, banging it away with someone who has a deadly sexually transmitted disease, or landing in jail because of the big fight that eventually will happen.

Are the diseases of alcoholism, drug addiction, and other addictions worse than co-dependency? How would you measure it if the emotional and spiritual result is the same?

There is a joke that goes like this: "How do you know when an alcoholic is lying? ...His lips are moving." (Of course, you could substitute the word *alcoholic* for the word *lawyer*, as I learned in one of my law school classes when the professor asked, "How many of you think a little white lie is okay to tell?" About seventy percent of the class raised their hands, with only one female hand popping up. Then he asked, "How many of you think it's okay to tell a big lie to win your case?" About twenty-five percent of the first group's raised hands went up. He then asked, "How many of you are children of attorneys? Almost every one of them raised their hands. He then pointed out, "You know, if you're caught lying, you will be disbarred.")

See what I mean? The alcoholic is constantly put on center stage when the truth of the matter is that a shopaholic, a sexaholic, a pedophile priest, preacher, rabbi, teacher or coach, a smoker, someone who hoards, dry-drunk syndrome (someone who does not drink but has the same behaviors as an alcoholic), the child of an alcoholic, is co-dependent and so on, including the children of these addicts, will lie rather than tell the truth even if telling the truth is easier to tell.

I heard on TV one day a reporter say that a newly deceased singer had a "degree" of recovery from addiction. There are no "degrees" of sobriety. You are sober, or you are not sober. When I use the word *sober*, I refer to the cessation of all addictions and free of addiction behaviors.

I knew I had to let go of my co-dependent behavior. I knew I was spiraling dangerously to the edge, even in my sobriety. I found that alcoholism was just a symptom of a bigger problem than an elephant sitting in the middle of the room. And that elephant's name was Co-dependent. I found that when people told me that I had the above problems, I did one of three things: I got angry and defensive that they would say such things that were untrue in my opinion, I said I know someone else who does those things—good thing I'm not like that, or I was in flat-out denial that those things were addictions and were in my addiction table of contents. How dare they? After all, my problem was alcohol, and I was no longer drinking—ergo, dry-drunk syndrome.

The key for me was to back myself down from alcoholism, other addictions, and co-dependency to depression, to anger, and then to fear. Ha! I wasn't afraid of anything—or so I thought. When I got to the fear part and *really* started looking at my life, I was surprised to learn that I had spent most of my life in fear. Another word I chose for *fear* was *hate*. My childlike illusion that I wrote about in Chapters 1 and 2 clearly shows how I kept myself totally in the dark about what was going on in my life and how I chose only to remember the silly fun observations because I could not look at the pain of the reality that went on between the lines and behind the closed doors.

When my family's modicum of cohesiveness went into shred mode, I immediately went from illusion to alcoholism. There was no middle ground because the reality of the truth hit me squarely between the eyes, and I did not want to acknowledge it. Also, I had learned in my family that there was no such thing as a middle ground. I also tried to remedy the pain of the truth by doing "geographics"—if I move over here, everything will be fine. If I move over there, things will be better. I found fault with my neighbors or where I moved every time. After all, if I acknowledged what was happening, it would make it real, and my illusion bubble would pop. The fault I was seeing was a fault in me. I needed to learn that the next time I pointed my finger at someone, I needed to do so in the mirror.

When I finally got serious about my recovery, I learned I was "only as sick as my secrets." Besides, why would I want people to know that mine was not a "golden family" like many people perceived them to be? Again, our parents told us not to discuss anything outside the family. When the door closed after a guest left and mom put away the cut-glass party dishes, the actual dynamics came out, like in every family, whether the dynamics were healthy or unhealthy.

People also told me when I got sober, I now had choices. I repeat: choices. I could not comprehend having any option on or about any decision or thing in my life until I stopped drinking as I had always been told as a child when to jump and how high. As I said before, I was told by every male in my family, "No one cares what you think" or "You don't know what you're talking about." (Intriguingly, later in my life, I grew benign nodules in my throat that I had to have surgically removed. These blocks closed down any words I had so I would not speak my truth. Why would I even want to? No one cared what I thought, and I also didn't know what I was talking about anyway!)

One morning after I left detox, I woke up and asked myself, "What should I do today?" I was surprised to find that I could even ask the question. I felt thrilled that I was asking my opinion about something. At first, I did not understand how I could suddenly have a choice. Then I faced a problem—I could do a plethora of things. I held out my hand, and when I saw my fingers, I realized I had at least five and possibly ten paths I could choose to go down that day. The event caused the spark inside my solar plexus to re-ignite and grow.

At about that same time, I started noticing how I would be going along on the path and suddenly start circling back with the same old behavior—the self-castigating, self-destructive verbal loop set into me by/with my family. I realized I could recreate my internal conversation. Upon this realization, I talked my way out of the loop and got back on the straight path by holding my hands out and saying, "I have all these choices today." Even when I was going to work, which I needed to do, I had numerous choices about how I perceived my job, my co-workers, and my tasks. Then I started questioning where the path was going. I didn't know, and it didn't matter. I knew it was leading away from the hell I had lived in until then and toward a future of self-respect and self-esteem.

I realized it *was* confirmed: "If I always do what I always did, I will always get what I always got."

And, what had I done to my children, family, and friends during my selfish self-indulgence and self-pity? These addictions and this co-dependent behavior had to go, and I needed to make amends.

CHAPTER 13

Splicing the Broken Tapes

As we grow up, there could have been an event that was so traumatic to our young minds that we "forgot" consciously what happened. If someone says to you, remember when blah, blah, blah happened, and you say, "I don't remember that," or you say, "It didn't happen, " you had a break in the memory tape. When those memory tapes break, they often do not splice back together squarely, like in a movie reel that breaks. When the projectionist joins the film back together, there is a click or a tiny chunk (or a big chunk, depending on the splicer doing the splicing) that we don't get to see. If we don't see it, we can't possibly remember what occurred in that chunk or click of the movie. In our real life, that chunk represents the disassociation.

Later, I would understand these breaks in the tapes as broken timelines. For example, we are going along, and someone molests or smacks us around, or we just decide on our own or via a life contract to change to another timeline. Our timeline is going along like this________________, and suddenly it looks like this:______---__---_____, with the upper hyphens representing the altered timeline where the conscious memory has broken. When the hyphens occur, you suddenly feel "spacey," or you feel like you have "stepped out of your body" (disassociated). That is why you sometimes do not remember the event, or it is an event that is not in keeping with what others remember or not in keeping with your own misperceived reality. Now, the key to putting your life back together is to bring those hyphens back down into the line of the underscored lines. Once the line is corrected, the memory line is re-established without a click. That is the integration of timelines.

Sometimes, the hyphen does not come back with the same "memory" as the underscore line because that part may have an experience in another "realm" of time travel, hence, the term "quantum timelines." Usually, the person comes back to their primary time "changed." Those who return may be cantankerous, moody, enlightened, or suddenly "grown up." Or, in some cases, the person does not come back at all and has switched bodies with another physical person, but that phenomenon is rare.

What happens to us within the hyphen of time? Where do we go?

In the case of dual souls, the lines could be even more complex and, quite frankly, I do not have the keys on the keyboard to demonstrate this adequately but suffice it to say that the original line may look like this============= with the two hyphens being the two souls. It's almost as if the person is an identical twin within one body. How farfetched is this? As Aunt Voula said in *My Big Fat Greek Wedding*, "Now, you are family. Okay. All my life I had a lump at the back of my neck. Right here." She points to the back of her neck. "Always, a lump. Then I started menopause and the lump got bigger from the "hormonees." It started to grow. So I go to the doctor, and he did the bio… the b… the… the bios… the b… the "bobopsy." Inside the lump he found teeth and spinal cord. Yes. Inside the lump was my twin."

Let's say an event occurs that one soul is unequipped to deal with, and one of the soul lines drops off while the other's soul line continues straight. The fragmented part could also fragment from itself and does so many times. When the line returns, if it does, one soul part of you will not remember what the other soul in you remembers. It takes a long time for dual-soul people to work in tandem, and most don't even know that they have two souls within them. They always seem "torn" with decisions, can't remember things, tell you that you never said that to them (because you didn't tell that soul), might feel they don't "belong," or always watch from the outer perimeter of the circle. They are the people who just don't fit in anywhere or may fit in with a group one day and not the next.

Many alcoholics and drug addicts are dual-soul people. To combat their constant non-communicating "Siamese twin" brain, which is what I will call it, they anesthetize with alcohol, drugs, sex, religion, gambling, or with an eating disorder or some other self-destructive behavior. (For those who cannot understand why I keep listing religion as a self-defeating behavior, it is because the psychiatric diagnosis manual lists it as one and also because religion is based on faith, which is not fact, therefore it is considered something a person does in a superstitious way to feel better. Religion is based on the outside of the body, whereas spirituality is based on the inside and is a *knowingness*, not a belief. Also, spirituality is not monetarily-based, nor is it a religion.) Once a dual-soul person understands they have two souls living in them, they can begin to communicate with each other and not have so many blank spots.

What does this have to do with this book? It's simple: As you have seen and will soon see, most people on Pan Am Flight 110 had massive splices in their memory tapes that were filled in only after speaking with others on the plane.

One night after I had completed my personal integration work and meditated, I saw a slide show of my past lives. The slide show went on for about an hour. The next night the same thing happened. These shows went on for several nights. I would later understand I was seeing my Akashic Record—my history on the Earth plane and other realms. Yes, other *realms*. The Bible calls the Akashic Record "the book of life." At any rate, I could see why the airplane incident happened, why some people died, and why others didn't—they were fulfilling their karmic contracts. As for the terrorists, they were victimized in a past life by those who died on the plane. If that was not the case, they had contracts with the terrorists to ensure they killed them for the simple reason they had fulfilled their life contract.

What in the world was happening to me, I wondered. Had I moved from the physical material world of "eternal agony" into another world?

Was I poking my finger into the veil that kept me "unconscious" and underwater? Was Plato right? Had I crossed the River of Lethe—the River of Forgetfulness, when I came to earth, and that is why I had no conscious memory of what had occurred before I came to earth and no memory of what was going on beyond my earthly life? Had I somehow been given a glimpse into another dimension of understanding (died), and what would that glimpse mean for my future? It felt like I was looking at something I wasn't supposed to see but couldn't help but look at. Although it was scary, it was tantalizing, and I could not stop my curiosity.

I heard about a professor who taught a class about near-death experiences and went to see him. He interviewed me about my experience and told me he would call me to schedule a date when I would speak with his class. I waited and waited, and no phone call came. Finally, I went to his office and talked to the secretary.

She told me the professor was teaching one day and suddenly fell on the floor. The students just sat in their chairs, waiting for the guy to jump up and yell surprise or something and tell them that he was demonstrating what death looked like. The irony was that the man was deader than a doornail, and it wasn't until several minutes later that the students figured out he wasn't kidding.

A few months later, my friend Kathy started making bi-weekly sojourns from Wyoming to stay over-night at our house. We rented the movie *Empire of the Sun* by Stephen Spielberg.[33] In the film, the Japanese captured a boy named Jamie and put him in a concentration camp during World War II. Outside of the fence was a school that trained kamikaze pilots. Jamie "befriended" a Japanese boy training to be a pilot. Whenever they saw each other through the fence, they always waved and smiled. Jamie reminded me so much of me that it was frightening. He was the one in the concentration camp who always ran from one spot to another, helping everyone else and putting out the fires, making everyone else smile.

---

33 Tom Stoppard, *Empire of the Sun*, Amblin Entertainment, Warner Bros., 1987.

At the movie's end, Jamie was on the other side of the fence with the boy, happy and acting like a relieved boy his age should have. American airplanes had dropped trunks of food from their bellies. The Japanese boy gave Jamie a mango that he had picked up and raised his sword to cut the mango in half. Three Americans who knew Jamie from the camp thought the Japanese boy would kill Jamie with the sword and shot the boy dead. Jamie started CPR on the boy, frantically repeating, "I can bring everyone back...everyone."

I lost it. My heart split wide open, and I cried inconsolably. I finally understood why I had become an EMT and then a Drug and Alcohol Counselor. I thought if I tried hard enough, I could bring everyone back, everyone—if I just had the right tools. No one on that plane would have died. I never did EMT work again after that. I understood my motivation and realized that I could not bring everyone back.

* * *

During my last year at the U of U, I took a required English class from a professor named Tom Malloy, one of my Psychology professors. Tom was a crack-up. He wore Berks and had long hair; you could tell he took advantage of the '60s. Sometimes Tom would stop in the middle of a sentence, amble to the window, and stare out the window for several seconds or minutes. He would then turn around, complete the sentence, slowly walk toward the podium, and continue his lecture. He certainly knew how to get the students to pay attention. Tom's theory was that students could not possibly learn how to write using textbooks as written. He convinced the English department to let him teach a writing class so he could prove that his theory was correct. It turned out that he was right.

He handed out a questionnaire asking how we felt about writing and what we experienced when we did write. I answered that I could not stop writing once I started and that I developed tunnel vision and heard and saw no one else in the room or the general vicinity. I could not stop writing, even when prompted by those around me.

Tom started with a story that he told for about five minutes. He suddenly stopped and said, "Now finish the story."

He taught us to "mind map" words and how to apply those words to the story. Sometimes we used a column with three or four words and wrote sub-words under those words. Sometimes we wrote a word in the middle of the page and wrote words around and around and were able to make a story out of the words in the round. In other words, we took the words and laid them in a straight line with other words filling in the spaces.

Tom continued to test a handful of students. After seeing the results, he then tested students throughout the university system. Tom called a handful of the students who described the same above tendencies "natural writers," and I fell into that category. Of course, when pushed, I backed away and wrote substandard papers. Heaven forbid I should succeed at anything out of my comfort zone. I had a duality of wanting to excel and to strive forward, but the old programmed tapes in me still whirled and clicked in my mind's dysfunctional tape recorder.

By the end of four years, besides the Drug and Alcohol Counseling Certification, I received Bachelor of Arts and Bachelor of Science degrees in Psychology and Sociology and a Certification in Criminology and Corrections. I had 36 hours toward a master's degree and wanted to know more. I applied at Willamette Law School's Center for Dispute Resolution and got accepted.

The girls and I moved to Salem, Oregon. I couldn't believe my eyes when we arrived at the rented house. By then, I had traded a car for a truck to move with and had towed my other vehicle. Now I had 2.2 children, counting the deceased baby and a dog. Believe it or not, the 3-bedroom house had a white picket fence. I had arrived!

The first thing I did was start the process of legally changing my name. I worked part-time with heroin addicts while in school and used the integration technique that was, by that time, second nature to me. My patients had the highest clean urinalysis tests of all counselors. Many approached me about the possibility of getting off of methadone, and a few of the addicts got off of both heroin and methadone. As you will recall, I stated earlier that in my drug and alcohol classes, statistics told us no one ever got off of both, and if they did, the addict usually died of alcoholism. But does this have to be a reality if one completes the integration process?

After I started working in the methadone clinic, I was amazed to find that several of the patients told me they remembered someone programming them to commit suicide or go on an alcohol or drug-induced binge when the part of the programmed memory tape came back that told them which drug to become addicted to. This memory came back with the details of them that were re-integrated.

Many people who are on heroin were programmed to use that specific drug. Others may be programmed to use cocaine, crack, alcohol, etc. When I discovered this, I was startled. (Later, I worked in a methadone clinic in California, and my life was, quite frankly, in danger from the owners of the clinic, who were both psychiatrists and doing the programming. One of them told me there were places for people like me. This threat was genuine because the co-owner of the methadone clinic was also the director of a psychiatric hospital. My boss said also to stop doing therapy on patients and do only counseling. In other words, only tell them to attend an N. A. meeting (Narcotics Anonymous). They were making a fortune "hooking" people on methadone through hypnotic suggestions. Taxpayer money primarily paid for this drug program because the addicted have no financial means to buy their own.) The sick part of the whole thing was that a quart bottle of pure methadone at that time cost about $40. They diluted the bottle, got dozens of servings from it, and charged the patient/taxpayers $40 a month for the patient's 20-30 milligrams of the methadone dose-a-day fix. Quite profitable! The good news is that both doctors will be old enough to die by this book's release.

There was something about Oregon that further enhanced my psychic abilities. My sixth sense expanded, and I liked it. I wasn't afraid of it for the first time in my life. I could use it in my work and could, as an example, see houses patients lived in as children before they brought it up. The house number was right in front of my eyes. I could see patterns on the curtains and where the furniture was. Initially, I was mesmerized by what I saw and would be quite startled when the patient started talking about the house they grew up in and described it exactly as I saw it, including the number on the front.

Then, another realization occurred to me. This knowingness was not a psychic ability. This knowingness was just that—a knowingness. If we already know everything when we come to Earth, and knowingness fragments off of us through disassociation, how do we get the knowingness back? Simple—the integration of those parts of us that hold the memory of what we know.

* * *

That Christmas, the girls flew to their dad's, then to Arizona to visit his family. I went to Iowa to mine.

At Christmas dinner, my cousin asked me about law school and what classes I was taking. I told him, and then I couldn't help but look over at my brother as he was sending out a vibration that almost paralyzed me. He resembled a turtle, and I thought, "*Oh-oh, someone's toes got stepped on. How dare I go to law school? He was the "smart" one in the family.*" I had stepped out of my family role, which was a no-no. Besides, no one cared what I thought, and I didn't know what I was talking about anyway.

Off to the other room I went. The women were gossiping about people, and I thought, *This is like a bowl of spaghetti. I don't know where one noodle starts and the other ends. So, this is what true co-dependency looks like*! *No wonder I was so sick*!

My mom dropped me at the airport on New Year's Eve, 1990, and as I watched her walk away without glancing back at me, I knew I would never see her again. I wanted to get well and knew that I had to leave my family to do so. I wrote my mother a letter telling her I had to sever all family ties. My determination for spiritual healing was so great that I accepted no words or excuses from the letters she wrote me for her behavior or what had happened to her while growing up. She suddenly started sending me $20 or $40 at a time, and I gave it to people who needed the money even though God only knew how much I needed the money. I did not want her energy anywhere around me, as I did not want anything to hold me to her energy field. I hadn't seen or spoken to my dad for several years because when he finally divorced my mother, he divorced the whole family, so he was a moot point.

The girls returned from Christmas and began telling me their "secrets" and stories about their dad. They wanted to sever ties with him and told me things he had done and they had watched him do. They wrote him a letter telling him they wanted nothing more to do with him.

I knew that for my daughters ever to have a chance of having a healthy life free of addiction and co-dependency, I had to make drastic decisions, even if those decisions involved never seeing family again. I was willing to go to any lengths for this to happen. Every day I said an affirmation for my daughters and myself. I set a dish of sea salt on my open Bible, read the 23rd Psalms and Psalms 91 daily, and talked with my guides. My determination and guidance were so great then that nothing could stop me from doing what I had set out to do. Once I took over my destiny, my fear lessened, my intuition expanded, and I finally started to leave my co-dependency behind and grow up. I had finally followed the advice of A. A. and turned my will and my life over to the care of God as I understood Him.

To add even more protection from the *was*band, we moved in with an elderly couple and gave no forwarding address. Fortunately, I only had one semester left of school. I walked my daughters to the door of their school and met them at the door every afternoon. I instructed the school that they were not allowed to leave with anyone other than me and that if their father showed up, they should call the police immediately. A detective came to the school, met with us and the principal, and we filed a police report. That set up a horrible, terrifying howl of denial from him, along with threats and pleadings.

I adjusted my hours at work and my classes and ensured they were never alone and could not be kidnapped by their dad if he suddenly decided the police were no longer watching him. My employer offered me a full-time position with nearly double the money and full benefits. I had to turn it down because I knew we needed to leave the area.

After I finished my classes, we went on the run. Several months later, we called the girls' dad to let him know we were okay, as I thought that was the right thing to do, but I refused to tell him where we were. Before he hung up, he said to the youngest one: "When I find you guys, I'm going to kill all three of you." Changing my name had been the correct call.

I knew that he meant it when he said he would kill us. I also knew it would be unsafe to practice using my licenses, so I returned to menial jobs and did personal counseling work with clients. Within months or weeks of moving somewhere, I would feel a tap on my shoulder and hear a voice say, "It's time to go now." I would tell my daughters it was time to go, and they would start packing. We'd move within 24 hours. What a way to live, but I knew to trust that voice keeping us safe and alive. Each time we moved, we told no one where we were going.

One day we held hands over an atlas, and after going around and around several times with our eyes closed, we landed on a town that we thought was about the most bizarre choice we could have landed on. We did it again and landed on the same city. When it happened the third time, we just shrugged, raised our eyebrows, and started packing.

Each move got harder and harder. My girls were pulled away from their friends, and the no contact with their friends they were leaving tore them apart. Somehow they always pulled themselves up by their boot-straps and made new friends. For some odd reason, every time we moved, we ran across an older woman who helped us either with a place to live or knowledge of a job.

* * *

One day the strangest thing happened during my daily meditation. I felt torn out of my body and floating in the ether. I was devoid of body and conscious mind. Gathering quite close to me was a cloud-like being that grew and grew and took up the space before me. From within that cloud came a voice whose timbre was so resounding and loud that I would not have been able to take it if I had not been in a meditative state. The voice rumbled in the most unambiguous terms, "You are loved. Do not fear again. I am watching over you." I was surrounded by and held by unseen arms that were so safe and secure that I would have cried if I was not still paralyzed. The "Ah-ha!" in me resounded through me, and I understood that a God-like presence was holding me and would always be and that I never need fear again unless I chose to fear. I knew then that I was completely safe, but I still needed to continue listening. Of course, this had side effects, as I just smiled at people who were trying to bully me—whether at a stop-light or on the street. This non-fear scared my girls half to death, and they feared that one day someone would pull out a Glock and shoot me. I just looked at them and said, "Been there. Done that."

I could not move for over an hour when I returned to my physical body after hearing this rumbling voice. I felt like a tuning fork's vibration was still rippling through me. I knew that I could tell no one. I knew people would not believe me. After all, who was I to have been shown the face of God?

* * *

Years later, I was between the double doors at the metro stop of Union Station in Washington, D. C. My daughter and her boyfriend had sped ahead of me as they were afraid we would be late for the movie. Three black guys cornered me. One guy shoved me up against the wall and sensually rubbed against me. I just smiled at him. This reaction seemed to confuse the heck out of them. Little did they know, I was smiling because the guy was so fat that I couldn't feel his dick. The smile seemingly threw them off because they furrowed their brows and ran to the incoming train. When I caught up with my daughter and told her, she was appalled. I was laughing. She seemed to miss the missing dick part.

CHAPTER 14
Starting Over

I went to work cleaning at a one-hundred-ten-year-old church that had just been placed on the National Historical Register and picked up two other low-paying jobs. Later on, the church hired me to do more restoration work. I could feel some nasty entities when I walked into the church. I opened all the doors and windows and told the creatures, "Out. Out. You have to leave now." It took about three days to accomplish, but the church's inside seemed no longer dark. I know—it sounds unbelievable. Doesn't it?

One day when I was outside working, an older lady came to me and asked me what I did to the church. I asked her why, and she said, "I heard that you made the darkness go away." I told her I told the dark entities they were no longer welcome there. She thanked me and said it felt so much brighter there. I was astonished! I figured she would think I was nuts. Heck, I thought I was nuts.

* * *

My youngest daughter befriended a girl in high school whose parents had a friend who was retired from one of the government watchdogs and had started a security company. My daughter told her friend's mom about their dad, and the mom said she had to help us. She took me to see their friend to find out about my ex-husband. Within two minutes of my story, he stopped me and said, "I know what's going on. I'm going to call a friend of mine who's in the FBI and see what I can find out. I'll call you on Monday."

He didn't call me on Monday. He called me on Tuesday. First, he apologized for not calling me on Monday. He had forgotten that it was a holiday. Then he said, "What the hell? This guy's got a one-and-a-half-inch FBI file and gotten involved in some pretty awful stuff."

I asked him, "What kind of stuff?"

He said, "You don't want to know, and I'm not going to tell you."

I told him the worst thing I could think of was kidnapping babies and selling them. He said, "Not even close."

I asked him if it was worse than that, and he said, "Yes."

He told me to continue working minimum-wage jobs and move at least every six months because "This guy wants you dead and has told everybody he knows he will pay them to do it."

The little voice in the back of my head had been right. I knew the guy wanted to kill us. He had indeed become psychotic! That is why I would feel the taps and suddenly tell the girls we had to move.

The man also told me the FBI had been watching my ex-husband for years and would use him to get to those above him, namely the man for whom he had been working for several years when we lived in Salt Lake City. (No wonder he gave me the creeps and wanted me to keep drinking!) He said, "This is a bad man, and you do everything you can to keep those little girls safe even if you have to live on the street because he does want to kill you. Make no mistake about this. He wants you dead."

Because the government had yet to arrest my ex, they would not place us in protective custody, nor was this a federal case. We were mostly on our own, but the man assured me that someone would be watching my ex-husband all the time so that he couldn't get to us. He also told me to have no contact with family members, past friends, or co-workers and that my children could not contact past classmates or tell them when or where we were moving. I had been right! Although this was a mixed bag of news, I still felt like I was in one of those real-life crime TV shows where the wife had no idea that her husband was a criminal. How can anyone be that blind? With this news, for the first time in years, I stopped looking over my shoulder every ten seconds and allowed my daughters to be kids again. I hoped they could get their childhood relived and resolved by the time they reached adulthood so that they wouldn't still act like children and instill their dysfunction onto their children. Unfortunately, they had lost so many years to running and to the sickness of addiction and co-dependency that they had a lot of making up to do.

* * *

Along with my intuition, my physical intuition was also peaking to an excruciating degree. Several months before the Northridge earthquake happened, I started to feel nauseous. At about the same time every day, I had to stop what I was doing and lean against something. It reached the point that my eyes would lose focus, and I felt like the earth was shaking under me. The Northridge quake happened; amazingly, I was fine the next day. I started putting two and two together and realized the correlation between the two—feeling nauseous, and then I felt the earth shaking, my eyes lost focus, then the actual earthquake would occur. Another bizarre thing would happen shortly after.

My youngest daughter came to the church one afternoon after school. On our way home from work, a homeless man riding his bicycle was hit by a car. The man driving took off. The crash threw the man into a 3" tree. My EMT training kicked in, and we exited the car to help the man. I went over to him and knew that it was a question of CPR or let him go as he was dead.

A whispery voice loudly and clearly said, "Let me go." My daughter and I both looked up. The man's essence was rounding the corner of the grocery store, and he turned around and waved at us. (I waved back). He turned away from us and kept walking. I said to my daughter, "Did you see that?"

She answered, "Yes."

I told her I wouldn't do CPR on the "body" because he didn't want to return. When I told the EMT that the man didn't want to come back, that his soul had already left, he looked at me like I was a total nut job.

The ambulance took the dead man away. They put his body on life support for three days and finally unplugged him. They either realized he had no insurance or realized his soul was gone. It would have been much cheaper if they had listened to me, and the soul's wishes would have been honored. As Kurt Vonnegut wrote about the people on the planet Vicuna in his goofy book entitled *Jailbird*:

> The judge from Vicuna in the story tells us that the way the people on his native planet said "hello" and "good-bye," and "please" and "thank you," too. It was this: "ting-a-ling." He says that back on Vicuna the people could don and doff their bodies as easily as Earthlings could change their clothing. When they were outside their bodies, they were weightless, transparent, silent awarenesses and sensibilities. They had no musical instruments on Vicuna, he said, since the people themselves were music when they floated around without their bodies. Clarinets and harps and pianos and so on would have been redundant, would have been machinery for making clumsy counterfeits of airborne souls.[34]

I couldn't help but think of that paragraph when I saw the man who had doffed his body because when I looked down at his bike, I noticed it had a bell and wondered if the ting-a-ling that rang out as the bike hit the tree was the man's body's way of saying "hello" and "good-bye."

* * *

I found a healing group that met in an old bunkhouse on a ranch. As usual, all of the attendees were women. The first time I went to the

[34] Kurt Vonnegut, *Jailbird*, (Dell Publishing, New York, NY, 1979), 98.

group, I felt like I had entered an alternate universe. What in the world was this group all about?

The facilitator Vicki, a retired RN, had been trained in Hawaii to teach this new-to-me, seemingly bizarre technique. She used one of the attendees for muscle testing. After doing a specific meditation to release our physical self (Mer-Ka-Ba) and to open our third eye, she asked questions of the middle person and pumped one of their arms to get the answer. If the arm stayed strong, that is the area the group would be working at. If the arm became weak, the answer was a no for working in that area. (The Greeks used muscle testing centuries ago.)

Vicki started by asking if we needed to work on the physical body, which represents the mineral kingdom and the earth elements; the life force body, representing the plant body and the water element; the emotional body, representing the animal kingdom and the air element; the mental body, representing the human body; and the fire element or the psychic body, representing the spiritual world and the ether elements. We then needed to know which sacred mineral (metal or tin, for example), which direction, flower, and sacred geometrical form, such as the tetrahedron, or Akashic record, we needed to focus on. She broke that down further into past, present, future, generational, lower and higher dimensions, Earth, and the universe, and asked which planet or universe to go to.

The first night the muscles showed a strong yes for working in another universe. At first, I thought this was beyond weird and couldn't figure out how we could go to another universe and work on their dimensional issues and do healing work there. The next thing I knew, I could feel myself floating at the speed of sound through the darkness to another galaxy. The air felt cool and soothing on my skin, and suddenly, there I was. It was not unlike what I experienced on the plane in the "dead" state.

The "people" in that universe looked different than we looked, and I could see they were distressed by something from another galaxy. We "worked" on them using the sub-sets, and the next thing I knew, the "people" were no longer in distress. When I flew suddenly back into my body, I looked around, and everyone else looked as startled as I did, even though I was the only newbie in the group. It took us several minutes to digest what had happened, and then we shared our experience. Amazingly, we all described the same thing!

The following week we worked on a specific person in the group who had cancer. The next week we worked on a future generation and on and on. I started working alone using the technique, flew off to some pretty amazing places, and went to some awful places to do healing work.

I started spending more time on the ranch with my girls and found it safe and cathartic for our healing from living in constant fear and moving. The ranch owner's wife, Linda, had a miniature pony that wore little rubber boots, followed us around like a puppy, and went in and out of the house with us. The pony loved watermelon and barbeque potato chips and would plop its front hooves on the picnic table bench and help itself to the food. I often had to look twice at it to ensure it was a horse. Linda raised Arabians and cold-blood horses, and the girls helped with the horses and the bronzing studio. They were in pig heaven on that ranch and felt free and happy.

One day a friend of Linda's stopped by while we were planting a tree and started talking about a seminar that he had gone to given by a (supposed) "walk-in" named Melchizedek. He told me I should visit the Taos/Santa Fe area or Sedona. He loaned me the Melchizedek videos he had purchased, and I sat mesmerized while watching. Melchizedek talked about sacred geometry, The Flower of Life, the Mer-Ka-Ba, Pi, Phi, the Golden Ratio, the Mysteries, the spiritual Jesus, "walk-ins," UFOs, Machu Pichu, indigenous people, spirituality instead of religion, and on and on. I felt like I had stepped into a whole new level of learning and felt liberation and an expansion of awareness. Years later, I learned the man who called himself Melchizedek was merely regurgitating what he had learned and taking credit for mysteriously discovering age-old information. Regardless, the information he passed along was irrevocably vital.

I found another group studying the Book of Enoch, the great-grandfather of Noah and the son of Jared in the Book of Genesis. Enoch was the seventh generation of Adam. Enoch was also Noah's teacher. Enoch is one of the books of the Bible removed by the Church and mentioned in the book of Jude. It is an apocryphal and believed to be a pseudepigraphical (falsely super scribed-written under a pen name) collection of second-century Jewish texts. Enoch spoke about the Mysteries that I would re-learn about several years later. Frankly, Enoch couldn't be left in the Bible because he talked about things the Church Fathers either couldn't not understand or didn't want parishioners to know. After all, it would take away their power over them. I wondered if that meant Noah's teachings were moot or bad since his grandfather taught him. It just happens that the clergy cast him out.

When I spoke with one of the priests where I worked about the Book, he told me that it was blasphemous and he looked frightened. Of course, he did! The church had forbidden him to read it, and they called the Book heresy. The Book is full of prophecy, not just about the Mysteries/Magic. The next thing I knew, my boss entered the room and ordered me not to discuss the Book of Enoch again. What in the world was going on here? Why were these men so afraid of this one re-found book of the Bible? That is when I knew all the new things I was learning were true, even if I did not understand them. People do not become frightened of false things; they laugh at them. Shortly after that, my relationship with the priest changed dramatically.

I was three years into the job at the church, and one day the priest and I were putting in flower beds. He was being pushy and bossy, and I flippantly said to him, "Jeez, you're such a slave driver."

His face turned red, and he tore into me verbally and said that he had never mistreated me even though, at that moment, he was. I was shocked that I had said what I did and was even more amazed when I suddenly started singing the old Negro spiritual, "Nobody knows the troubles I've seen, nobody knows my sorrow…."

He became livid and stomped off. Clear as a bell, I saw us in a past life. I worked in a cotton field; he was my white master. I was his reluctant lover.

Pretty soon, he returned to the flower beds, stood with his hands on his hips, and glared at me. I looked at him, tucked my upper lip behind my lower lip, widened my eyes, and said, "Whoops." It was when the song started that he no longer liked me.

By the fourth year, he was poking me in the chest with his finger, accusing me of things I didn't do (at least not on purpose, such as accidentally using Round-up on a wide swath of the lawn), and ridiculing me. One day he told me that he loathed the sight of me and couldn't stand being in the same room with me. I usually just grinned at him. I'd heard all that crap when I was a child and had learned that words, such as he was spewing, were his problem, not mine. He cut my hours a little each week, eventually taking away my benefits, and I, in my ornery fashion, just held out.

A few months later, we agreed that I would quit, and I told him that if he ever wanted to go to an A. A. meeting with me, give me a call. He blinked at me and looked confused, and said, "Sure. Okay." He thought I was asking him to go so that he could support me. I wasn't. One of the brothers living at the rectory told me my boss got rip-roaring drunk at night and was abusive. His most fun thing to do was to poke *him* in the chest with his finger and belittle him! When I asked him why he didn't file a complaint, he said it was because the priest would transfer him to another site. If this happened, he would have to start over with his college classes in a new location. He also said the priest would stop his ordination into the priesthood. I wasn't about to back down from this guy. I filed for unemployment with the justification that I had been emotionally, verbally, and physically abused. He fought it and lied to the judge when we had our on-phone court date. The state ordered me to pay back the unemployment money I had received at 10% interest if I missed a payment. Now, how in the world would I pull that one off when I had not found a replacement job?

Of course, he won the case! The city where the judge was is where the regional Catholic Church is located, with a Catholic college and heavily Catholic influence. The town is the Salt Lake City of that state, only Catholic. Not only that, but it was at the beginning of the lawsuits against the Church, and the legal system still believed priests over those victimized by priests. It wasn't until 2002 that *The Boston Globe* brought the abuse to national attention.

Right after I lost my job and insurance, I had a physical. The nurse practitioner found a lump in my breast. I had a mammogram, and the lump was the size of a silver dollar and appeared metastasized. The nurse practitioner found a surgeon who would do a biopsy pro bono—or, as Aunt Voula would say, "the bobopsy." I told the doctor I saw that I was going to heal it.

I went home.

I had just completed massage school and had learned numerous hands-on-healing modalities. I did Reiki on myself, and my Reiki teacher Gertrude worked on me also. (She made bullets for the Nazis in World War II and said she left out the gunpowder on every other one as she didn't believe in the war even though her father was, albeit unwilling, an officer in the S. S.). I also had friends who had a Rife machine, and I used that. I changed my diet and threw my body into an alkaline state. (Some studies show that cancer cannot live in an oxygenated, alkaline state. Of course, western medicine won't tell you that because there's no money in oxygenating someone.)

When I returned for the biopsy in November, the radiologist snapped another picture. The doctor entered the room, jammed the previous and recent X-rays into the light, and said, "What did you do?"

I said, "What do you mean, 'what did I do'?"

He said, "It's gone."

My younger daughter, who was with me when the "ting-a-ling" guy died, said, "That doesn't surprise me."

I told him, "Reiki. Why?"

He said, "Because it's gone. Look." And, sure enough, the tentacle-looking lump was gone.

He leaned against the counter and said, "Will you please tell me how that works? You're the third person I've seen in three months who has healed their cancer. Explain to me how Reiki works."

I told him, "It's just Universal Light that flows through your hands."

I knew a woman, one of the three he was talking about, whose breasts were full of cancer. They told her she had less than six weeks to live and immediately needed surgery. Why perform surgery if she only had six weeks to live? Anyway, they told her to get her affairs in order. She was a young woman with young children. She went home, and when she returned a few months later, her cancer was completely gone. She started wearing bells on her shoes.

I started to wear a new awareness.

CHAPTER 15
Manifesting My Needs

When my youngest daughter graduated from high school and went to college, I got the itch again—not to run but to explore and learn. I bought an R. V. and headed for Sedona, but as I was heading down the road through Idaho, I kept hearing that I needed to call my old friend Kathy, who I hadn't spoken to in years. Every time I tried to ignore the message, it came louder and louder. Besides, too many people in that small town knew my ex, so I didn't feel it was safe to go there. I finally pulled off the road and called her. She asked me to make a detour to her house. She was at the town's hotel for a birthday party and told me she needed to talk to me before I joined the group of old acquaintances and new people. After some debate, I agreed. I pulled into the hotel parking lot, and she met me at the door. She pulled me into the bathroom and told me what had happened. Her twenty-three-year-old daughter had dropped dead of a stroke, and she didn't want me to ask about her and be embarrassed. She asked me to stay with her for a while. We talked and talked about her daughter, and she cried and cried. A few days later, she told me she had prayed that someone would come and help her through her grief. The mysteries of synchronicity amazed me again.

Back on the road again, I stopped in Salt Lake City to see Dr. Ralph. He told me he had been to Sedona and that I needed to stop at a bookstore on the west end of town and get a map of the vortexes. Vortexes? When I got to Sedona, I was pleasantly surprised to find people like me—people who also saw "people" and could hear what they were saying and somehow could "heal" others (some just thought they could).

I wanted to exchange alternative healing trades with people to learn their modalities. People told me to be careful what I wished for in Sedona because "she" would manifest what you asked for, and I may not like it. I leaped anyway. I wished for a great spot to park my R. V., to meet like-minded people I could make bodywork trades with, to find a group studying Melchizedek's teachings, and to find the vortexes.

I walked into Crystal Magic Bookstore and went to the back, where, at that time, a juice bar was. I asked the girl behind the counter where a good spot to camp was. She pointed to a white-haired, bearded Santa Claus look-alike sitting at the bar and said, "Ask Traveler." "Traveler" told me to go up Dry Creek Road, turn right at the T intersection, and go about a hundred yards. He said there was a large red rock there, and it was the flattest spot. Then I asked where the vortexes were, and the lady handed a map to me.

Okay! Two out of four.

A few seconds later, a guy came storming in and asked me if that was my "rig" parked out front. I told him it was, and he said he was considering moving to that area. He cricked his neck, and I asked him if he had neck problems. He said yes. I told him I would work on his neck, and we made an appointment for the following evening. I asked him if he knew of a group studying Melchizedek. He said a group met on Tuesday nights and that if I met him at a deli the next night, he would introduce me to the man who held the group at his house. Wow, Sedona did seem to manifest what I asked for—all in five minutes.

The next night I met the guy at the deli and also met the man who sponsored the Melchizedek classes; he invited me to the potluck. After that, I worked on my new friend's neck. Later he told me that he could feel hands on every part of his body. When I entered the deli the following morning, the people there knew me and asked if I would work on them, as my new friend's neck was now okay. That town had quite a line of communication.

I camped in my R. V. out by Long's Canyon. Just up the road was a hill called Rachel's Knoll. From Rachel's Knoll, there is an unimpeded 360-degree view of the area. When I stood out on the edge of the Knoll, I felt like I was overlooking the best that creation had to offer. Even though the wind was quite exuberant, there was a quietness that I had never experienced anywhere else on Earth. The knoll had numerous medicine wheels built and used by the Native Americans. The medicine wheels represent moving into the future and a rebirth (born again)—not living in the past. Rachel's Knoll is said to be the primary energy "vortex" site of Sedona's five main energy vortexes.

A mandate was put into place shortly after I left the area that camping would not be allowed anymore outside of a privately-owned or state-run campground. A barbed wire fence now mars the landscape to keep out the "riff-raff," even though the barrier looks more riff-raff than the people. Later, they put in a cross-buck fence to hide the barbed wire. They also parked NO PARKING signs along the fence. We would soon understand why they forced out the "riff-raff." The word was that a development company called Seven Canyons had its eye on Rachel's land. Rachel refused to sell to them, but that didn't mean her children wouldn't.

I'm sure the development company jumped in the air and clicked their heels when Rachel finally died in 2001 because her family sold the property below the Knoll to the development company. However, they kept the Knoll. The company proceeded to terrace the hillsides and ripped up the soil even though hundreds of Native Americans and white people picketed and sat in defiance of the contractors and their bulldozers. They put in a gated, locked community with a golf course touted as something "smart people" buy shares in (www.travelgolf.com). Of course, the "smart people" didn't want anyone to cross their private domain to get to Rachel's Knoll and tried to bypass their agreement with the children. Rachel's children and attorney went to court and fought to allow people to get up to Rachel's Knoll. The courts declared that Seven Canyons must comply and allow people access to the Knoll.

Here's the kicker: When I moved to Sedona years later and tried to get to the Knoll, a guard stopped me at the gatehouse and told me I couldn't go onto the private property. He never mentioned that I could sign a waiver. Disappointed, I went back into town and told someone what happened. That's when I learned what Seven Canyons was pulling. If you only say the first part of a sentence, are you breaking a court order? I learned you could get to Rachel's Knoll via the gated community but must sign an agreement to stay on the designated road. The gatekeeper left off that part of the sentence. Unfortunately, when you hike in any part of the area, the once astounding serenity is marred by the buzz of golf carts and people yelling across the greens to each other about the surprising acrobatic things their balls unexpectedly did. (Not sure which balls they're referring to.)

The Natives did the same thing at Boynton Canyon to no avail. A group of wealthy people built a locked, gated community there. The Natives said the land was sacred and harm would come to those who built on that land. I don't know if the "smart people" have figured it out yet, but I know that several of the "smart people" went bankrupt, and their lots sat empty as of 2001. The gash the bulldozers left on the hillside for future roads and houses was a testament that the Native Americans were probably right. We must remember that all of this sacred land to the Native Americans was taken from them by white men with no compensation. Is that fair?

Would the United State Supreme Court support this taking of land for private use? If you go back to the Takings Clause of the Fifth Amendment to the Constitution, which says "private property" can be seized for "public use" after providing "just compensation," the answer is yes. Or is it? As a rule, governments employ this rule for projects such as highways and power lines, but using eminent domain to take land from a private owner and transfer it to another private owner is another thing. This scenario takes us to a woman named Suzette Kelo, who bought a dilapidated house in New London, Connecticut's Fort Trumbull area. Shortly after completely renovating the house and painting it pink, the corrupt Republican governor of the predominantly Democratic state, John Rowland, wanted an even higher position. How to do this? Revitalize an area where a major submarine research lab used to sit. It just happens that Suzette's house and about eighty-nine other houses sat in the way of this grand scheme.

Rowland worked through the New London Development Corporation (NLDC). They found an interested party—namely Big Pharma Pfizer. With big promises of jobs, all but seven homeowners gave in to the NLDC and sold their homes. The remaining seven refused to sell, and the war was on. After receiving eviction notices, the Institute for Justice came into the picture. They asked Suzette to lead the fight. Under Suzette's name, they filed a lawsuit to stop the taking of the homes with the argument that the "public use" ruling did not support the taking of their homes for "private use" (Pfizer).

They lost in the Connecticut trial court, which struck down most, though not all, of the rulings. Both sides appealed to the Connecticut Supreme Court, where the homeowners lost in a contentious 4–3 ruling. The dissenting opinion was strong enough that they appealed to the U. S. Supreme Court. This time the homeowners lost 5–4. Shockingly, "Ruth Bader Ginsburg, the celebrated social justice warrior, sided with the majority to throw a working-class woman out of her home. So did Justice John Paul Steven, who wrote the opinion." This ruling did not have a horribly negative side, as Steven's opinion said, "… the Court should have a light touch in applying the Takings Clause, deferring instead to state and local legislatures to enact eminent domain restrictions. On the second, he cited two prior Supreme Court decisions that upheld the use of eminent domain for private development… He quoted from *Berman* [*v. Parker*], "The concept of the public welfare is broad and inclusive. …The values it represents are spiritual as well as physical, aesthetic as well as monetary."[35]

Spiritual? How spiritual is it to build a factory with two looming smoke stacks painted red and white-striped that belches smoke?

---

[35] Matt Purple, "The Little Pink House, 15 Years Later," *The American Conservative*, Jul 3, 2020, https://www.theamericanconservative.com/the-little-pink-house-15-years-later/#:~:text=As%20for%20Susette%20Kelo's%20little,despotism%20and%20very%20nearly%20won.

In her dissent, Justice Sandra Day O'Connor used these words: "… maybe even aesthetic pleasure." Clearly, there was no aesthetic pleasure.

The good news is that "Rowland resigned as governor after being convicted of corruption charges. He spent a year in prison, got out, became a radio host, was convicted of more charges, and went back to prison."[36] Guess what Pfizer did. It moved into New London and moved back out in 2009, never having completed the development. Why did they leave? Their tax incentive ran out. The site where the Fort Trumbull homes sat became a barren field.

Suzette's little pink house was disassembled and reassembled on another street with no waterfront or dock.

Many states and the federal government were unhappy about the U. S. Supreme Court ruling. Fortunately, legislators passed laws to protect private homeowners. You'll be surprised when you see what happened to the Pan Am pilots when Pan Am went bankrupt. Those who went to work for United were retired shortly and got no retirement. As John Holmes of the Clipper Pioneers said, "We got zip, zilch." He told me United took the playbook from Delta [Abdu Brisson III v. Delta Air Lines, Inc.] and filed bankruptcy so they wouldn't have to pay the pensions. The pilots who went to work for Delta and TWA didn't fair any better. They sued for back benefits, and the courts found in favor of Delta. The only ones who made money off of these mergers were the attorneys. Why was this decision made? There are two reasons: The first is because federal law over-rules state law; the second is that "states laws would have a direct economic impact on the price it charges consumers." In other words, even though many of these pilots served the customers for twenty to fifty years, consumers owed them nothing for getting them to and from their destinations safely.

When I lived in Sedona the second time—2007–2011, one of my friends was an older woman named Mary. She worked at Sedona's history museum. Her husband "Slim" played a cowboy/wrangler in many of John Wayne's movies filmed in the area. In the 1940s, the land owner along Dry Creek Road offered "Slim" the property for

---

36 Ibid.

fifty cents an acre. He considered it worthless since he couldn't graze his horses or cattle on it and declined the offer. As of June 24, 2023, a 4.64-acre lot at 700 Dry Creek Road lists for $389,738. Ah, hindsight. How much of that money goes to the Native Americans? Quite frankly, the white man did what Putin is doing in Ukraine and what China is doing in Africa—if I stroll in, I can take your land. As for the Sedona area, a man named J. J. Thompson was the first to claim land in the Sedona area using the 1862 Homestead Act. He didn't pay the Native Americans a cent.

Now, back to the story.

One day a friend told me to go up on the Airport Vortex, where I could see all the main vortexes from one spot on the hillside. She also said I would feel something I had most likely never felt. I asked her what the feeling was. She just smiled and, with a twinkle in her eye, said I needed to experience it myself.

So, my dog and I hiked up the path at the Airport Vortex, which the twist of the trees shows as masculine energy. I noticed the wind was blowing from the south on the right side of me and from the north on the left side of me. While hiking along Dry Creek in the Long's Canyon area, I saw the same phenomenon. Below, flipping around on the red rocks, was a collection of baseball caps that the wind had ripped off people's heads. I got to a place where I could tell many people had sat. I noticed something peculiar as I stepped onto the circle of rocks laid by human hands. There was no wind in just that spot, but I could see the twisted branches of the Juniper trees leaning in opposite directions on either side of me, flipping around in the wind. I sat down, and my old, arthritic dog suddenly started bouncing around like a puppy. I sat and sat and wondered what I was supposed to feel.

And then it dawned on me. For the first time, I felt nothing. I felt no love, hatred, fear, joy, craving, fulfillment, anger, or other afflicting states. I was completely balanced and out of the causes of human suffering—desire and ignorance. I had achieved what the Buddha described as the perfect peace of the state of mind or "Nirvana." Years later, I would learn that I had mastered a level of *jhana* or *dhyana* without knowing it.

(*Jhana* is a Pali word, the same as *dhyana* in Sanskrit, *samadhi*, *samatha*, or *serenity*, and means "meditation." Both refer to withdrawing the mind from automatic responses to self-impressions. Another way to describe *jhana* is: "burning up the defilements." Defilements include a desire for sensual pleasures, unwholesome states, unwholesome thoughts, and discursive thoughts. Upon releasing defilements, one is born of concentration, knowing but non-discursive awareness, and the buried latencies of *samaskras* (latent mental impressions, recollection, and psychological imprints) are brought into full view. When this occurs, stillness, tranquility, and unification of the mind without applied thought, inquiry, or investigation of what has been focused on without conscious thoughts come forth. The third jhana is the fading away of pīti (joy, delight, pleasure, rapture counteracts ill-will (malice)), where one abides in equanimity, affective detachment, and mindfulness with fully knowing and discerning awareness. Upon achieving this state, one enters and abides in the third jhana, where one is equanimous and mindful. When one completes the third jhana, one moves to the fourth jhana. Here, one abandons the desire for pleasure and has an aversion to pain. Along with the previous disappearance of the inner movement between gladness and discontent, one enters the space of *adukkham asukham*, which is "neither painful nor pleasurable, freedom from pleasure and pain, and enters a place of complete purity of equanimity and mindfulness." Arbel describes this space as "non-reactive and lucid awareness."[37] The fourth jhana is where liberating insight is attained. Schmithausen says liberating insight suffices.[38] The fifth jhana is infinite space; the sixth is infinite consciousness; the seventh is infinite nothingness; and the eighth is neither perception nor non-perception.)

What had I stumbled onto in that tiny circle bordered by rocks, sticks, and gifts to the gods? I had learned to clear my mind, which brought me into a state of equanimity. That's what Christianity calls

---

37 Wikipedia, "Dhyana in Buddhism," https://en.wikipedia.org/wiki/Dhyana_in_Buddhism.

38 Ibid.

"the mind of Christ." To explain how this works, picture a teeter-totter. On one side are the yummy feelings—praise, gain, pleasure, and fame. On the other side are the yucky feelings—blame, loss, pain, disrepute. Suffering arises when one gets too mired on either side. You read that correctly—suffering also occurs when one gets too mired in praise, gain, pleasure, and fame. What happens if you're on a teeter-totter and the person on either side has more weight? You end up stuck up in the air or smack-dab on your bottom. Does the Bible talk about equanimity? It sure does. Read Ecclesiastes 4. These verses are known as the "Vicissitudes of Life." The Bible also mentions *peace* several hundred times, yet many religious people say those who travel to Sedona to find peace are heathens. Does it matter how or where one finds peace? One might fight it working in the garden, on a piece of art, fishing, or reading a book.

The next day I went to the Cathedral Rock vortex, a feminine energy vortex. I lay down on a water-washed soft red-rock indentation and felt a very emotional tide ripping throughout me. I felt as if I couldn't move. After the wave ebbed, I got up and moved to a stool-like rock beside a gentle waterfall. I pulled up emotions that I had buried for decades. I silently spoke to the people I felt had offended me and told them how their actions had caused me harm—my perception of harm. I cried, spit, and snarled words at them, and when I finished washing away the anger toward them, I got up and walked to a sandy beach area. I scooped up handsful of sand, and as I sprinkled the sand into the water, I released my anger toward them and from my life. I felt cleansed of my rage toward them and the need to hold onto them any longer.

A few days later, I went to the Bell Rock area. I climbed up as far as I could go and as far as my dog's claws would allow her to climb without me giving her a lift against her rear end and an accidental goose, which she gave me dirty looks for. As I looked over the valley, I felt awash with peace and realized that my craving for more was gone.

I wondered if the people born in Sedona left there if they would feel oddly out-of-place energetically. Now how in the world could those of us who were not born in the Sedona area feel an energy that was so different than what we were used to, and those born there think people are nuts who say they feel the additional energy? To explain this question, if you hold a simple ring on a chain necklace or other type of pendulum from your fingers in the vortex area, the ring will spin clockwise or counter-clockwise, just as the juniper trees spin. (Years later, when I moved to the Sedona area, I went to a dowsing potluck and discovered my doctor was a member of the Dowser's Club! Not only that, but a friend of hers, a nun, was visiting her. When I heard her last name, I said, "Huh, your last name is the same as my brother's best friend in high school." When I told her his name, she smiled and said, "His dad is my brother." What a small world we live in! Also, who would ever dream that a nun would belong to a Dowser's Club? That goes against the rules of the Church, which condemns dowsing, among other things, as "of the devil.")

Numerous people believe Sedona is a portal site to other realms. Some think the rocks' red iron creates energy. The Native Americans understand that Sedona's healing has to do with healing on a deeper dimension. Many scientists worldwide have studied the vortexes in Sedona, and everyone I have talked to concurs that there is something different about the powers in the Sedona area. Other areas with equally peculiar energies are Stonehenge, England; the pyramids of Egypt and Bosnia; formations in New Hampshire, Machu Pichu, Peru, etc. Why do the powers in these places draw out emotions that we have stored within us for years and years? It would be years before I would begin to understand why those energy or portal sites are located in certain spots on Earth, how and why the energies alter or stop, and how the location of those energies can be and are changed.

Some claim that Sedona is an ancient colony of the Lemurians. Author David Icke in his book *Children of the Matrix* wrote that the magnetic energies felt under the Boynton Canyon area can be registered on instrumentation and attributed to underground bases where aliens work with human or part-human puppets in the Illuminati on the scientific and genetic agenda.[39] (He also says the "Native Americans call

---

39 David Icke. *The Children of the Matrix—How an Interdimensional Race has Controlled the World for Thousands of Years-and Still Does*, (Bridge of Love, 2001).

America 'Turtle Island' after their reptilian ancestors." This assertion is incorrect. They call it that because it is turtle-shaped.) Although Icke's claim might be a stretch of the imagination, numerous people I have talked to have run into an armed guard at the door leading into an underground area, and several friends have said they have seen this and heard the same thing from others, usually tourists.

Interestingly, wealthy people have built a gated community called Enchantment Resort right on the vortex of Boynton Canyon and right above the underground base. What exactly is Enchantment Resort, and who exactly lives there? Do the people living in that gated community work in that underground area? (As of July 2023, the U. S. government is finally acknowledging that they have "bodies" that are not "biologically human.") What are aliens? Are they something to be feared, or are they a more intelligent society from another dimension? From what I've seen over the years, a society more intelligent than ours wouldn't take much.

The Native Americans say that no one is to live in Sedona because it is a sacred place for healing. They also say Mother will remove the energy if it is misused, so they adamantly oppose people building in the area. (Notice that the Native Americans are smart enough to realize that a Mother is necessary for Creation.) There is also a saying about Sedona, "She'll kick you out when she's done with you." One morning at precisely five weeks, I got up, felt a tap three times on my shoulder, and heard a voice say, "It's time to go now."

I looked around like a dunce, and, of course, no one was there. I packed up my R. V. with my Springer Spaniel perched in the passenger's seat (she would get a snotty look on her face and, perhaps, bite anyone who tried to take her seat) and headed up the canyon toward Flagstaff. I thought, "Huh, I didn't see my friend John on my way through town."

I had seen the same man daily for five weeks, and on that day, when I drove past *New Frontier* grocery store, his car wasn't there. About five miles up the canyon, I saw a maniac coming down the road with his arm flailing out the window. I pulled over. It was John. I got to say goodbye.

* * *

I found a beautiful deserted campground on top of a mountain in Utah and stayed there for four days. It's the only campground I had ever been to that had tables forty feet long. Most of them had reserved signs for the following weekend already stuck to them with a family's name. However, my daughter's urgent voice pierced my serenity because I kept hearing her say, "Mom, call me!"

Finally, the voice got so loud and annoying that I packed up and went back down the mountain. I found a pay phone and called. As soon as I heard my daughter's voice, I said, "What's wrong?" She told me that she had been sick for five days and had been telling me to call her.

I drove for fourteen hours, and when I walked into the house and saw her, I said, "Get in the car. We're going to the hospital." They admitted her immediately. They hooked her up to IVs. She had a virus that had seriously dehydrated her.

I was getting pretty good at the listening thing.

* * *

One night I dreamed I was in a room filled with tomes. The room glistened in bronze, copper, silver, and gold colors embedded in a shimmering iridescent background. Loving books, I reached up for one of the books, and a "being" with long hair, a beard, and wearing a long robe pushed my hand aside gently and carried the tome to the dais. When I tried to open the book, I heard him think, "Just lay your hands on it." I did, and a wealth of information flowed into me. Later, I would learn that this was my Akashic record or the "book of life" (Phil. 4:3). (I only quote the Bible so that the Christians will read this and possibly understand the true meaning of the word *Akashic* that the Bible speaks of, which is an ethereal record of every soul's journey to realize the Divine.) There are numerous times in the Bible that the "Book of the Lord" is mentioned. In Luke 4:17–19, Isaiah handed the "book" to Him, and He told him what was in his [Akashic] record. *Webster's New Universal Unabridged Dictionary* says: "akasha…n.: (in the philosophies of India) the ether, regarded as including material and nonmaterial entities in a common medium." We all have an Akashic record. And some of us can see the material entities, and some can hear the nonmaterial entities.

Akasha comes from the Sanskrit word *kash*, meaning "to radiate, to shine," or "ether," believed to be the medium of movement. Some mystical doctrines think it is "a mystical (vague/mysterious) spiritual substance where memories are stored since the beginning of time." In Theosophy, the Akashic Records or Book of Life are the historical records of all world events and personal experiences of all thoughts and deeds which have taken place, are taking place, and will take place on Earth. No one can change one's Akashic record. They are a part of your Earth contract, but I would not understand that for some time.

What had I stumbled onto? For the first time, I felt that my life had some meaning, however bizarre, and now I was not as fearful of my future. The irony of the situation was the timing of what I knew my future held in store for me. When was the timing to occur? What if I made a mistake and zigged instead of zagged? How ridiculous was that? I became almost obsessed with not making a mistake that would mess up my life's purpose. I had no choice but to get a result lined up like a Rubik's Cube.

* * *

The following spring, I went to Taos, Santa Fe, and then the Gallup area, where I worked at an Indian Boarding School. I learned a lot about Native American customs, some Navajo language, a laid-back lifestyle, and what was important in life. When I returned home in the spring, I knew I had to somehow get my daughter out of the area where she was living.

While she was balking, I went up in the mountains to live. I spent my days studying the Fibonacci Law and discovered that there is no randomness in nature, and everything is in perfect order. Fibonacci said that all plants have an absolute number of leaves, stems, etc., and the numbers are an integer sequence—0, 1, 1, 2, 3, 5, 8, 13, 21, 35, 55, 89, 144.... In other words, 0+1 is 1. 1+1 is 2. 2+1 is 3. 3+2 is 5. 5+3 is 8. 8+5 is 13. 13+8 is 21. 21+13 is 35. 35+21 is 55, and so on. As this sequence continues, the ratio between each number becomes closer and closer to 1.68—the Golden Ratio, also known as Phi. The Golden Ratio is the ratio nature relies on to maintain balance. It describes the proportions of everything from atoms to planets. Fibonacci introduced India's Arabic mathematical system to Italy after he spent time in India learning their numerical system. That system was the stepping stone to our numerical system of today.

God instructed Noah to build the Ark using the Golden Ratio. A man in California created a model of an ark using the Golden Ratio and used the arcs of the Earth, Sun, and Moon, and the arcs of the Moon's orbit around the Earth and the Earth's orbit around the Sun on each edge. It was built to the precise scale of 120 cube cubits and was 300 x 50 x 30 by 3 stories tall. The model I saw looks a little goofy, but if you spin it in one direction, it spins freely and keeps spinning until you stop it. It also self-corrects. If you turn it in the opposite direction, it will not turn and correct itself.

He put the ark out into the ocean. From a helicopter, they filmed the ark. It went all over the place, around the waves rather than up and over them, and only would go in a circle rather than go in its opposite direction. The people inside the ark said they could not feel the boat going all over the place like a bobbing, spinning cork, and it felt like they were going straight. Why?—because the builder built the ark according to the Golden Ratio and, therefore, the ark was compatible with the universe. I would lay odds that if the Noah's Ark story happened, rather than just a symbolic lesson on mathematics and physics, Noah most likely built the Ark using arcs, not straight lines like how many people make replicas of the Ark.

The name *Noah* means "calm, peace, and balance." And what did the ark do? It balanced and became calm and peaceful when it landed on Ararat. But did it? Ararat is a fascinating word because it doesn't mean anything in Hebrew. *Jones' Dictionary of Old Testament Proper Names* says *Ararat* comes from the common Hebrew word רה (*har*), meaning "hill" or "mountain," and the common Hebrew verb ירד (*yarad*), "to go down, descend, march down." This would make the word *Ararat* "Mountain Mountain" or "Mountain of Descent" if it weren't for the final letter *teth*. Unfortunately, that *teth* changes the story to mean a mountain and future in a flash laid out with a curse and a trembling.[40] Was the Ark story true, an allegory for spiritual growth, or a conveyor of consciousness? Maybe the story of the Ark was just a story directing humans to balance the three aspects of the psychic (water) with his conscious mind (physical) and his soul. What happened on the airplane? In a flash of exploding grenades and firebombs, with a curse and a trembling, a terrorist sneered, "Pan American. Pan American." Who was teaching whom in this attack? It certainly opened me to spiritual growth and consciousness and also opened the three aspects of my psychic with my conscious mind and my soul. Before the bombing, I hadn't seen or heard the "scary" man standing in the corner since childhood, and we moved from that house.

Numerologically speaking, God told Noah to take specific numbers with him on the boat, including the three sons, which correlate to the many threes of the Ark and all of the threes used in future Biblical lessons. After learning these things, I started listening to people discussing the power of numbers. However, I had trouble believing people who said words have power. They often misunderstood what they were talking about and felt the words themselves were the power rather than the numerical energy of the word, thus causing the terms to take on superstitious energy. Which one of us was correct? Or was the problem in semantics?

Then I started questioning whether there was any randomness in my physical/soul journey. Did I have a choice about what happened in my life? Was there a choice in what I did, or was it that I would perhaps get to the result in different scenarios that gave me an illusion of having an option? I also wondered if I would arrive at the result in another timeline because of the strategies chosen.

I worked on issues regarding my mother and let go of much of my extra "baggage." While living in that forest, I spent days listening to

---

40 Abarim Publications, s.v. "Ararat meaning," 2006-04-19, www.https//: abarim-publication.com/Meaning/Ararat.html#:~:text=The%20word%20ararat%20is%20...

a poor misguided frog hopping up and down under my RV, hitting its head, and never figuring out why he kept smashing into the undercarriage. The day I left there, I backed out and heard a squish. When I looked through my windshield, I saw the frog smashed flat. I guess he had not learned about proprioception or vehicle tires. This event was a perfect example of equanimity in practice.

* * *

My daughter finally surrendered and transferred to another job site. I helped her move and discovered that there were pages of jobs that paid pretty well. I decided to stay for a while. A while became a year and then two. I was not used to being in the same place that long but sensed that I was safe from my ex-husband. I miserably and erroneously bounced between metaphysics and the material world and started chasing money and the security I thought it could bring me.

I worked for a temp company that sent me to a place where I did some painting. The part-owner decided to befriend me. I ended up living five houses from her a few months later. She stopped by when she saw me outside and tried convincing me to go to a movie or dinner with her. Even though everything in my being told me the woman was trouble, I ignored the voices. That would be one of the biggest mistakes I had ever made that turned into a blessing and a checkmark next to a box on my karmic balance sheet. It was like what I had heard before the airplane hijacking. I knew something terrible would eventually happen, but I also knew I was supposed to go.

I was about to start the third phase of my life, and it would be a ride that I could not have dreamed of, even for a movie. My life would now split into two realms—the realm of returning from the dead into the physical, or the subconscious, the unconscious, and the realm of the ethereal spiritual. Fortunately, I found that Naga was still with me—still protecting me.

CHAPTER 16
The Miracle

While re-writing this book with the information I've gathered over the years, I went online to do some research about Pan Am Flight 110. I ran across an article in the *Hartford Courant* triggered by a lady named Ann Blumensaadt. Ann, a flight attendant for Pan Am from 1969–1991, sought information from anyone who knew what happened to Purser Diana Perez. I contacted Ann. I told her some of my experience on the plane and said much of what was in the Pan Am articles was false—no one deployed chutes, and only the flight engineer helped me, then he ran away. I didn't have the heart to tell her that two flight attendants hid in the lavatory. As it turns out, it's a good thing they did, and you'll soon see why. I told Ann that my friend Barb said someone had opened the emergency exit and shoved her out the door. Barb didn't know who. They jumped off the wing and ran to a field. Was it a flight attendant, or was it someone else? I was about to find out who it was.

Ann also said she was assigned the New York to Rome flight a few days after the bombing, and they passed the burned-out hull of Flight 110 pulled off to the side of the runway. She said the whole top of the plane was missing, and it was a sight she would never forget. My cousin happened to land in Rome on the same day and said the same thing.

Ann told me a reporter from Italy had contacted her about doing a fiftieth-anniversary article about the bombing since Ann worked with World Wings International, a charity group for retired Pan Am workers. Ann gave the reporter, Viviana Mazza's, name to me. Viviana ended up contacting me. I told her my story. I left out one significant detail, which I did not know about at the time. Viviana wrote an article using the information I gave her and posted it in her newspaper *Corriere.* It was not until days later that I learned that some of what I told her was inaccurate. One thing she did write that was inaccurate was that Robyn's child had died. I told her the child was injured. Now comes the fun part.

I found the "Unclassified" U. S. Embassy cable from December 18, 1973, on July 24, 2023. As I read through the records, I realized the "Deceased" records of Pan Am and the Embassy did not match. Who was mistaken? I knew I had little time to resolve this discrepancy because the publisher needed this manuscript pronto so the book would be ready for the Frankfurt Book Fair. The name in question was Randy Kirby. I had grieved his and my other acquaintances' deaths for forty-nine years and needed to find out if he was still alive. I typed in his name. No luck. I typed in his sister Jane Kirby's name, along with the name Harding College. Bingo! I found a story about a forty-year remembrance for Janie at Harding College. The article said her brother Randy, his wife, and three children attended, and he said the memorial touched him. What? I reread it.

I could find nothing about Randy online, so I typed in his wife's name. Her name came up on Linkedin. I sent an email to her at that address—MAILER-DAEMON! However, her link gave me another clue. It named the town they lived in. I typed in Randy's name along with the name of the city. Bingo! Found his name and an email—MAILER-DAEMON! I wasn't about to give up. I needed his story! I needed to know if I was wrong about the deployed chutes, and if he was alive, how did he get off that plane? Did he leave with Barb's group at the very beginning? He certainly wasn't on the wing when I exited.

The Linkedin site gave information about their church. I wrote a long-winded letter to Randy, jpeg-ed it, and attached it to a letter to the church asking them to forward the email to Randy. Within fifteen minutes, I got a text from Randy saying I could call him anytime, and he gave me his number.

I didn't know whether to cry or what to do. After gathering my emotions, I phoned Randy. Imagine my surprise when this man I had known forty-nine years ago and thought was dead not only worked at the church but answered the phone. We talked for quite some time, and he said he would try to find the talk he had given at his church about the airplane ordeal. He said it might take some time because he was moving from one office to another and wasn't sure which box it was in. I received the document he said I could post in this book within three hours. Here it is, in part.

YOU WERE THERE

> New York Times – Dec. 18, 1973
>
> "Arab Terrorists Attack US Jet in Rome"
>
> On Dec. 17th Pan Am Flight 110, The Clipper Celestial, was scheduled to fly from Rome, Italy to Beirut, Lebanon then to Dhahran, Saudi Arabia.
>
> At approximately 1:10 PM local time, just as Flight 110 was boarding approximately 8 Palestinian Terrorists made their way through the terminal building armed with automatic weapons and grenades. The terrorists removed their weapons from handbags and began firing throughout the terminal, shattering windows and killing two.
>
> The crew, in the cockpit of the aircraft, was able to observe travelers and airport employees in the building running for cover. Captain Erbeck announced over the plane's public address system that there was some trouble in the terminal and ordered all on board to get down on the floor.

Several of the gunmen ran across the tarmac toward the Pan American jet, throwing phosphorous hand grenades through the open front and rear doors, of the aircraft. The explosions knocked crew and passengers to the ground, and the cabin filled with thick, acrid smoke from the resulting fires.

Flight engineer Kenneth Phrang was knocked to the galley floor by the first grenade. "I got hit by the concussion" he said later," and I thought, 'Why aren't I dead?' Then I realized it was some sort of incendiary device and smoke was pouring out of the canister." Within second, there was more flashes as two phosphorus grenades went off inside the forward section. Two other grenades were thrown in the rear; suddenly the entire plane was filled with roiling black smoke. [It actually took a while for the whole plane to fill with "roiling black smoke."]

"It was a miracle that so many people did get out," said first officer Davison. "I flew C-123s in Viet Nam, but I've never experienced anything that happened so fast or in which you were so helpless."

Somehow, 40 passengers and crewmen managed to escape. Many suffered burns, including one passenger who died later [Bonnie Presnell]. But 29 more were trapped inside, including all eleven passengers in the first-class section. Among the dead were 4 Moroccan officials, 14 relatives of employees of Aramco Oil Co and Mrs. Bonnie Erbeck, wife of the plane's captain.

Two of the passengers that day were my 19 year old sister, Janie and me. I had turned 21 two days earlier and we were traveling from Harding to visit our parents who lived in Saudi Arabia.

We had flown to Rome the day before and spent a day sight-seeing. This was a trip of a lifetime and we were excited about the opportunity to see the world. Janie had bought two presents that day for mom and dad for Christmas over my protests about spending money. Some things never change.

As we boarded for our flight to Saudi Arabia our seats were in the middle of the plane. I had a window seat on the flight in so Janie was to sit by the window today. I had the middle seat and an elderly lady with a walker sat in the aisle seat.

The capacity for the 707 was 197 passengers. I asked the flight attendant if I could move to an open seat by the window and she told me to stand at the rear of the plane until everyone was seated. [He told me that because he was only 21 years old, he felt special standing in the back of the plane with the flight attendant.] I was at the back of the plane visiting with her when the announcement was made to get on the floor.

[He told me he moved to the third or fourth row from the back and laid flat on the floor with his feet to the wall and his head toward the aisle. One flight attendant crawled past him and lay in the next seat aisle. He said he saw the other one move forward and then back toward the galley.]

Soon after lying down the explosions began and the next thing I remember was waking up in darkness and a blinding, burning smoke. [He told me the terrorist I encountered ran past him through the plane. The terrorist threw a farewell bomb as he exited the plane, knocking Randy and others unconscious. That is the same terrorist who came through the first-class curtain and stepped over me.] I could barely hear because the explosion had ruptured my eardrums and I was struggling to see. Since I was near the rear exit there was light shining through the haze and I could see one of the flight attendants struggling with the door. The explosion had blown the door all the way open and she could not pull it into position to deploy the slide. A woman passenger was screaming and wanting to jump. While holding her back I was able to pull the door into position so the attendant could deploy the slide. Once I was on the ground and cleared my lungs, I noticed that the plane was on fire. I don't know how long I had been unconscious but it must have been several minutes because the trucks, ambulances and rescue personnel were already present.

The rest of the afternoon was spent in complete confusion while being held and regrouped [in a building away from the terminal]. By evening we were transported to a downtown hotel. At that point my only concern was finding Janie. A local reporter agreed to take me to the area hospitals that were treating the wounded and eventually around 3am—I discovered she had not survived the attack.

IT was in the MOMENTS that the loss of a loved one, the announcement of cancer, the reality that your baby has serious medical problems, an attack that steals your innocence, abuse that robs you of your childhood, a natural disaster or a betrayal and divorce is when you ask—WHERE ARE YOU GOD!

SO WHERE WAS GOD?

The first glimpse came within a few weeks. After days of untold grief, confusion and pain, we gathered ourselves with friends and family in Little Rock for

> Janie's funeral. It was during this time our luggage from the trip was found and returned to us. As difficult as this whole event must have been for mom and dad they now had to unpack Janie's suitcase. What they found were the two gifts Jane had purchased in Rome.
>
> The first was a printing of the Serenity Prayer.
>
> "God grant me the serenity to accept [the] things I cannot change
>
> Courage to change the things I can
>
> And the wisdom to know the difference."
>
> This was the first hint that God WAS There.
>
> There was something about these two items that touched Janie's heart. They proved to be perfectly timed reminders that God too had suffered the loss of a child and understands our pain—as well as giving a message of encouragement—to be strong and trusting of God's promises.

Randy's story continues and lists the many people who knew Janie at Harding College and named their daughters after her. One story, in particular, caught my eye. A girl named Memory Jane wrote that after hearing the story of Janie, she feels honored to have received the name Janie and the first name Memory in memory of such an incredible role model.

Remember: God, a Higher Power, or whatever name you might choose to call It, works in mysterious ways. The writing is in the sky, and sometimes that writing is shown to us in the placement of the planets or where we are at a specific time. The answer might be answered in a dream, a psychic reading, hypnosis, or therapy. It might come to you from the clear blue sky or during meditation.

Why didn't more of us die that day? Is it because our work was incomplete? Why did so many who died mention that they could die and be okay with it? Did we have lifetime "contracts" to fulfill? Why didn't the terrorist shoot me and the couple in the corner at the first-class doorway but throw the bomb into the fuselage on his way out? Is that why my concept of time was so far off, and I couldn't figure out how and when the people ended up outside on the plane's wing? Is that what happened to Lari? Remember: she told me she stayed under the people until she thought it was safe but told others she was unconscious. Why the discrepancy? Or was there a discrepancy? Did those who stayed alive do so because they were in an altered state or on the floor? Later claims would say the terrorists went after Pan Am and those in first class because of their "opulence."

Later in the day, Randy called me again. He found the piece of paper with the names of the flight attendants trying to stabilize the back door on the 2R side of the plane. Their names were Linda Jacobson and Sharon Dyer. As stated, they went to an outbuilding away from the terminal after escaping the aircraft. From there, the people were either taken by ambulances to hospitals or bused to the Metripole Hotel, where Randy sat in the lobby for hours, trying to figure out what to do next. An Italian reporter named Umberto Gerardi came to the hotel and spoke with Randy. Randy was desperate to find Janie, and Umberto offered to help him. Umberto drove Randy to the three hospitals where the injured survivors were. Unable to find her in any of those places, they finally drove to the morgue. Sadly, that is where they found Janie.

As it turns out, some of the Pan Am people did help that day, ran away, then reappeared. How did I figure out the timing of all of this? As unsavory as this might be for some of you to swallow, I have a friend in Tucson named Kim Pfleuger. Kim is a gifted medium who has helped me figure out some rather daunting puzzles. I asked her why the terrorist didn't shoot me when he came through the curtain. "Spirit" showed/told her it was because he thought I was dead. I didn't understand what she meant, and neither did she. She said the only way she could describe it was that Spirit put me into a shock or trance state so that it looked like I was dead to him. That made sense because as the weight of Muriel pulled me down, I remembered my eyes were open—not wide, not closed, but also staring as if not seeing. She also said he was hurrying to get through the plane to throw the last bomb. I asked her why I couldn't find Muriel. Spirit told her it was because I wasn't where I thought I was. My final question was, why didn't I know about Randy and the chute deployment in the back of the plane? I told her that Bonnie and Robyn had checked and said no one was alive. She said it was because Randy and the others were still unconscious, and Bonnie, Robyn, and I were already inside the terminal when they woke up, so we did not know this was happening on the other side of the plane.

That same night was my Buddhist meditation night. During the meditation, I was able to piece together what Kim told me and so was able to see where I was when I suddenly went from being in gray smoke to being in black smoke when I "came to." I was in first class, but Muriel wasn't. She was on the other side of the bulkhead wall, still in the economy section. I asked Kim if I had also "died" in the ambulance. She said yes, but it was more of a "shock" on the plane because the silver cord didn't break. I told her I could see the attached cord and had actually written about it. (The silver cord in Hindi is called the sutratma thread.) In other words, you aren't dead-dead if the thread doesn't break. As Miracle Max said in *The Princess Bride* about Westley, who appeared dead,

> It just so happens that your friend here is only MOSTLY dead. There's a big difference between mostly dead and all dead. Mostly dead is slightly alive. With all dead, well, with all dead there's usually only one thing you can do.[41]

At that point, Miracle Max took a fireplace bellow, blew air into Westley, and gave his friends Inigo and Fezzik a golf-ball-sized lump of clay to give to Westley just before they stormed the castle. The lump was supposed to bring him back to life for an hour. Max realized later that the pill he made would only bring Westley back to life for forty

[41] William Goldman, *The Princess Bride*, 1987, directed by Rob Reiner.

minutes. Is that what they did to me in the ambulance? If they did, the clay pill they gave me was only the size of a marble because I don't think I lasted that long before my lights went out. I think it was more like twenty minutes.

What is the difference in the smoke in the plane, and why is it important? Petroleum products, rubber, and many plastics cause black smoke. Remember that I said earlier the side panels, ceiling panels, and today's baggage compartments are plastic? "Although crude oil is a source of raw material (feedstock) for plastics, it is not the major source of feedstock for plastics production in the United States. Plastics are produced from natural gas, feedstocks derived from natural gas processing, and feedstocks derived from oil refining."[42]

Wow! So all of the plastic in an airplane, an aluminum tube, creates something like a can of charcoal lighter fluid.

Black smoke also tells us the fire in first class was well-ventilated. The 1L door was open, and the first-class roof had a hole blown in it. Not only that, but the crew in the cockpit removed the windshield. Plus, add the opened overwing exits, the open 2L door, and the hole in the roof at the rear of the plane, and there was plenty of ventilation. This color of smoke tells me I was in first class. Slow, white, dissipating smoke, which I saw as I was going down at the first-class door, indicates steam and the early stages of heating. I must have been in first class for a while because as I felt my way back through the economy section, the black smoke had infiltrated the plane back to at least the emergency doors. Considering that Randy said he "woke up in darkness," he was out longer than I was, meaning the black smoke had infiltrated further back.

We know the flames did not reach the middle or back part of the cabin because the fire did not incinerate the people beyond the emergency door exits. Their bodies were intact except those blown up

[42] U. S. Energy Information Administration, "How much oil is used to make plastic?" Accessed July, 2023, https://www.eia.gov/tools/faqs/faq.php?id=34&t=6#:~:text=Although%20crude%20oil%20is%20a,derived%20from%20crude%20oil%20refining..

and burned by the grenades and bombs in the back rows. Fortunately, the fire seemed to have crept along the ceiling, sparing the cremation of those between the emergency exits and at least a few rows back. Using Kim's information, the smoke signs, and what Randy told me about the explosions I didn't hear but that he heard enabled me to piece together what happened to me in the missing time. But that's not the end of the story because, as you'll soon see in the next chapter, there's more to it.

Randy spoke of how lucky he was to have married a therapist who helped him through this horror, which he said he couldn't talk about for forty years. I was not as fortunate as he. I married a madman. Was there a reason for it? What was I to learn? I think I laid that out pretty well in this book. In case you didn't figure it out, I needed to realize that there is much, much more beyond this physical realm.

CHAPTER 17

More Questions Answered

Miracle of miracles. Through a chain of people, former Flight Attendant Barbara Marnock passed her phone number to me. For years, she refused to talk about the bombing and had never spoken to someone about the attack not affiliated with Pan Am. She seemed eager to speak with me.

According to Barbara, the 747 from New York we were to be on was so delayed Pan Am diverted the Celestial Clipper from its scheduled itinerary. We were loaded onto the plane as soon as Pan Am completed the required paperwork for the different aircraft. She was to work the bulkhead area. The bulkhead is the wall dividing first class and second class. Some French-speaking nuns had been picked up in Nice, France, and were on the plane. Because Barbara spoke French, she was the interpreter, so she went into the second-class area to translate what the pilot said. Barbara started toward the front of first class when the pilot told everyone to get on the floor. When he saw her move forward, he yelled for her to "get back into the center of the plane." She turned around, went toward the plane's center, and laid down two or three rows back from the bulkhead. As you will recall, from the back of the aircraft, one of the female flight attendants told us to move to the front.

That would guarantee all of us running into each other or converging in the plane's center where the plastic incendiary device that didn't go off would have blown all of us to smithereens. (Barbara said the "guerillas" used this same technique in a later attack. They herded everyone to the plane's center, where they would die from the white phosphorous poison, the toxic seat material, and the bomb they attached to the belly of the aircraft. Of course, the "guerillas" did not count on someone opening the overwing exit doors and the 2R door thwarting their total death and destruction plan. They also could not have conceived that the plastic incendiary device they attached to the belly of the plane would not go off.)

I also brought up how muted the bombs in the front and the back and the gunshots in first class were inside the plane. I told Barbara that I was shocked at how quiet they were. She was equally surprised at the muted sound. Is this because the sound couldn't expand? It must be, because the gunshots outside the plane when the guerillas were shooting at us and the police surrounding the Lufthansa plane were quite loud.

I asked Barbara if the smoke was gray or black when she exited the plane. She said the smoke was gray, meaning she got off before the black smoke entered the second-class cabin. She told me the emergency doors were already open when she got to them, and when she got out on the wing, people out there were "frozen." Barbara stood at the door repeatedly, saying, "Come to my voice." I did not hear her saying this while moving toward the door. No one inside was making a sound. Was this because I was the only one still alive, or was I the only one conscious or hiding in the lavatory? I told her when I exited the plane, Mr. Wilson's arms flailed as he headed toward the wing tip. She didn't remember that. The odd thing is that Mr. Wilson's arms flailed slowly and jerkily like a marionette, and his steps were "wooden."

Later, I remembered Barbara was walking toward the middle of the wing when I exited, telling people to jump because the plane would blow up, which is why I didn't hear her saying, "Come to my voice."

Barbara also remembers two people catching people jumping off the wing. I told her, "That other person was me." That surprised her, and she asked, "That was you?" I assured her it was, and she said, "Oh, my!" among other things.

She said she stayed on the wing next to the door, saying, "Come to my voice," even after Lari came out. I was confused when she said this because I thought we had everyone off the wing. Lari's story only mentions her and Dominic leaving the wing area and hiding behind the barrel. Lari never noted Barbara running with them, and Barbara said that was because she didn't. This statement takes us back to Lari Hamel's report, where she said, "The surviving crew stood near the wing and shouted, "Jump, jump!" Had Barbara already jumped, and her time-line was out of whack? Or was she still on the wing coaxing Lari to jump?

Once again, I conferred with Kim to find out why I didn't remember Barbara on the wing. Kim assured me that Barbara was still on the wing. Kim said I have the answers in the back of my mind. She was right. After calming my mind, I saw a woman crouched near the emergency exit saying something. Barbara did say she wanted to go back inside but was too afraid of the fire and the smoke and was worried the plane would blow up. Perhaps we all stupidly thought we wouldn't blow up with the plane if we were merely on the wing, going up the stairs, or standing next to it. That's ridiculous because we were standing on top of the full fuel tanks when we were on the wing.

How did Barbara get off the wing, and why didn't I consciously remember Barbara still on the wing? When faced with a predicament much worse than someone standing next to a door repeating a mantra, the mission to get back on the plane to find friends and others, or what is standing in front of them and needs help immediately overrides someone still on the wing. What was standing in front of me? The horribly-burned Bonnie and Robyn.

Ironically, after speaking with Barbara, I started remembering more details. For example, I remember passing her lying in the row while carrying Muriel up the aisle.

Then she told me Dominic caught her. I asked her if she was sure it was Dominic, and she assured me it was Dominic Franco. She also told me Dominic is the one helping me catch people off the wing. I told her the man said he was the flight engineer. She assured me it was Dominic. Which one was it?

When I told Barbara that Bonnie and Robyn said two Pan Am attendants hid in the lavatory, Barbara said Dominic told her he hid under a server cart because it was empty. This statement means the statement saying Dominic tried to hide under the cart but couldn't get under it was a misprint, she misunderstood him, or he did not tell Barbara the truth. This statement also means Sharon Dyer and Linda Jacobson are the two who hid in the lavatory, which is impossible if one was lying in the seat aisle in front of Randy. Randy said he only saw one creep back toward the galley. Could it have been off-duty pilot John Parrott hiding in the lavatory with one of the female attendants? I'd have to wait for the answer to that question.

Although Dominic caught Barbara when she jumped, she still hurt her heel and could barely walk. After jumping, she hobbled to a room in a building away from the terminal where other escaped victims gathered. This room is probably the same room Randy said he went to. I spoke with him a few days after my conversation with Barbara and asked if he remembered Barbara. He said he didn't remember much about who was in the room except that his sister wasn't there.

Barbara said that later, Pam Am shuttled them to the Metripole Hotel. They took the pilots to a luxury hotel near the Embassy. Barbara said she spent a day in the hospital, and her foot bothered her for a long time.

Here is the thing about shock: You will go into a protective mode out of fear of dying and having to accept that someone is shooting at you. Needless to say, Bonnie, Robyn, and I were not in shock mode because we remembered the terrorists' last barrage of shots very clearly. Barbara doesn't. Once again, I was surprised when she said she didn't remember that. Did she jump sooner than she thought or block the shooting from her memory? More than likely, Barbara blocked it because she jumped after Lari, and Lari very clearly remembered being shot at and the cowardly carabinieri behind the barrel, saying he didn't want to get killed and "they're crazy." After the shooting stopped, Lari took the child immediately to the Alitalia desk. This statement means

Dominic was still on the tarmac, which means he could have gone back to the wing after the shooting stopped and caught Barbara jumping off the wing.

According to Barbara, the 1R door (first-class door) was not opened because the door was too badly damaged to open, and the area around the door was too badly mangled to get to the door. This is backed up by what Lari said. That area is the location of the galley ovens and has a shelf that lies down in front of the door to use as a counter. If the front of the plane was that badly mangled, how did someone open that door and deploy the slide? Remember how Lari said she tried to deploy the slide but couldn't because her hands were shaking too much. I know the pilot and co-pilot were in the cockpit because I saw them crawl out the window and down the side of the plane, and Capt. Erbeck said he couldn't get to Bonnie because of the flames. Ken Pfrang said in the *Time Magazine* article (Chapter 6) the concussion from the first grenade was so great that he was "knocked to the floor."

> "I got hit by the concussion," he said later, "and I thought, 'Why aren't I dead?' Then I realized it was some sort of incendiary device and smoke was pouring out of the canister." Within seconds, there were more flashes as two phosphorus grenades went off inside the forward section. Two other grenades were thrown into the rear; suddenly the entire plane was filled with roiling black smoke.

How and when did he get to the economy section to open those emergency doors?

Return to the *World Wings International* story that said Ken Pfrang opened the 1R door—"Flight Attendant Barbara Marnock and Flight Engineer Ken Pfrang opened the overwing exits and lead passengers to safety. Flight Attendants Sharon Dyer and Linda Jacobson armed the 2R [Economy right side aft] door and deployed the slide."When I asked Barbara who opened the overwing emergency exits, she said a woman from ARAMCO opened them.

Oh, boy! Another conflicting story.

I asked Barbara if she knew where John Parrott, the off-duty pilot was. She said he was in the back of the plane. She said he deployed the slide, was the first down, and caught people. This is contrary to the World Wings article and to what Randy said. She also said she heard that John traded his first-class seat with the Captain's wife. I knew I would have to find John Parrott to get clarification. Ann emailed John's son John telling him I wanted more information about what happened that day.

Through the craziest maze of phone and playing email tag, I finally connected with John Parrott, Jr., who had been off sailing. While in high school, his daughter had interviewed "Pappy" about his hair-raising ordeal on Pan Am Flight 110, so they both remembered what "Pappy" had told them. The incident impacted John Jr. so much that, in his email to me, he wrote,

> the whole family was supposed to be on the plane as we were starting our Christmas holidays. We all arrived the next day and I will never forget even at my young age the look on the captains face. Dad [John Parrott] still smelled of smoke and I too remember seeing the plane out on the tarmac.

Captain John was on his way to evacuate people from a war zone. As rumored, he traded seats with Captain Erbeck's wife, Bonnie, so that she could be in first class near her husband. According to John Jr., John was standing in the galley area, "probably flirting with the flight attendants," as his son told me, when the Captain told everyone to get on the floor. John stayed in the galley area. He said he couldn't escape out the 2L door because after the terrorist tossed the grenade in the back, he was standing at the foot of the stairs shooting at anyone who tried to leave. Within seconds, he saw the terrorist running down the aisle from first class. He believes the bomb the terrorist threw ended up in the overhead baggage area, which is why the bomb blew a hole in the roof. That is very credible because if he had dropped the bomb on the floor, the death toll would be much higher. This would have included Randy and the flight attendant lying in the seat row before him.

Somehow John got the 2R door open, jumped, and began catching people who also jumped out the door and off the wing. What stuck in Senior's mind is that he also caught children jumping.

Linda and Sharon then closed the door so they could deploy the slide. This is where Randy comes into the picture. When I told him Barbara said John deployed the slide, he said he never saw John helping with the slide. Now I understand why this statement was so puzzling. John was already on on the ground.

So, did Ken Pfrang open those doors, or was it an ARAMCO woman? John said Ken told him he had to jump over people lying in the aisles and climb over seats to get to the doors. And, you know, the crazy thing is that, as I write this, as clear as a bell, I remember a man in a uniform climbing over the seats as I started moving forward. John said Ken was also helping get people off the wing on the starboard (right) side. Was it Ken or Dominic who came to the other side, ran up the stairs to see if they could get into first class, and then ran back to help me pull people off the wing? Barbara swears it was Dominic. Senior says it was Ken Pfrang. After seeing pictures of both men, I know it was Ken Pfrang. John Parrott, Jr. also said his father said Ken talked about how he jumped over the seats to avoid people lying in the aisles and between seats to get to the exit doors. It was definitely Dominic Franco running up the aisle toward me and leaping out the right emergency exit as I was groping my way down the aisle to the exit. Dominic is also the one I saw hiding behind the wheel of the plane.

Why this conflict on who opened the doors, where people were, and what they did? There are several types of grenades. They are stun, gas, M67, smoke, EMP, and RG-42. A stun grenade releases shockwaves. People use it for crowd control and to cause disorientation, and I was certainly disoriented, as were the "frozen" people on the wing. Also known as a "smoke grenade," a smoke grenade will cause people to lose their vision. Also included in this arsenal of destruction used on us is the white phosphorus grenade. The irony of the word *grenade* is that it comes from the French word of the same, meaning "pomegranate." Others call it a "pineapple." It is called a pomegranate because it is reminiscent of the many-seeded fruit in size and shape and contains many "seeds" of fragments that injure or kill people. What is so horrible about the white phosphorus grenade (M34 a. k. a. "Willie Pete") used on us and that newspapers and reports called an "incendiary device"? It burns up all oxygen, is toxic to humans, is quite unstable, and suffocates the enemy. In other words, it sucked the air out of the airplane, as well as out of our lungs. That is why it felt like my lungs were collapsing when I tried to breathe. They were collapsing. In some forms, it "catches fire at just 10-15 degrees above room temperature in reaction to oxygen."[43] The fragmentation grenades used is why Lari said she grabbed a shoe with only a foot in it and a hand.

Here is why Bonnie and Robyn's burns were still smoking, why I smelled garlic, why my lungs continued to close down, why I was also in the first triage group sent away in an ambulance, and why I stopped breathing on the way to the hospital:

> White phosphorus bombs can have a worse effect on human health than other weapons of similar explosive power.
>
> On the skin, white phosphorus causes very painful burns that may be second-degree (partial thickness of skin) to third-degree (full thickness of skin). The burns typically have a yellowish color and a garlic-like odor. You may notice smoke coming from the injury as the white phosphorus continues to burn.
>
> In addition, because white phosphorus dissolves easily in fat, it gets absorbed easily through the skin and into the body, where it can cause other serious symptoms.

43 Wikipedia Online, s.v. "White phosphorus," https://en.wikipedia.org/wiki/White_phosphorus_munitions.

In fact, burns from white phosphorus on less than 10% of your body could lead to death because of damage to the kidneys, liver, and heart. [Remember that Robyn had burns over 35% of her body.]

In addition, white phosphorus can cause serious injury and death if you inhale or swallow it.

In the short term (acute effects), if you ingest white phosphorus in a large enough dose, you'll notice signs and symptoms in three stages:

- Stage 1: You may notice an upset stomach or other effects on your gut.
- Stage 2: This is a quiet period -- typically about 48 hours without noticeable symptoms.
- Stage 3: This starts a fast decline in your condition, with serious symptoms in your gut, like vomiting, stomach cramps, and lots of pain. You or medical personnel might start to see signs and symptoms of damage to your liver, kidneys, heart, blood vessels, or central nervous system. [Remember how I said I hurt all over when I arrived in New York? Of course, this pain could have also been caused by six grenades exploding, jumping fifteen feet off the plane's wing, having people jump on me, running across the tarmac, under a truck, up and down the ramp, crawling through the terminal through broken glass, dying—only God knows how many times, and staying in a rigid post-trauma state for hours.]

Along with the above symptoms, you may notice irritation in your breathing passages and coughing if you breathe in white phosphorus.

> Regular exposure to white phosphorus can make the bones of the jaw start to break down (necrosis, or "phossy jaw"). You might notice a bit of swelling and irritation at first that gets worse. Eventually, this can lead to open sores and the destruction of the jawbone as well as damage to the sinus and nasal passages.[44]

Unfortunately, some of these symptoms never go away. I have chronic stomach, lung, larynx, pharynx, sinus, jaw, and neurological problems. I have often said I will die from choking or a common cold because when I catch a cold, it always turns into ear infections, then bronchitis and or pneumonia.

The next question I asked Barbara was her theory on why they attacked our plane. She said she heard a rumor that Henry Kissinger was supposed to be on the plane. If true, it would be no wonder they attacked our aircraft, considering Nixon and Kissinger's foreign policy. This debacle was about America's insatiable need for Arab oil and its ongoing war against Russia. What? That's right. According to Henry Kissinger, in his meeting with the Jewish Leaders (Klutznik Group),

> We had to consider the following factors during the 1973 war: First, what would be the impact of the oil crisis on Western Europe and Japan? And I must tell you that every European leader that I have seen has told me that under no circumstances will he allow his country to undergo a domestic depression due to an oil embargo. Secondly, our impression is that Israel must be strong, but Israeli strength does not prevent the spread of communism in the Arab world. Israeli strength provides for Israeli security. The best defense against the spread of communism in the Arab world is to strengthen the moderate Arab governments. So it is difficult to claim

44 Paaauuul Frysh, "What to Know About White Phorsphorus Bombs," March 25, 2022, https://www.webmd.com/a-to-z-guides/white-phosphorus-bombs-overview.

that a strong Israel serves American interests because it prevents the spread of communism in the Arab world, lt does not. It provides for the survival of Israel. This was our perception in October of 1973.

What was our strategy in 1973? First, we sought to break up the Arab united front. Also we wanted to ensure that the Europeans and Japanese did not get involved in the diplomacy; and, of course, we wanted to keep the Soviets out of the diplomatic arena. Finally, we sought a situation which would enable Israel to deal separately with each of its neighbors. We told the Israelis they could go to the Europeans if they wanted proclamations, but if they wanted progress toward peace they would have to come to us. Thus, the step-by-step process began.

The step-by-step led to two disengagement agreements. But then we had to make a basic strategic decision: Shall we go now for an overall settlement or continue the step-by-step? An overall effort has its advantages. Most importantly one can put everything on the table; one can argue the framework of final settlement with full knowledge of the objectives of all sides involved. But the disadvantages are that it would bring all the Arabs together, and when this happens the radical Arabs would have the upper hand. Then the Soviets would always be able to outbid whatever else was on the table and the radical Arabs would, of course, have to opt for what the Soviets had to offer. Of course, the Soviets would not make an offer in the interests of achieving peace but rather in the interest of assuring that there was no progress.[45]

[45] Kissinger memorandum: "To Isolate the Palestinians," 96 (May/June 1981), https://merip.org/1981/05/kissinger-memorandum-to-isolate-the-palestinians/

All you have to do is look at the title of the Kissinger article to understand why any Palestinian would want to blow up our plane if Kissinger was supposed to be on it—"To Isolate the Palestinians." The fact is, Kissinger wasn't supposed to be on that plane. It was just a rumor. That rumor wasn't nearly as dangerous as the rumor Al Qaeda would pass along as being in the Qur'an—namely, 72 virgins would await them in Paradise if they slaughtered innocent infidels. As John O'Neill of the FBI quipped, "So, this is a war about pussy?" when referring to the many Al Qaeda-motivated terrorist attacks. Al-Qaeda also left this out: Chapter 5, verse 32 states, "We ordained for the Children of Israel that if any one slew a person—unless it be for murder or for spreading mischief in the land—it would be as if he slew the whole people, and if any one saved a life, it would be as if he saved the life of the whole people." In fact, based on the Islamic teachings, killing a human is forbidden. The Holy Qur'an also forbids fornication, which includes rape, a tool used by Al-Qaeda soldiers to gain power.

Who was the wife of Islam's prophet Muhammad? She was an exceptionally beautiful Jewess who received the title Umm-ul-Mu'mineen, or the "mother of Believers." Her real name was Safiyya. When she was 17, she was married to Kenana ibn al-Rabi. She had a dream in which the moon fell from the heavens into her lap. When she told Kenana about the dream, he interpreted it to mean she had a desire to marry Muhammad. He struck her in the face, leaving a mark still visible when she had her first contact with Muhammad. After a bloody war, Muhammad conquered Kenana, married Safiyya, and bedded her that night. Muhammad told her that if anyone insulted her Jewish heritage or were jealous of her beauty, she was to respond, "My father (ancestor) Harun (Aaron) was a prophet, my uncle (his brother) Musa (Moses) was a prophet, and my husband (Muhammad) is a prophet."[46]

46 Wikipedia Online, s.v. Rayhanna bint Zayd," https://en.wikipedia.org/wiki/Rayhana_bint_Zayd#:~:text=Rayh%C4%81nah%20bint%20Zayd%20(Arabic%3A%20%D8%B1%D9%8A%D8%AD%D8%A7%D9%86%D8%A9,627%20CE%20(5%20AH)..

In a way, Safiyya got the last laugh because when she died, she left her estate to her sister's son, who followed Judaism. Safiyya was not entirely happy in her situation because she was known for the moon miracle, her suffering, and her reputation for crying. Was she crying because that falling moon had hoodwinked her? You'll also have to wait for the answer to that question because things aren't always what they seem.

* * *

In case you wonder what happened to Linda Jacobson and Sharon Dyer, a car hit Linda while she was crossing the street in Boston. Linda was thrown in the air and landed, hitting her head on the concrete. However, her daughter's wedding continued as planned. The doctors temporarily released Linda from the hospital, and she was wheelchaired to her daughter's wedding, which Barbara attended and told me about in detail. Although Linda survived, she had serious health issues—many of them cognitive. Linda worked for Pan Am for 35 years and then Delta Airlines before retiring in 2004. According to her obituary, "she was an enthusiastic world traveler, bonne vivante, connoisseur of flowers, and lifelong lover of art." She died in 2013.

Sharon passed away in 2018 after a long battle with Alzheimer's.

Barbara Marnock is the sole surviving flight attendant of Pan Am Flight 110. As I earlier stated, she had not spoken to another survivor until she spoke with me. She would not even talk about it with co-workers. Recently, she did a podcast, but in the podcast, she didn't talk about the plane incident. After a brief chat with Barbara about her life today, the commentator briefly said that Barbara helped people get off the wing of the plane. Unfortunately, he repeated much misinformation published in many outlets, such as how many people were on the plane. Some journalists gave the number of passengers as the number of people the plane could hold rather than the number of people on the plane. He further stated that Barbara helped save eighty people. There weren't even eighty people on the plane—fifty-five passengers and nine crew members. Of those crew members, only one died, and one was the off-duty pilot John Parrott. Just like many of us, Barbara had nightmares.

We must remember that when any country, tribe, or person attacks another, those attacked also have nightmares, including when the United States and or its allies attack any entity. Rather than turning the other cheek, as Jesus said to do in Matthew 5:39, Luke 6:29, and seventeen other Bible verses, most think we need to create more mayhem than the original injury. This type of thinking creates a snowball effect that creates a bigger and bigger snowball. Pretty soon, all-out war breaks out. Where's the logic in that? Does the Qu'ran teach something similar? It does. It says, *Nor can goodness and evil be equal. Repel evil with what is better: then will he between whom and you was hatred become as it were your friend and intimate* (Q. 41: 34). Perhaps Gandi summed all of this violent nonsense up best. He said, "An eye for an eye makes the whole world blind."

Afterword

This book now splits into several parts. As you may recall, I earlier discussed the physical body, the life force body, the emotional body, the mental body, and the psychic body. To adequately understand what the conscious, the subconscious, and the psychic part of me needed to do to become balanced, I needed to become *un*conscious for several years with only short bursts of consciousness thrown into the mix. The five parts of me became separate at times and many times enhanced.

Within the unconscious time frame of head injury, which I was about to experience on a grand scale, I spent many hours in a catatonic, seizure-like state. During that same time, I spent many hours in a meditative, ethereal state. The result was an awakening into another dimension of higher consciousness—not of human brain consciousness but of ethereal consciousness, where my human senses and ethereal senses were awakened and became so unfiltered that everything, earthly and non-earthly, poured into me. During that time, I wrote the book *Headache: How to Survive a Head Injury and the Headache Caused by Insurance Companies, Doctors and Lawyers* by B J Geisler. The book *The Mystical Marriage—Opening the Sixth Seal of the Revelation—The Doorway of Vision* by C. S. Warner followed. The books are about the journey I took during and after the auto accident into the realm of the ethereal, spiritual, psychic world on the other side of the veil, where I started to understand the differences between spirituality and religion and the steps to enlightenment or rebirth (born again without ego—not the Christian version of "born again," where one simply believes that a supernatural character can and will make them happy). Both books are available on Kindle and paperback through Amazon.com, Apple, Diesel, and other electronic venues. *The Mystical Marriage* is also available through iUniverse Publishing.

Notice the change in names after the book *Headache*.... I thought the name change was appropriate because I never believed I was given the correct name at birth, and I also needed to hide from the *was*band.

Headache takes the reader on an unbelievable journey through the quagmire of head injury and what to expect and not expect. It talks about brain injury symptoms, different healing modalities, the legal aspects of the injury, the insurance company's manipulations, "bad faith" and stalling tactics, and what to do with the money you might receive in a settlement. If you think your car insurance will take care of you if you are injured personally, think again. After reading *Headache* and *The Mystical Marriage*, you will never look at the veiled world the same way again.

I learned several valuable things during my oddball life. One is that I was born on the south node of the Moon, meaning this incarnation is a time to repay karmic debts or to make sure others repay their debt. In the case of the airplane incident, the terrorists were receiving remuneration for something that occurred several centuries ago. (Yes, I went back and saw what happened.) In other words, the terrorists were the victims in that lifetime, and the victims in this lifetime were the aggressors in that lifetime. You might have trouble believing this if you are a Christian because it has been drilled into your head that you get one life, and you'd better get it right, or else you will go to hell. That is true, but hell is not a place we go to after death; it is a place we go to in an incarnation. We have many lives until we get it right, and I will explain how this works in upcoming books. In the meantime, understand that the ancients said the Underworld is where the Sun goes at night; it is not a flaming pit inside the Earth, as churches teach us.

Another term for the south node of the Moon is a Lilith Moon, which is the point along the Moon's orbit when it's farthest from Earth. Yep, good old Lilith, the name Christianity fears so much they don't mention her, and the same Lilith that Judaism said was Adam's first wife. Some legends say Adam cast Lilith out (farthest from Earth) because she refused to submit to Adam and "lie beneath him." For this reason, the gods kicked her out of the Garden of Eden. Oops! Christianity also left this out of their Bible.

In the Jewish Bible, there are two serpents in the Garden, but in the Christian version, there is only one serpent. A Lilith serpent and an Eve serpent? You'll have to wait for the answer to that question. Unfortunately, Lilith, in my natal chart, is why I constantly tried to bring balance to relationships and why I chose people in relationships who I romanticized. Of course, I was always disappointed when the person did not meet my high standards and unrealistic expectations. Heck! My dog couldn't even reach those high standards and unrealistic expectations. Neither could I. These expectations set up a pattern of self-defeating behavior that I had to overcome repeatedly.

In Old Hebrew, *Lilith* translates to "night monster" or "night creature." They even said she cursed pregnancies and stole children and men's semen. Today, we know that's ridiculous, but not more ridiculous than believing that Donald Trump can single-handedly "Make America Great Again." (I didn't realize it wasn't great.) Lilith wasn't all bad, as she wanted to understand and connect emotionally to humans. To accomplish this, she gave up immortality. Tie the last two sentences into my life. Did I move from person to person and from place to place to learn how to connect emotionally to all types of humans? Did I give up the comfort of mortality to do so?

Had I been born on the north node of the Moon, known as an Eve Moon, I would have been one of the people living a golden life. However, a problem arises in an Eve Moon when someone is given many gifts and blessings and does not share them with those who are not as blessed. Guess what happens to them in the next life. Bingo! Lilith Moon! Those gifts and blessings are taken away until the piper is paid back for being stingy.

One good thing about a Lilith Moon is that she is associated with intuition, psychic abilities, one's hidden desires, and exploring new aspects of one's self. This description leaves me wondering: What was Adam so afraid of? Was he fearful that Lilith could see through him?

Add the Lilith Moon to Mercury sitting almost on top of my Sun at the time of my birth, as well as Neptune, and it is no wonder I can see things others can't see. Mercury is said to be the planet that brings messages from God to humans (goes retrograde and then direct). Neptune is the planet of psychic abilities and visions, intuition, the connection of the spirit, clairvoyance, seeing auras, crystal gazing, dowsing, omen reading, and telepathy. Give me a willow stick, and I can find water (dowsing). Toss all this into the ninth house of philosophy, religion, publishing, legal and academic matters, emphasizing the higher mind and mental exploration. The ninth house is ruled by the fortunate Jupiter and by Sagittarius's philosophical and scholarly sign, so it is no wonder I am a perpetual student majoring in these areas and continue to study them.

How crazy is someone talking about astrology and the psychic world? Today's field of psychology has much of its basis in Carl Jung's theories, so the fact that Dr. Ralph delved into the metaphysical world should have come as no surprise to me. In Jung's memoir, he wrote, "Human consciousness created objective existence and meaning, and man found his indispensable place in the great process of being" (p. 256).

Jung's biographer Gerhard Weber tells about an interview between Jung and BBC reporter and deputy editor of the *New Statesman* John Freeman. Freeman asked Jung if he believed in God. Jung thought a moment like one of his subjects on the hot seat and admitted, "I know." He paused another moment, then said, "I don't believe. I know." This statement backs up what he said earlier in his writing "Spirit and Life," where he wrote, "God is a psychic fact of immediate experience, otherwise there would never have been any talk of God" (1926, p. 328). Even more peculiar is that Jung compared God to the unconscious and said, "I prefer the term "the unconscious," knowing that I might equally speak of "God" or "daimon" if I wished to express myself in mythic language. I am aware that "mana," "daimon," and "God" are synonyms for the unconscious" (Jung, 1961, p 336-337). When we say something like "God wants me to...," we are saying, "My unconscious wants me to...."

Hm. So, this means that when God sent mana/manna from heaven (Exodus 16:4, 1, and John 6:30–32), He sent psychic information. Deuteronomy 8:3 and 16 say manna is something "previously unknown." Numbers 11:9 tells us it fell "at evening." What happens at night? We have dreams. Within those dreams, we see three things: 1) the past, 2) the present, and 3) the future. What did I say earlier is the thing that animates the hand within the glove? The Spirit The Spirit is the same as Jung's unconscious, daimon, mana, and God.

Jung also had a tear in his veil because, before WWI, he dreamed that legions of bloodied men would march into the lake where he lived. His dreams and psychic awareness would so overwhelm him that he eventually had a nervous breakdown. We also find many other famous people who predicted the horrible war. Wassily Kandinsky, in 1912, wrote of a coming universal catastrophe. Ludwig Meidner painted a series of "apocalyptic landscapes" with scenes of destroyed cities, corpses, and turmoil (1912 to 1914).

Another very curious thing about Jung is that he also studied astrology and was good friends with one of the founders of A. A. Astrologer Steven Forrest wrote that some believe the Twelve Steps and Twelve Traditions of A. A. are based on the houses of the zodiac. If you compare the characteristics of the lessons taught in the zodiac houses, you will see the correlation between the Steps and Traditions.

Does one need to have an artistic bent to be psychic? There is a correlation between people who are right-minded thinkers and psychic abilities, which I outline in *The Mystical Marriage....* As scientists tell us, the left brain is analytical, and the right brain is intuitive. Amazingly, almost every one of the predictions I made in *The Mystical Marriage* has happened or is occurring as I write this.

Jung had a theory on why some people can see things. He wrote, "Perhaps my unconscious is forming a personality that is not I, but which is insisting on coming through to expression." He believed a woman represents the unconscious in dreams. Does this mean God is a woman? Many religions do.

Jung's comment takes us back to water, representing the psyche. I often have dreams of water rushing toward me, such as last night. In the dream, four animals appeared, surrounded me, and helped me not be afraid. Strange? Not really. The first to appear was a rooster. Roosters are spirit animals admired across various cultures, faiths, and religions. They protect the flock and present spirituality, bravery, honesty, courage, prudence, pride, strength, positivity, enthusiasm, punctuality, observance, masculinity, and sexuality. They teach a person how to use their voice for good.

Most importantly, they are protectors, symbols of vigilance, and warn people to be overly cautious. Remember how the cock crowed at 3 a.m. in Matthew 26:34? It reminded Peter never to fall away from his spiritual beliefs.

The next animal to appear was a dog. Dogs represent family, devotion, adaptability, friendship, loyalty, patience and devotion, bravery, protection, sensitivity and insight, purpose, and joy.

The third animal was a cat. Cats represent grace, agility, stealth, intelligence, independence, sense of purpose, and a sixth sense guiding them. The Egyptians revered cats as gods.

Rabbit was the fourth animal. Rabbits symbolize luck and creativity and remind us that life is full of possibilities. They help us get back on center if we feel out of balance and are the animals of people who are natural-born leaders. Rabbits represent people's kindness and niceness but don't mean the person is a pushover, but instead that they love with all their heart. For this reason, the people with rabbit spirit around them are good listeners and make people feel comfortable confiding in them.

Most importantly, they can be a powerful ally if one starts a new life chapter. Am I starting a new chapter in life? I sure am. As for the fertility aspect of rabbit, it doesn't mean I'm going to pop out a litter of six to ten babies; it might mean I will come up with new ideas, begin a new project, travel to a far-off place, start a new relationship, meet new people, etc.

As you can see, this dream came at a very opportune time, as I am doing the final edit on this book, have purchased a ticket to the Frankfurt Book Fair, will be traveling to see my family in France, and who knows what else might happen in the future. What I know is that these animals have shown me that my intuition will return to me full-bore, which I have been asking for recently.

So, why was my life such a train wreck? Astrologically, my rising sign and Moon were both in the twelfth house at the time of my birth. The twelfth house contains afflictions, death, sorrow, loss, enemies, poisoning, and explosions. As one psychic told me, "Most people come to Earth and choose to learn lesson A, K, or another letter. You chose to learn all letters and added a few more."

There is a Japanese word that sums up my seeming train wreck of life with one word. That word is *kintsukuroi*, meaning "more beautiful for having been broken."

What You Can Do to Combat Gun Violence

For more information on how to make a difference in gun safety, contact my friend Mike Martin at www.https.//springs.rawtools.org. Mike arranges a time and place that is convenient for you to meet to turn your gun/guns in. It only takes about 5-10 minutes per gun. Suppose you don't live in the Colorado Springs area. In that case, he has a nationwide network of blacksmiths and pastors trained according to federal safety regulations and equipped with the necessary tools to decommission guns. He also does workshops where victims of recent shootings speak about how the violence has affected their lives. Mike's dad. Fred, then demonstrates how they turn the guns into garden tools, jewelry, and what they call "talking pieces." As Mike says,

> No talking piece is the same. Each has been made from an existing circle as it was designed for use in a firearm. Each has been reformed by changing its orientation. From one perspective it can be seen as a circle. From another perspective it can be seen as an oval, or a widened circle. It's designed to be tactile as you hold it, using your thumb and fingers to push at its edges

> as if they are widening the circle as it's being used for mediation or meditation.[47]

Pictures of a dove made by our friend, C. Bryan Miller, are on the following page. Bryan is a gifted metal sculptor who takes bicycle parts and or gun parts and turns them into works of art. In the case of the dove, notice how Bryan uses all parts of the gun for the dove's body and a bicycle chain wheel for the stand. Do you think this is a better use of a gun?

[47] Mike Martin, "Talking Pieces," https.//springs.rawtools.org.

Acknowledgments

There are innumerable people to thank for getting me to where I am today. This very long list includes different types of therapists, body workers, doctors, nurses, EMTs, surgeons, and friends.

In the present day, were it not for Ann Blumensaadt of World Wings International, the last few chapters of this book would not have been possible. She helped me find Barbara Marnock, John Parrott, John Parrott, Jr., and his daughter Anna. They all helped fill in some blanks. A misprint by Pan Am helped me find Randy Kirby, who filled in even more blanks.

Thanks to Writers Book Fair Publishing—Charles Brown, Jade Howards, Fay Turner, and Macey Rogers, who I worked with on the book cover to keep the airplane from looking like it just came through a car wash.

To my friend Rev. Kim Pfleuger, I'm always grateful for her insight. (For more information about Kim, her classes, spirit readings, or to join her email list, go to: churchofmankind@msn.com.)

To Lauren Weaver, photographer extraordinaire. She and her dad Rodger also answer and repair many of my tech questions and problems.

And, of course, to my girls, who have given and still give themselves each day to make the world a better place, whether it be at home, in a church, a Buddhist retreat, in Novosibirsk, Russia, the jungles, mountains, or cities of South or Central America, Singapore, Malaysia, India, Rwanda, Nigeria, Kenya, Lesotho, South Africa, or wherever their jobs and their spirit take them.

Excerpt from *Headache—How to Survive a Head Injury and the Headache Caused by Insurance Companies, Doctors, and Lawyers*

Chinle, Arizona, is a magical place. The town is steeped in poverty with a landscape of dirt yards, tumbleweeds, tumbling cans, newspapers, and candy wrappers blown up against chain link fences. But it is home to Canyon de Chelly, one of the most spiritually inspirational places I have visited.

My new friend Pam, her dog, and I rode in her SUV to Chinle (Chin-lee') one weekend in 2001. We drove on post-snowstorm roads for hours, through treacherous snow-packed mountain roads, until we reached Arizona and the bright late-afternoon sunshine.

We marveled at the buttes and spires that turned from deep red to rose pink to denim blue as the setting-sun shadows cast their signature. Although we planned to arrive in Chinle sometime in the late afternoon, Pam missed the turn-off to Canyon de Chelly (pronounced Shay) and ended up in New Mexico. I kept telling her that she had missed the turn-off and needed to go back, but she wouldn't listen.

We were sixty miles out of the way and running low on gas when we finally saw the bright lights of a solitary gas station, seemingly out in the middle of nowhere. The lady at the gas station told us to turn around, return, and turn left at a tiny brown sign that most people missed the first time.

We backtracked through the now-eerie forested mountains and found the little carved wooden sign at an unlit junction that was the entrance to the canyon.

We finally reached the town of Chinle late that evening.

When we got out of our beds on Saturday morning, we ate breakfast at the motel restaurant, then drove to the visitors' center at the mouth of the canyon. We hired a Navajo guide to ride with us for two hours since no one could enter the canyon without a Navajo present.

Pam drove the SUV into the canyon through the constantly shifting, tire-sucking sand that was the non-road. She was having a great time gunning the engine and fighting the wheel. She told the guide about her days as a "professional" driver and how she missed that.

The guide told us the history of the canyon's Anasazi people. We viewed the petroglyphs up close and the tiny-looking cliff dwellings from hundreds of feet below. It was cold in the canyon that morning with a crisp, blue sky and a strong breeze. Blowing golden leaves swirled through the air and splashed flashes of dancing shadows on the ancient cliff walls.

We shopped for jewelry and pottery at the lean-tos set up at the canyon's halfway point, then plowed back through the sand to the visitors' center.

I paid the guide and said, "Yah-te-he" (hello) to a weatherworn, wizened Navajo grandmother trying to sell her hand-woven rugs near the front door. I told her that her rugs and the turquoise jewelry adorning her hands and neck were "na-zho-ni," meaning beautiful. She beamed from ear to ear while gesturing with her gnarled, worn hands and spoke with me in broken English interspersed with Navajo about her rugs.

By mid-afternoon, billowy clouds began rolling in, chased by a determined wind. We drove along the winding road that hugged the canyon's rim, parked the car, and walked down into the canyon on the only walking path available to non-Navajo.

I stopped numerous times to marvel at the richness of the sheer red cliffs and to watch the colors change on the cliff walls as a cloud danced by, painted its charcoal image on the wall, then erased itself. I held my breath and watched the shadows deepen as the sun lowered itself deep within the canyon's folds.

We gorged on Navajo fry bread laced with honey at the motel restaurant that evening, then returned to our room. I read for a while and went to sleep.

Sometime during the night, Mother Nature sent us a gale-force snowstorm.

On Sunday morning, the flag on the pole in the courtyard was hanging on for dear life, its frayed tips snapping and bucking in the wind. The garbage flattened and quivering against the fences the day before was tossed upward during an updraft and blown and tumbled to a new resting point.

The minuscule snow the storm brought had turned the concrete and asphalt surfaces into skating rinks. The icing on the cake for the morning, or so I thought, was when the electricity blinked once, then twice, and finally went out.

By eight o'clock, the motel room was getting cold. Because the power was out, the Motel restaurant was closed. We were hungry for hot food, and Pam had not had her coffee. I had a packet of nuts and ate a handful. I offered some to Pam, but she declined.

We decided to head north toward home, hoping the next town would have its electricity on and a place to eat. When we went outside, the sun barely peeked through the clouds, and the wind was losing some of its blusters. It was still bitterly cold.

Pam mentioned that she wondered if a stick or something had gotten stuck above one of the tires while we were driving in the canyon because she had heard an odd noise the day before. She looked up under the right rear wheel well and decided it was too cold to look further. She commented about how icy the parking lot was as she skidded her feet around to test the slickness.

We loaded our suitcases into the backseat of the car, took our coats off, and put her dog in the back end of the vehicle.

Pam backed the car out of the space and headed for the street. I noticed an ambulance creeping along on the icy road toward the canyon, the opposite direction we would go. I mentioned the slowness to Pam and said the road must really be icy.

The car's tires spun as we pulled out of the driveway, turned left onto the road, drove to the stoplight, and turned right. All the business windows were dark, and their doors firmly said, "Closed."

At the edge of town, I saw a Highway Patrolman parked along the side of the road. I mentioned this to Pam, who had a propensity for speeding and getting tickets. She asked me what the speed limit was. I told her it was fifty-five. She checked her speed.

I picked up my one-liter water bottle from the console between us, noticed I had only taken a few drinks, and set it back down next to her cell phone, which she had found useless on the reservation.

Out in the open country, the wind was whistling from the west. The buttes and spires, whose color resembled freshly washed blue jeans as the sun set behind them the day before, now looked a dull, filmy rose color. Crystals of icy snow, or perhaps sand swept up from the desert by the wind, swirled up and spattered the car's paint and windshield with a rat-a-tat-tat.

The road was obviously quite icy and glittered and twinkled where the peeking sun shone on it.

Driving north, I noticed Pam was going much faster than I thought she should have been. I thought about saying something to her, but I was sure she would inform me, as she had numerous times that weekend, that *she* used to be a professional driver and that *she* knew what she was doing.

She was looking off to the west at something. I looked at the speedometer. From where I sat, it appeared we were going between fifty-five and sixty miles per hour. Up ahead of us, I saw an old burgundy Chevy full of people rolling slowly down the road and wondered if we would go around them or run over the top of them.

The sun had just started to pierce through the skittering clouds, and the wind was losing some of its bluster.

Pam was slowly accelerating the car while she still looked at the buttes.

We were slowly creeping toward the edge of the road. I was feeling agitated when—lo, and behold—I sensed my dog jump up on my lap, lean back against me and brace herself against the dash with her front paws. My dog died the week before our trip!—but there she was. I could see her clear as could be.

Pam looked down at the speedometer and let off a little on the gas. I heard a clunk, like a tire flipping a rock up against the undercarriage, or of something jarred loose and falling from the bottom of the vehicle.

Suddenly, the car fishtailed clockwise, then counter-clockwise, and then back again while Pam frantically turned the wheel from one side to the other. We were sliding backward, with the front of the driver's side of the car closest to the ditch.

"Don't hit the brakes," I told her, thinking that she would lock up the wheels if she slammed on the brakes.

The front tire caught the road's edge first, then the rear tire. The car hurtled into the air.

She said, "We're gonna flip!"

I said, "Yep."

I grabbed the grab handle with my right hand and braced the console with the other when I heard someone say, "Relax," and then, "Don't brace yourself. You'll get hurt worse." I relaxed like a rag doll.

We smashed down on the driver's side of the car with a thunderous explosion of bursting tires and crushing metal.

My head and body flew left and back between the seats. My left arm slammed down hard into the console. The seatbelt grabbed me, and my head snapped back to the right like it had been slung out of a catapult.

Don't disassociate, I kept telling myself. *Don't disassociate.*

The next voice I sensed was saying, "Don't hit your head."

I tipped my head just as it hit the window so that the impact was blunt instead of sharp. My right leg smashed into the armrest. My head glanced off of the glass shooting to the left and slightly forward, then to the right, where the back of my head slammed into the post. Stars and a haze overtook me. Then I felt myself hurled out of my body. . ..

* * *

I stood with one foot on the third step down and my right foot on the second step down of the three-tiered stairs. In the background were filmy-looking beings that looked like they were in absolute peace, calmness, and serenity. I felt confused and wasn't sure where I was, but I knew I was where I was supposed to be. A much larger angelic being came forward and spoke with me in words I could not hear. Then the being quite clearly said. . .

Excerpt from *The Mystical Marriage: Opening the Sixth Seal of the Revelation—The Doorway of Vision* by C. S. Warner

One night at the end of this phase of my journey, I went to a meditation. In the meditation, a man whose essence shimmered with gold and silver and gems, and had long brown hair that flowed like ocean waves, and who wore warrior's clothing, complete with an exquisitely gilded blouse, came to me with a gift. I asked him what I was to call him, and after much thinking, he silently said a name without moving his lips. I couldn't quite understand the name and asked, "Brutus?" He shrugged his shoulders and silently "told" me that humans think there must be a name for everything in the Universe and this infatuation and obsession with names is not necessary, and frankly, gets in the way of hearing their "guides". He said that true communication is done through telepathy, not words, and that all things have an "energy" attached to them. When he "told" me that, the oddest thing happened. Right before my "eyes" I pictured strings of synapses firing away in my brain that were not banging against a wall of black doubt.

The gift he gave to me was a little box that matched his essence. It was beautifully adorned with shimmering bronze, gold and silver wrap and was tied with an opalescent-colored, shimmering bow. I was awestruck and didn't want to open the box and disturb the stunning ornamentation. I asked him what was inside the box, and he said, "It's a gift for a job well done."

I was humbled by the gift, and when I lifted the lid, I felt a warm lavender flood of pure love flow out of the box and into me. I felt my heart open and fill with this new radiance and knew that I was one step closer to finding my way out of the corn-field maize.

I did not want to leave the essence of Brutus' amazing, loving energy, but I was pulled reluctantly back onto the earth plane by the mediator's human voice. Begrudgingly I re-entered my body and lay as perfectly still as I could. I did not want the essence of what I had just experienced leave my now warmth-filled body, and I wondered, had I actually left my body or had I simply risen to a higher level of Consciousness within myself? Is that what happened in the car accident when I visited the Beings?

I wouldn't be able to ponder these questions long because the mediator's voice asked each of us to share our experience. I avoided talking for as long as I could because I really didn't want to share what I had seen, as I felt it was so divinely personal. After several attempts to avoid talking, however, I was prodded into it by the mediator, who happened to be named Angel.

I described Brutus and everyone "o-o-h-ed!" and "a-a-h-ed!" and excitedly said that they wanted to meet Brutus—mostly because of his looks. I was chagrined at the debasement that I felt was being given to Brutus as He was beautiful because of His energy field, not because of His looks. His eyes were filled with nothing but pure love and I knew His communication with every fiber of my being. I also knew that this was the Being that Daniel of the Bible had seen.

To be continued.

Printed in the USA
CPSIA information can be obtained
at www.ICGtesting.com
LVHW040513090424
776774LV00001B/45